CANYONING IN THE ALPS

About the Author

Simon grew up in Sheffield, spending much of his free time mountain biking and climbing in the Peak District. In 1998 he took up caving at Bristol University and was pretty content until discovering canyoning a year later. He was glad to discover a serious mountain sport that didn't take itself too seriously and seemed to combine everything he loved about the outdoors. Since then he has been canyoning enthusiastically (bordering on obsessively) all over Europe and beyond, taking in a handful of first descents along the way.

Caving remains a major interest of Simon's, and over the years he has helped to make significant discoveries both at home and abroad – in the deep systems of alpine Europe and in more exotic karst further afield. Trekking (and an apparent desire for navigational difficulties and personal hardship) has also taken him to some interesting places, including the Tien Shan in China and the Alborz mountains in Iran. Now back in Bristol after several years away, he can often be found running over the moors and ridge-tops of the Mendip Hills or squeezing through the caves beneath. Or perhaps down the pub plotting his next trip...

CANYONING IN THE ALPS

NORTHERN ITALY AND TICINO
by Simon Flower

2 POLICE SQUARE, MILNTHORPE, CUMBRIA LA7 7PY
www.cicerone.co.uk

© Simon Flower 2012
First edition 2012
ISBN: 978 1 85284 683 1

Printed in China on behalf of Latitude Press Ltd

A catalogue record for this book is available from the British Library.
All photographs are by Andrew Atkinson unless otherwise credited.

Acknowledgements

A big 'thank you' to my trusty canyoning team, who frequently turned up to find a boot-camp in place of a holiday – Juliet Morse, Tom Holden, Ed and Helen Hodge, Johan Bengtsson, Euan Major, Mylène Ragioneri, Pete Talling, Fleur Loveridge, Dickon Morris, Becka Lawson, Julian Todd, Bill Miners, Holly Bradley and Noel Snape.

A special thanks must go to Andrew Atkinson for his spectacular photographs and tireless proofreading. He has been a major driving force – always full of enthusiasm even when my own was waning.

Also thanks to Mum and Dad, Tim Haynes, Tony Seddon, Portishead Medical Group and the Severn Deanery, who all helped in one way or another.

Most of all, though, to Ginevra, without whom the idea for a book would never have left the beermat, and who, once it did, gave me a bottomless well of patience and support to draw from.

Advice to Readers

While every effort is made by our authors to ensure the accuracy of guidebooks as they go to print, changes can occur during the lifetime of an edition. If we know of any, there will be an Updates tab on this book's page on the Cicerone website (www.cicerone.co.uk), so please check before planning your trip. We also advise that you check information about such things as transport, accommodation and shops locally. Even rights of way can be altered over time. We are always grateful for information about any discrepancies between a guidebook and the facts on the ground, sent by email to info@cicerone.co.uk or by post to Cicerone, 2 Police Square, Milnthorpe LA7 7PY, United Kingdom.

Front cover: The exhilarating final pitch in Zemola (Route 66)
Front inside cover flap: The toboggan in Nero Inferiore (Route 88)
Back cover: (top) The delicate 50m pitch in Osogna Inferiore (Route 35)
(bottom) A calm moment in Grigno (Route 54)

CONTENTS

Map of areas covered 9
PREFACE 11
INTRODUCTION 13
Canyoning – a brief history 15
Geology of the Alps (for canyoners). 19
Weather and when to go 22
Getting there 23
Getting around 24
Waymarking, access routes and maps 25
The risks of canyoning. 26
Canyoning rope techniques 30
Equipment and clothing. 34
Canyon safety – precautions and pre-trip preparations. 39
Cameras and photography 41
Mountain rescue, local healthcare and insurance 42
Canyon etiquette 43
Using this guide. 44
Key facts 48

VAL D'OSSOLA   49

Route 1	Massaschluct 56
Route 2	Gondo. 60
Route 3	Rasiga Superiore 63
Route 3a	Rasiga Inferiore 69
Route 4	Variola Superiore. 70
Route 5	Mondelli 2. 75
Route 5a	Mondelli 1 77
Route 6	Mondelli 3. 78
Route 7	Bianca. 81
Route 7a	Segnara 84
Route 8	Toce 85
Route 9	Rio d'Alba 88
Route 10	Antolina 93
Route 11	Isorno Finale 97
Route 12	Antoliva. 101
Route 13	Ogliana di Quarata 104
Route 13a	Menta Inferiore 109
Route 14	Ogliana di Beura – Parte Finale 110
Route 15	Marona 112

TICINO   115

Route 16	Serenello. 123
Route 17	Bignasco 125
Route 18	Sponde 128
Route 19	Giumaglio 132
Route 20	Salto 135

Route 21	Val di Gei Inferiore	140
Route 22	Val Grande Inferiore	142
Route 23	Loco Inferiore	145
Route 24	Ticinetto Inferiore	148
Route 25	Barougia	151
Route 26	Malvaglia Inferiore	153
Route 27	Combra	156
Route 28	Pontirone Superiore	160
Route 29	Pontirone Inferiore	164
Route 30	Iragna Superiore	167
Route 31	Iragna Inferiore	171
Route 32	Lodrino Intermedio	174
Route 33	Lodrino Inferiore	176
Route 34	Osogna Intermedio	179
Route 34a	Osogna Superiore	183
Route 35	Osogna Inferiore	184
Route 36	Cresciano Superiore	188
Route 37	Cresciano Inferiore	193

LAKE COMO — 195

Route 38	Bodengo 2	206
Route 38a	Bodengo 1	208
Route 39	Bodengo 3	209
Route 40	Pilotera	212
Route 41	Mengasca	215
Route 42	Casenda	219
Route 43	Bares	224
Route 44	Borgo	230
Route 45	Perlana Inferiore	232
Route 46	Bondasca	236
Route 46a	Drögh Grand	240
Route 47	Lesina	241
Route 48	Ferro	243
Route 49	Cormor	247
Route 50	Valle di Scerscen	252
Route 51	Val Brutta	255
Route 52	Esino Inferiore	258
Route 53	Boazzo	260

THE BELLUNO AND FRIULI DOLOMITES — 265

Route 54	Grigno	273
Route 55	La Soffia	279
Route 56	Forti	284
Route 57	Pisson	286
Route 58	Clusa Superiore	289
Route 59	Clusa Inferiore	296

Route 60	Mus Inferiore	298
Route 60a	Mus Superiore	302
Route 61	Fogarè Superiore	303
Route 62	Fogarè Inferiore	307
Route 63	Maor	310
Route 64	Maggiore	313
Route 65	Tovanella	317
Route 66	Zemola	321
Route 67	Pezzeda	325
Route 68	Ciorosolin	330
Route 69	Torrente Chiadola	333
Route 70	Ciolesan	335
Route 71	Alba-Molassa	338

CARNIA AND THE JULIAN ALPS 341

Route 72	Lower Rötenbach	349
Route 72a	Upper Rötenbach	353
Route 73	Frauenbach	354
Route 74	Novarza	360
Route 75	Lumiei	364
Route 76	Rio Negro	366
Route 77	Viellia	370
Route 78	Picchionis	378
Route 79	Chiantione	382
Route 80	La Foce Inferiore	386
Route 81	Cosa	388
Route 82	Leale Inferiore	391
Route 83	Lavarie	395
Route 84	Tralba Inferiore	398
Route 84a	Alba	402
Route 85	Simon Inferiore	403
Route 85a	Simon Superiore	406
Route 86	Cuestis	407
Route 87	Rio Nero Superiore	411
Route 88	Rio Nero Inferiore	413
Route 89	Brussine	415
Route 90	Mlinarica	418

Appendix A	Canyon summary table	421
Appendix B	Further information and resources	428
Appendix C	Campsites	430
Appendix D	Tourist information offices	433
Appendix E	Glossary of technical terms	436
Appendix F	First descents	438

ROUTE INDEX 440
ROUTE PLANNER 442

Aquatic and encased, Bares (Route 43 in the Como region) is a long, committing alpine descent

WARNING – CANYONING CAN BE VERY DANGEROUS

The canyons described in this book are often long and aquatic in nature. Many are sparsely rigged and almost all are flood prone. Canyoning is a dangerous sport with very real risks and hazards, most of which relate specifically to the sport. Practising it safely requires good judgement based on previous experience and a realistic understanding of your personal skills and limitations. Even those with extensive caving or mountaineering experience should hesitate before attempting certain canyons until they are sure of their canyoning ability.

This book is aimed at an experienced audience – either dedicated canyoners or mountain enthusiasts looking for a different twist on their sport. Few canyons described here are suited to people fresh on the adventure-sport scene. Good rope skills, level-headedness and a good degree of physical fitness are essential and assumed.

While the information in this book is as accurate as possible, it cannot keep you free from danger. By their nature canyons change. Hazards multiply in high water conditions and anchors are damaged by floods. Pools silt up and even landslides occasionally occur. Flow rates in dam-controlled rivers may change completely at the whim of hydroelectric companies. You must be prepared for changing circumstances and have the skills to adapt appropriately. Legislation also changes. Canyons that are now freely accessible may be out of bounds by the time you get there. Seek local advice where there is doubt. See 'The risks of canyoning', 'Canyoning rope techniques', 'Equipment and clothing', 'Canyon safety' and 'Mountain rescue' in the Introduction for information on a range of hazards and how to prepare for them.

Except for any liability which cannot be excluded by law, neither Cicerone nor the author accept liability for damage of any nature (including damage to property, personal injury or death) arising directly or indirectly from the information in this book.

IN CASE OF ACCIDENT

To contact the mountain rescue service in any of the countries covered in this guide, dial the international rescue number 112.

If you call out the rescue services, you will be charged, usually a considerable sum. It is therefore essential to be adequately insured.

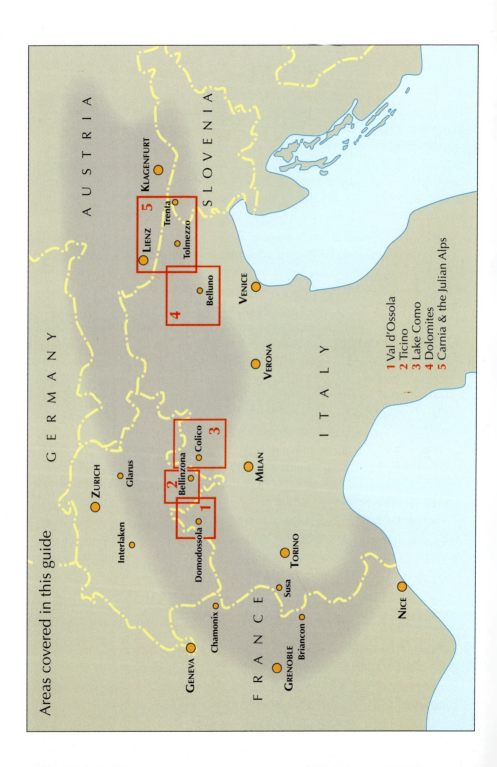

PREFACE

Offering a stunning selection of routes in the best areas, this guide to canyons in the Alps of northern Italy or Ticino is not an exhaustive one.

Canyons of mediocre quality have been excluded, as have some better canyons in mediocre areas. The latter category includes Val Susa (west of Torino), Aosta and Lake Garda, all of which contain a number of fine canyons, but too few to justify a week away. If, having tried some of these routes, you find you wish to explore the Italian-speaking Alps in greater depth, there are a number of foreign-language guides available (listed in Appendix B).

Remarkably, despite a firm following on the continent, canyoning remains a relatively unknown sport in the British Isles, even among the outdoor communities. Few people really know what the sport entails, believing it to be something akin to gorge walking or white-water rafting. Ignorance stems from the lack of opportunity to practise the sport. In these islands there are no canyons of comparable quality to the continental ones, and with a lack of English-language guidebooks on the market, few people venture abroad to try it. Those that do will often give it a go on 'rest days', in areas celebrated more for climbing or caving than canyoning, while others visit the more publicised canyons of southern Europe. The canyons in these sunnier climes are better known for beauty than for sport, and their ease ensures that many are overrun with private and professional groups alike.

It is therefore hardly surprising that the smattering of British or Irish people who have tried canyoning have a fairly neutral view of it. The aim of this guide is to shake you out of that neutrality. If you get half as much enjoyment out of these canyons as I did, then it will have fulfilled its role.

Simon Flower, October 2012

Deep pools in Mondelli 2 mean that much can be jumped or tobogganed

The delicate 50m pitch in Osogna Inferiore (Route 35 in the Ticino region)

INTRODUCTION

No room for error – a technical 100m pitch in Sponde (Route 18 in the Ticino region)

Frequently hidden among a backdrop of lofty mountain peaks, the canyons of the Alps are wild and forbidding natural reserves, where rivers, waterfalls and clear-green pools nestle between towering walls of rock and vegetation. They are the awesome product of tremendous erosive forces, scored deeply into rock over millennia by the movement and melting of glaciers that have long since disappeared.

Unlike the mountains around them, with their bold, universal appeal, the canyons attract a more select crowd, prepared to tackle a unique variety of hazards and challenges. Certainly, mountaineering ability will be called upon, but the fast-flowing alpine streams demand additional skills more familiar to white-water enthusiasts. At times the current can be an intimidating barrier to descent. Very often abseils are under the full flow of water or into plunge-pools seething with waves and undercurrents. Many waterfalls must be (or at least should be) jumped or tobogganed. Some control has to be abandoned to the river – a concept not everybody will be comfortable with. This makes canyoning in the Alps a serious mountain sport, but one punctuated by moments of child-like thrills.

In this book you will find some of the best descents that the Alps (and the sport) have to offer. Many are long, technical and aquatic in nature, geared towards physically fit parties unfazed by white water, rope work and hard labour. While previous canyoning experience isn't necessary, a background in other mountain sports (such as mountaineering, caving or climbing) is. A number of canyons are suited to people who have never canyoned before, provided they are in the company of more experienced team mates. **It is fundamental that you develop your understanding of canyoning hazards and safety and its special descent techniques with experienced canyoners.**

The canyons are grouped into five Italian-speaking areas across northern Italy and Switzerland, outlined below. Sitting at their peripheries are the best canyons of Slovenia, Austria and the Valais Alps, which have been included as a bonus. Most are within easy reach of a single base (usually under an hour's drive), making each

CANYONING IN THE ALPS

The 45m pitch of Lodrino Inferiore (Route 33 in the Ticino region)

INTRODUCTION

area a perfect destination for a week or fortnight's canyoning holiday. The book also contains practical information needed for organising your stay, including details of walking, climbing and via ferrata possibilities in each area (this is the Alps, after all). Finally, as this sport remains so little known in the UK, some advice regarding the precautions, equipment and techniques specific to the sport is also given.

Val d'Ossola

An area of wild alpine rivers carved into the gneiss and granite peaks west of Lake Maggiore, this region spans from the rugged terrain of Val Grande National Park to the towering giants along the Swiss border. Two canyons in the Swiss Valais region are also included.

Ticino

Switzerland's sunniest canton is a canyoner's paradise, famous for its lofty, theme-park-like canyons. The canyoning is only a stone's throw east from Val d'Ossola, in two broad valleys snaking north from Lake Maggiore. With the canyons so closely

huddled together, Ticino probably has the greatest concentration of superb descents anywhere in Europe.

Lake Como

The area around Lake Como offers a mishmash of different mountain ranges and canyoning styles. It encompasses the mighty Bernina and Lepontine Alps on the Swiss border, along with the Orobie Alps and limestone pre-Alps further south. Their differing geology affords the canyons very different characters, ranging from beautiful gneiss playgrounds and sunlit granite cascades to cave-like limestone and serpentinite tombs almost totally devoid of light.

The Belluno and Friuli Dolomites

These wild mountains fall largely within the national and regional parks around Belluno, on the quiet south-eastern edge of an otherwise busy mountain range. The unique, rugged Dolomite terrain is reproduced in the canyons here, which are frequently long, remote and technical in nature.

Carnia and the Julian Alps

The little-visited limestone mountains of northeast Italy offer an excellent introduction to alpine canyoning. The canyons are scattered throughout the Carnic Alps, the Julian Alps and the pre-Alps to the south, with a handful over the borders with Austria and Slovenia. Aside from one or two notable exceptions, their canyons remain within the reach of most cavers and climbers.

High water levels in Grigno (Route 54) meant that it was several years before the first successful full descent was made

CANYONING – A BRIEF HISTORY

The beginnings

Canyoning in its modern guise is a relatively recent sport, but its origins can be traced back a century or more to the exploits of a handful of French cavers and explorers. Armand Janet is usually credited with the first technical descent. In 1893 he made a partial descent of the Gorges d'Artuby, a tributary of the Verdon, armed with only a rope and a few planks of wood. In 1905 an expedition led by Édouard Alfred Martel, a man widely regarded as the father of modern speleology (caving), set off in boats to explore the Verdon Gorge itself. At over 20km long and up

15

CANYONING IN THE ALPS

to 700m deep, it was a serious prospect, with few possibilities for escape or retreat. Janet, who was on his team, had already made an attempt on the gorge nine years earlier but had been pushed back by the Verdon's considerable current, which was then many times what it is today. The current caused problems for Martel's team too:

> So formidable was this passage that, in fact, we can barely remember anything at all, too preoccupied with paddling the boats clear of rocks. The boulders create three crevasses of furious water, passed quickly and without injury. The boats are all but thrown ashore, where our assistants have just arrived, stunned by our audacity...and our luck. One boat is broken up somewhat.
>
> We are at the bottom of a veritable well; our outstretched arms can almost touch the walls, which loom 400m overhead, shielding us from the sky. Up above the sun is shining; down here, in this aquatic dungeon, it is nearly night; an awesome, unimaginable spectacle.
>
> ...More than once the ropes are required to avoid slipping into a water hole, where we would certainly be crushed. At least the splendour of the canyon is unrivalled. But the more it widens, the more the boulders block our way. We must clamber out, boats on our back, to gain a sort of 'track' 100m above the river. The going is terrible, virtually a virgin forest, but it seems excellent in comparison to the rocks below.

Several of the men gave up on the third day, tired and demoralised. The remainder of the team, which included Martel and Janet, arrived exhausted at the 'Pas de Galetas' on the fourth day, successfully completing the first descent of the gorge. Only the semi-subterranean passage of the Imbut remained unexplored. Here, for 150m, the raging Verdon waters burrow through the base of the limestone cliffs rather than take a surface route. The passage was dismissed by Martel as too risky a venture; he opted instead to carry boats and equipment along the dry river bed. It was another 23 years before Robert de Joly, Martel's friend and disciple, returned to investigate.

Wearing a flotation jacket and lead weights around his ankles to keep him upright, he took to the water:

> I entered the water and was carried along swiftly. Before long I was in a calm, level passage, surrounded and boxed in on all sides by the mountain. The roof was at least 36 feet high, and the channel width varied from two to five yards.
>
> All of a sudden a kind of wall came into view. Did this mean there was no way out, that the water exited through a siphon? I was seized by fear. It was absolutely impossible to fight back against the current. Should I have heeded the wise, reasonable counsel of my companions instead of throwing myself into such a risky adventure?

Very probably, but he was hauled to safety, lead weights and all, by his team mates as he eventually emerged on the far side.

De Joly clad ready for the Imbut (photo from Memoirs of a Speleologist, Robert de Joly (1975))

INTRODUCTION

A ground-breaking descent

In 1906 Martel made the first descent of the Daluis Gorge before making an aborted attempt on Clue d'Aiglun, an imposing and aquatic cleft in the Maritime Alps. In the following year he turned his attention to the Basque Pyrenees, focusing much of his efforts on the imposing Canyon d'Olhadubie. Even by modern standards the Olhadubie retains an air of seriousness, and despite a series of expeditions probing its upper and lower reaches nearly a mile remained unexplored by the time Martel departed from the scene in 1909. Interest in the gorge dwindled until nearly two decades later, when the rising popularity of caving and climbing produced a string of new challengers.

In 1933 the canyon finally fell to Henri Dubosc and a group of active young mountaineers from Pau – Roger Ollivier, Francois Cazalet and Roger Mailly, men who later became household names in Pyrenean climbing history. Ditching hobnailed boots in favour of flimsy fabric plimsolls and clad in just swimwear and a couple of woollen sweaters, they made a full descent of the gorge in just over 13 hours. They opted for a lightweight, alpine-style approach, employing ropes and a pull-through technique rather than the heavy rope ladders of old. It was a landmark in canyon exploration, and was described by Ollivier in his report:

> Our equipment, as picturesque as it is rudimentary, throws a note of gaiety into the expedition. No hobnailed boots this time, not even stockings or socks, but simple esparadilles [Pyrenean plimsolls], swim wear, two big pullovers and a pair of old trousers to reduce rope friction. Dubosc sports a pair of amusing red flannel culottes and a curious white hat.
>
> A sling is placed around an enormous block, a 50m rope uncoiled and Dubosc, protected by a life-line, confronts the first cataract. The water pummels his head violently, his pretty white hat carried away. Our companion finally reaches a sort of cauldron, seething with worrying eddies. But he's landed in water only shoulder-deep. We hurl the sacks unceremoniously down the pitch. The first, which lands with a resounding 'plouf', is greeted with a great burst of laughter from Dubosc, who wades off with fervour. I descend last, pull the rope through and rejoin my companions. All retreat is now cut off from above.

The golden years of exploration

Over the next couple of decades exploration quietly continued, but was severely impaired by a lack of suitable equipment and clothing. Although climbing hardware became more sophisticated with each year, protection against the icy waters remained limited until the appearance of neoprene wetsuits in the mid-1960s. With these modern materials the 60s and 70s were a boom-time for canyon exploration, and with vertical caving techniques becoming more widely used caving clubs again led the way. The Sierra de Guara in northern Spain became a hive of activity, culminating in 1981 in the first true canyoning guidebook (*Les Canyons de la Sierra de Guara* by Jean-Paul Pontroué and Michel Ambit). The book helped popularise the sport among the wider public and ensured an explosion of interest throughout France, Spain and then Italy. By the beginning of the 90s, most canyoning areas of France and Spain were represented by topo-guides, along with a handful of areas along the length of Italy.

The appearance of relatively light and affordable masonry drills during the 1990s meant that more ambitious projects became possible in the harder rock types of the high Alps. A new breed of explorer came to the fore, many of them alpinists and mountain guides willing to push the boundaries. During this time the grand classics of Val d'Ossola, Ticino and Lake Como were opened up, although, as in previous decades, the exact details of exploration remain scanty. Lake Como's history is perhaps the best documented, owing to Pascal van Duin's seminal guidebook *Canyoning in Lombardia*. Van Duin himself has been one of the most prolific modern explorers, as a glance through the list of first descents in Appendix F will testify.

The rising popularity of the sport paved the way for professional canyoning outfits, which could cash in on the improved safety margins of sturdier rigging. Even so, a number of companies had questionable standards and poor safety records. In 1999 the sport gained notoriety following the tragic deaths of 18 paying tourists (mainly

CANYONING IN THE ALPS

Val Zemola (Route 66 in the Friuli Dolomites), one of Italy's most famous canyons, was first descended in 1986

Australian) and three guides during a flood-pulse in Saxetenbach Gorge, near Interlaken.

The present day
Canyoning ethos in western Europe has shifted firmly from exploration to sport. Certainly, in France and Spain it seems unlikely that any great surprises lie in wait. Both countries have been thoroughly scoured for canyons and the more notable finds published in guidebooks or websites. Elsewhere, canyon details have taken longer to filter through to the wider canyoning community – northern Italy was virtually *terra incognita* until the first guidebooks emerged at the turn of the 21st century, and central Switzerland appeared on the map only in the last couple of years.

Undoubtedly, there is still more to be found. Of the areas in this guide, Carnia and the Julian Alps hold perhaps the greatest potential, yielding three classic descents during the time this book was written.

Outside Europe, away from the US, Australia and the French and Spanish overseas territories, there is enormous opportunity for making first descents. There are few places on the Earth's surface that remain as little known as canyons. Even in New Zealand, with its thriving outdoor community and majestic, canyon-rich mountain scenery, the sport has only just taken off. Travel to Asia, South America or almost any other mountainous land you can think of and the canyons are there for the taking. Pack your flags and get out there!

GEOLOGY OF THE ALPS (FOR CANYONERS)

A brief history of the Alps
The Alps, like all great mountain ranges, were created by the collision of continents. They began rising some 90 million yeas ago as Italy, inching slowly northwards, collided with the southern edge of mainland Europe. The ocean floor that once divided the two continents gradually disappeared, driven into the Earth's mantle as the gap between them closed. As the land masses collided, their margins buckled, folded and slid over each other to form immense overlapping thrust sheets, or nappes, which pushed northwards as

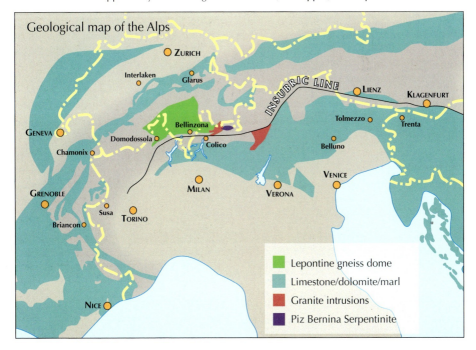

CANYONING IN THE ALPS

Beautifully shaped gneiss in Massaschluct (Route 1 in the Valais Alps)

Italy continued to advance. In this way, great rock masses from the Italian plate were displaced far to the north to create mountains in what are now Switzerland, Austria and France. As the Alps rose, the rocks of the ancient seabed were exhumed, now metamorphosised by the immense heat and pressure of the Earth's interior. Today these hard-wearing metamorphic rocks (the so-called Penninic nappes) form much of the backbone of the Western Alps.

Canyon formation

Although plate tectonics are responsible for the formation of the Alps and the distribution of its rock types, the rugged landscape seen today is largely due to glaciation. Over the last two million years there have been a number of periods of glacial advance and retreat that have done much to remodel the region. The last glacial period ended some 10,000 years ago, when the climate changed so quickly that the glaciers retreated into the mountains over only a few hundred years – a mere blink of an eye in geological terms. Colossal sheets of ice were set in motion across the mountains, scouring deep channels into the rock and forming conduits for billions of tons of melt-water – the canyons we see today.

Limestone environments are susceptible to another, more subtle process – karstification. Limestone is one of the few rocks soluble in rainwater (a weak acid), and it gradually dissolves over time to form a number of characteristic landforms, including caves, dissected plateaus and deep slot canyons.

The regions and their rock types

The canyons of Val d'Ossola, Ticino and the northwestern shores of Lake Como are for the most part formed in gneiss, a highly metamorphic rock of the Penninic nappes. At extremes of temperature and pressure within the Earth's interior, minerals of a similar type within the parent rock (here mainly granite) have migrated and aligned together. This gives the rock a beautiful decorative quality with swirls and bands of different colours, polished smooth by the action of glaciers and flowing water. These canyons are often sporting, with deep green pools and gently sculpted waterfalls ideal for jumps and toboggans.

INTRODUCTION

Impressive limestone scenery in Rio Simon (Route 85 in the Julian Alps)

CANYONING IN THE ALPS

The area around Lake Como is geologically complex, and gneiss is only one of a number of rock types in the area. Valtellina, a broad valley extending east from the northern tip of the lake, is part of a long fault line – a weak point in the Earth's crust – that runs east–west across the Alps. The fault, known as the Insubric Line, marks the boundary between the Italian and European plates. This weakness has allowed liquid magma to ascend from beneath, cooling slowly within the Earth's crust to form coarse-grained rocks such as granite and diorite. These have been exposed in a number of places along the fault, creating some of the youngest mountains in the Alps. Among these is Piz Badile, a granite peak on the Swiss border, where a couple of canyons reside. Although granite is hard it erodes quickly on account of its grainy structure, leaving well-rounded canyons open to sunlight.

Just east of Piz Badile is Piz Bernina, one of the most celebrated mountaineering peaks in the eastern Alps. Its southern slopes are formed of a distinct grouping of rocks that includes basalt, gabbro and serpentinite. These rocky assemblages are common throughout the Alps. Termed 'ophiolites' in the early 19th century (a word derived from the Greek for snake-stone), it would be another 100 years before their significance was understood. They are now believed to be fragments of the ancient ocean crust, scraped off as they dipped beneath the advancing Italian plate. Serpentinite, derived from the deepest layer, is the most significant from a canyoner's perspective. It has a mottled greenish tinge and waxy polished surfaces similar to soapstone (to which it is closely related). Serpentinite canyons are extremely rare. Perhaps the best known is Cormor on the flanks of Piz Bernina, famous for its sculpted cave-like passages, almost totally devoid of light. There is nowhere else in Europe like it.

To the south of the Insubric Line, from Lake Como to Slovenia, lie the Southern Limestone Alps, home to the limestone areas described in this guide. All limestone (and dolomite) in the Alps originated in the ancient seas that once separated Italy and Europe. It is formed from calcium-rich minerals mainly derived from the shells of marine organisms laid down throughout the Mesozoic Era (the 'Age of the Dinosaurs' – around 65–250 million years ago). Owing to the solubility of limestone in rainwater, limestone canyons tend to be narrow, twisting and deeply encased, resembling cave passages open to sunlight. Like their subterranean counterparts, karst features such as stalactites, flowstone and rock arches are common. Distinct bands are often visible on the canyon walls, each representing a different age of limestone formation, although the banding is now rarely horizontal owing to folding and buckling of the Earth's crust. Older layers underlie more recent ones, and a descent through a limestone canyon may take you through several million years of Earth's history.

WEATHER AND WHEN TO GO

Water levels in a canyon are a reflection of weather conditions (chiefly rain, snow and temperature) over the preceding weeks to months. Ideally, it would be possible to plan a holiday when water levels are sensible (or not so sensible, depending on your persuasion) during periods of fine, settled weather. Unfortunately, predicting both water levels and the likelihood of having good weather is difficult, as the weather conditions in any given month differ dramatically from one year to the next. For example, a snowy winter or a wet spring will mean water levels remain elevated in summer, even if the summer is hot and stable. In other years, the spring months will be dry and canyoning perfectly feasible. Recommending when to visit is therefore a little tricky, and the advice given here must be taken with a degree of caution.

In general, the summer months (mid-July to mid-September) are the best time for canyoning in the Italian Alps and Ticino. Days are frequently sunny and periods of prolonged rain unusual. August is the hottest month – often rising to 30°C in the middle of the day – and the cool mountain streams make very welcome retreats. However, this is the peak month for Italian tourism – accommodation is expensive and harder to find, and certain canyons can get busy with groups (although this is much less a problem than in southern France or Spain). Afternoon storms, the canyoner's nemesis, are also a feature of the Alps in the summer months. This is especially true in northern Italy and Ticino, where the warm, moist air of the Mediterranean meets the cool air of the mountains. More than at any other time of year, it is essential to check the weather forecasts

INTRODUCTION

Bouldery going in Massaschluct (Route 1 in the Valais Alps)

(details given in each chapter) and monitor the sky for signs of cloud build-up.

As the summer wears on, water levels usually decrease. Days cool off a little and the crowds go home. Good weather can stretch into October, although tourist facilities start to close down. Without the heat, any rain that falls tends to augment the rivers for much longer, and on the higher slopes it may fall as snow. Although certain canyons may remain feasible into autumn, canyoning in winter conditions is an entirely different sport. Rivers freeze over and narrow passages become choked with snow. Different skills and equipment are needed, such as ice axes, crampons and specialist clothing. It is not within the scope of this guidebook to describe canyon descents at this time of year. Nevertheless, it is a sport gaining in popularity.

Spring is generally too wet for alpine canyoning. Long periods of rain can render all descents impossible, and the canyons draining the higher slopes become swollen with melt-water. Additionally, dangerous pockets of snow can persist in sun-deprived canyons until early summer.

Visiting in early summer is a possibility. June, for example, is often a pleasant time in the Alps. The heat isn't as intense, the mountains are lush green and there are far fewer tourists around. Rainy days may be more frequent, but certain descents remain feasible or even preferable, depending on your level of expertise and thirst for challenge. Ticino in particular enjoys a slightly longer season than the rest on account of its many hydroelectric installations, which act to moderate the flow of water (see the Ticino chapter for details). Be warned, however – the more aquatic canyons will be very dangerous at this time of year.

GETTING THERE

By air

The Val d'Ossola, Lake Como and Ticino areas are all within a 90-minute drive of Milan. The plethora of cheap flights to Milan's airports makes it the first choice destination. These are, from west to east – Malpensa, Linate and Orio al Serio (in Bergamo). Malpensa airport is best for Val d'Ossola and Ticino, but there isn't a great deal in it, and there are also trains from Geneva airport to Domodossola. For the Dolomites, flying to Venice Marco Polo or Treviso are generally better options, as Milan is a three- to four-hour drive away. For Carnia and the Julian Alps, which are further east still, Trieste and Klagenfurt serve as well as the Venice airports. Zurich airport is also convenient for the Ticino area, being about a two-hour drive or train journey away.

CANYONING IN THE ALPS

By train
All areas are well served by rail (see individual chapters for details). Useful websites are www.raileurope.co.uk and the national rail websites of Italy and Switzerland, respectively www.ferroviedellostato.it (or www.trenitalia.com) and www.sbb.ch.

By car
Anyone intending to drive from the UK or northern Europe should bear in mind that the journey time from Calais to Biasca, in the Ticino region, is about nine hours (if you're lucky), and involves nearly 1000km of driving and multiple toll booths. Val d'Ossola, Lake Como and the southern Dolomites are about one, two and four hours further on respectively.

GETTING AROUND
For most areas, a car is essential given that most canyons are accessed by minor mountain roads not served by public transport. It is often better (and frequently necessary) to have two cars for shuttling people between start and finish, where a long walk would otherwise be necessary. Some canyoners opt for a car and bicycle. On busier roads hitch-hiking may be an alternative to two cars, and is generally quite easy in the Alps. The distance of any shuttle-run is given in the route description for each canyon to help you decide at a glance whether one or two cars are needed. Canyoning by public transport is only a possibility in Ticino, which has a frequent and reliable bus service and where canyons are close to main roads but the buses aren't cheap.

Almost all the motorways, or *autostrada*, in Italy are toll roads, and toll booths are reasonably frequent. Cash and credit cards are accepted. There are no toll booths in Switzerland, but all cars driving on motorways (recommended to reduce driving times) are required to have an annual toll sticker, or *vignette*, displayed in the windscreen. These can be purchased at the border for a modest sum and are valid for 14 months, from 1 December to 31 January the following year. See the Swiss Federal Customs Administration website (www.ezv.admin.ch) for prices.

It is also worth noting that Italian sign-posting is frequently inadequate and inconsistent. Having a sat nav can significantly reduce the amount of time driving aimlessly back and forth!

The approximate driving times and distances between the four areas are given below.

	Domodossola (Val d'Ossola)	Biasca (Ticino)	Maggia (Ticino)	Colico (Como)	Belluno (Dolomites)	Tolmezzo (Carnia)
Domodossola (Val d'Ossola)		95km 1h45	55km 1h15	210km 2h30	480km 4h45	550km 5h
Biasca (Ticino)	95km 1h45		60km 1h	159km 2h	476km 4h30	550km 5h
Maggia (Ticino)	55km 1h15	60km 1h		166km 2h30	480km 5h	550km 5h30
Colico (Como)	210km 2h30	159km 2h	166km 2h30		430km 4h30	550km 4h45
Belluno (Dolomites)	480km 4h45	476km 4h30	480km 5h	430km 4h30		200km 2h
Tolmezzo (Carnia)	550km 5h	550km 5h	550km 5h30	550km 4h45	200km 2h	

INTRODUCTION

Walk-in along Valle di Darengo (Route 44 at the north of Lake Como) (photo: Simon Flower)

WAYMARKING, ACCESS ROUTES AND MAPS

Approach walks vary from the very straightforward to the virtually invisible or physically brutal. Some approach walks make use of existing walkers' paths (many of which are numbered in the Italian Alps); others have breathed new life into paths that would otherwise have crumbled away. Splashes of paint are frequently used to make route-finding easier, although the sight of paint should not necessarily reassure you that you're on the right track. One marker that can be trusted though is the distinctive Associazione Italiana Canyoning (AIC) emblem – a blue spot on a white background (Italy only).

Owing to these route-finding difficulties, a necessarily detailed walk-in description is given in this guide for each canyon, along with a sketch map. Be warned that things change. Depending on a canyon's popularity, a walk-in may become more or less obvious over time, or may change altogether if a preferred route is found. Access rights change over time too, so what may be freely accessible now may be out of bounds by the time you arrive. Seek local advice if uncertain.

Access to canyons can be complicated – if in doubt (in Italy) look out for the AIC marker (photo: Simon Flower)

Detailed topographic maps are usually unnecessary, but those wishing to buy them will find details in the 'Practicalities' section near the start of each regional chapter. They will certainly be needed if you wish to do any walking or via ferrata in the area. On the other hand, a good road map is very useful (1:200,000 or better). There are many such maps available, but perhaps the most convenient are the 1:200,000 Touring Club Italiano maps. These cover the whole area of this guidebook in

25

CANYONING IN THE ALPS

just two sheets: 'Lombardia' (which covers Val d'Ossola, Ticino and Lake Como) and 'Veneto-Friuli Venezia Giulia' (which covers the Dolomites, and Carnia and the Julian Alps).

THE RISKS OF CANYONING

Although most trips will pass trouble free, accidents do happen. Understanding the risks can help prevent accidents and prepare for their eventuality.

High water

Drowning remains the number one cause of death when canyoning. Sudden flooding is the main culprit (see 'Sudden flooding', below), and in addition many people underestimate water levels even before committing themselves to a descent. Prolonged periods of rain or a wet spring mean that the canyons will be wetter than normal in the summer, thus increasing their difficulty above the grade quoted in this guidebook. Get an idea of the water levels in the area before attempting more difficult canyons. Keep an eye on the weather a week or two before you arrive, and bear in mind that the flow rate in dam-regulated rivers may change over time (see Route 54 Grigno or Variola Inferiore, in Route 4, for a case in point). Comparing current flow rates in rivers with historical data is a useful trick, but such data is hard to find and will not be easy to access when abroad. For Ticino, hydrological data is available at www.bafu.admin.ch.

The main white-water hazards are turbulent plunge-pools. The high air content in white water renders it very difficult to remain afloat or swim in, while downward currents at the base of waterfalls and at the pools' edges can actively drag a person underwater. Such hazards are better avoided than tackled head on. This can be achieved either by jumping clear of the danger (a solution with obvious risks) or by manipulating the abseil trajectory using deviations or guided abseils (see 'Canyoning rope techniques', below). Strong currents elsewhere may sweep people over waterfalls or dash them against rocks. If carried by the current, lying on your back, feet downstream, will reduce the chance of serious injury. Watch out for siphons, potentially lethal hazards that lurk hidden among submerged boulders. The gaps between the boulders create strong currents which can suck body parts in, trapping people underwater.

An unavoidable soaking in Clusa Inferiore (Route 59 in the Belluno Dolomites)

Sudden flooding

Flooding can be caused by heavy or prolonged rain, snow-melt, or the release of an upstream dam. It is important to assess the risk of each before setting out. If waters rise seek high ground (dry vegetation and trees are a good sign) and wait. Do not be tempted to push on downstream until water levels have returned to normal.

Rainfall

Significant rainfall is brought about by frontal systems and afternoon storms. Fronts may bring prolonged periods of rain to large areas of the Alps, whereas afternoon storms are short-lived and very localised, but frequently severe. The latter are brought about by cumulonimbus clouds, which develop from ordinary cumulus clouds as moist air rises throughout the day, a process accelerated by high temperatures and mountain relief. These storms are more common in northern Italy and Ticino than anywhere else in the Alps, owing to the

INTRODUCTION

Floods can make a huge difference to the condition of a canyoning route (left: before flooding, right: after flooding)

moist, warm Mediterranean air travelling up from the south. Unlike fronts, which are easy to predict, forecasting afternoon storms is difficult. It is therefore vital to get frequent weather updates and to keep an eye out for cumulonimbus development. Weather reports are available in tourist information offices, campsites and local newspapers. Relevant websites are given in each chapter.

Snow and glacial melt

Melting snow and ice can lead to dangerously high water levels as the day heats up. This is mainly a problem of canyoning early or late in the season. Few canyons in this guidebook have significant snow fields present in their catchment areas during the summer months.

Presence of upstream dams

Many canyons in the Alps have hydroelectric constructions somewhere along their length. Surprisingly, given the growing popularity of canyoning as a sport, it is difficult to find definitive information on their purge/opening patterns. Put simply, there are three basic types of construction

- a grill in the stream bed which pipes away water to a nearby reservoir or power plant
- a small dam that traps water first before piping it away
- larger-scale dams, holding back millions of cubic metres of water, which is piped off to the power plant. Water may be piped into the reservoir from a number of sources.

CANYONING IN THE ALPS

When a single river intake closes (due to obstruction, malfunction or maintenance purposes), the water normally diverted away will return to the natural riverbed. Unless the river is large this is unlikely to cause problems for the canyoner. If the whole power plant needs to be shut down, or if rainfall is especially heavy, even the larger reservoirs fill and may be forced to open their overflow gates. A release of such vast amounts of water would be disastrous to unwary canyoners downstream. The smaller dams are also dangerous. They may be 'purged' after rainy periods to flush away sand and other debris that could otherwise harm the system. In short, the flow of a river below a hydroelectric installation may suddenly increase without warning, even in times of good weather.

In Switzerland it is usually possible to ring somebody to determine the risk of the dam opening (although the hydroelectric companies still decline all responsibility). In Italy this sort of service is by no means standard, and a certain degree of risk often has to be taken.

Jumps and toboggans

It would be fair to say that anyone who wasn't prepared to jump or toboggan anything wouldn't be getting the most out of this sport. As well as being great fun, these techniques speed progression and, in certain circumstances, may actually be safer than abseiling (for example, if an abseil deposits you in the worst of the current). That said, the Fédération Français de la Montagne et de l'Escalade (FFME)

Jumping is a useful technique and great fun, but it carries obvious risks (Route 82 in the Carnic pre-Alps)

INTRODUCTION

When toboggans go wrong! The 20m toboggan in Combra (Route 27 in the Ticino region)

reports that half of all rescues arise due to misjudged jumps, with a smaller number attributed to toboggans. Injuries are more likely with jumps over 4m. Abseil to verify pool depth if there is any uncertainty. Note that canyons can change drastically over time – pools silt up or fill with detritus washed down by floods. To reduce the chance of injury, jump with legs together and slightly bent, flexing on entering the water. For toboggans, keep feet together and elbows away from the rock.

Waterfalls and abseils
Use a hand-line to approach exposed pitch-heads, and clip into the anchor while rigging. Tie long hair back to reduce the risk of it being sucked into the descender. Although sharp edges can damage ropes, the majority of abseil problems arise due to high water (see 'Canyoning rope techniques' below).

Slippery rock
Falls resulting from slippery or loose rock account for about a third of all canyoning injuries. Some rock types provide good friction but become slippery when wet, particularly when covered in a layer of algae. Good shoes are essential (see 'Equipment and clothing', below). Be sure to test out their grip when first entering the canyon.

Rockfall
Rockfall is a greater risk in drier canyons, where loose rocks tend to loiter at pitch-heads. Rocks also get thrown in from above and blown in on windy days (when it is better to avoid tightly encased canyons).

Hypothermia and exhaustion
A warm, well-fitting wetsuit is essential (see 'Equipment and clothing', below). The chances of hypothermia are increased if exhausted, so physical fitness, food and fluids are important; it is easy to forget to drink when constantly immersed in water.

Absence or failure of in-situ equipment
The quality and positioning of in situ equipment varies greatly from canyon to canyon and from one pitch to the next. Even good quality rigging may be damaged by floods or rockfall. The quality, state and position of all equipment needs to

CANYONING IN THE ALPS

be scrutinised before deciding whether or not you want to risk your life on it. Where possible avoid single-point anchors. Back up hand-lines with a belay or rig your own. In less frequented canyons, or those that are badly flood prone, be prepared to replace damaged anchors or slings.

Rope loss or damage

Losing a rope is a nightmare situation. At best it is an expensive mistake. At worst it prevents further descent and escape. A rope may get stuck when pulling through, or entangled in flood debris at the foot of a waterfall. Good rope management is key in preventing this (see 'Canyoning rope techniques', below). Ensure that all tackle-sacs have a flotation device (an empty bottle or waterproof drum) and take extra care in high water not to allow them to get swept downstream (do not throw them down pitches unattended!). Ropes also get damaged, for example when abseiling over sharp edges (a rope severs with surprising ease when under load). There are several methods to avoid this (also discussed below). Best practice is to carry a spare rope, so the canyon can be completed safely if a rope is lost.

CANYONING ROPE TECHNIQUES

It is assumed that the reader is able to abseil proficiently and has a thorough practical knowledge of basic rope techniques. Therefore they are not described in detail here. Alpine canyons are not the places to learn these skills.

Below is a basic summary of the techniques appropriate to canyoning. Further information can be found in the resources listed in Appendix B.

Single-rope technique

When abseiling, climbers typically use the whole rope, doubled over and thrown down the pitch (the double-rope technique). This technique is both time-consuming (as all the rope has to be paid out, then packed away again) and potentially dangerous in wet canyons, where

- turbulent plunge-pools will cause any excess rope to tangle, making the rope difficult to release from a descender
- the excess rope may get trapped around submerged branches and boulders
- the two strands of rope may twist around each other into a friction knot, making the rope difficult to pull down.

Using single-rope technique in Pontirone Inferiore (Route 29 in the Ticino region)

INTRODUCTION

Using a guide-line to steer clear of the current during a 'wet run' in Cormor (Route 49 in the Lake Como region)

Although double-rope technique has its place, single-rope technique is infinitely more suited to canyoning. The main advantage is that the rope length can be 'set' to the length of the pitch. Where pitch length is uncertain, the first person can be put on belay using one of the releasable rigs described below. They can then be lowered if the rope turns out to be too short (communicating this need may have to be through pre-agreed shouts, whistle blasts or hand gestures). The remainder of the rope, still in the bag, can either be brought down by the next person, zip-lined down the abseil rope or (if sensible to do so) thrown down to waiting team mates. The two ends of the rope can now be kept well clear of each other, ensuring a trouble-free pull-through.

Another advantage of single-rope technique is that it is easier to steer the course of an otherwise aquatic abseil by means of deviations (where the abseil rope is clipped into intermediate anchors) and guided abseils (a taut line secured between the top and base of a pitch, into which abseiling canyoners can clip their cow's tails).

The main disadvantage of single-rope technique is the risk of rope damage. Single ropes stretch and bounce more than double ropes, increasing the sawing action over sharp edges. If sharp edges are anticipated, the options are to:
- run the rope over a tackle-sac secured to the rigging above (a method which is effective only if the rub-point is near the pitch-head)
- pay out/take in rope between abseils to vary the position of the rub-point
- use double-rope technique.

Releasable rigs

Although they are more time-consuming to rig, releasable systems should be used when possible in technical canyons. If a team mate gets strung up mid-rope (for example if hair, a glove or wetsuit gets caught in the descender), they can be quickly lowered out of danger.

Methods include

- an indirect belay (very quick and simple)
- a direct belay (an Italian hitch is often used)
- the figure-of-8 block.

The figure-of-8 block works well (see photos 1 to 6 for how to tie one) and is the technique most commonly used on the continent. With the other two methods, the last person down needs to convert the belay to a non-releasable system.

The figure-of-8 block

1. Thread the figure-of-8.
2. Cross the rope (important: not doing so may result in the device being difficult to undo when loaded).
3. Pass a bight of rope up through the large ring
4. Pull the loop down and 5. pass it over the small ring.
6. Pull everything tight. To prevent people abseiling on the wrong end, a quick-draw could be clipped between the small ring of the figure-of-8 and the anchor (do not use an ordinary karabiner for this purpose – it will be difficult to undo under load).

INTRODUCTION

A clove hitch and locking karabiner (left) and a stopper-knot crabbed to the live rope (right)

Non-releasable rigs
- a clove hitch and locking karabiner (see photo) (important: ensure that the knot lies **away** from the gate and that the gate is **locked** – a twist-lock karabiner is recommended here), and
- a stopper-knot crabbed to the live rope (see photo). This may be safer in the absence of a twist-lock karabiner, but the knot can be difficult to undo. Also, the rope can be more difficult to pull through from an oblique angle.

All these systems are fairly bulky and have the potential to jam when pulling through. If this is anticipated the last person down can remove the knot or figure-of-8 device, then either use double-rope technique or have the live rope counter-weighted by team mates waiting below (the 'fireman's belay').

Whichever method is used, the last person to descend should be confident that the rope will pull-through.

A FEW TIPS FOR ROPE MANAGEMENT

- Pack the rope so that you can get easily at both ends in the tackle-sac. This will be useful when tying two ropes together or rigging traverses.
- Flake the rope into the tackle-sac rather than coiling it. A three-person approach will speed things up – one to pull down, one to hold the bag open, one to pack.
- While a number of knots are suitable for joining ropes together, a double overhand knot (see photo) is quick, simple, safe and easy to undo after loading. It is also asymmetrical, reducing the chances of it jamming. Tie two neatly laid overhand knots very close to each other, with a 30cm tail. **Warning** Do not use a figure-of-8 knot in this situation. It rolls back on itself, and those with short tails can completely undo at loads as low as 50kg.
- At intermediate ledges on multi-pitch abseils, thread the pull-down rope through the next anchor before pulling-through. This limits the chances of the rope getting dropped down the pitch.

A double overhand knot – a quick and effective method of attaching two ropes together (photo: Simon Flower)

CANYONING IN THE ALPS

ABSEILING INTO TURBULENT PLUNGE POOLS

If abseiling into turbulent plunge-pools, take the following steps to reduce the risks of entanglement and other problems.
- Do not tie stopper-knots in the end of the rope.
- Do not use prusik loops or shunts to control the rate of descent.
- Consider zip-lining tackle-sacs down the abseil rope, rather than abseiling with them.
- Try to release the rope from your abseil device before entering the water or, if this is not possible, swim away into calmer water first.
- If you anticipate submersion, taking three or four deep breaths beforehand will increase the time you can hold your breath.
- Those standing by at the bottom should have a throw-rope ready to pull people out of danger.

EQUIPMENT AND CLOTHING

Although canyoning requires relatively little equipment, dedicated canyoning equipment is quite difficult to obtain outside the canyoning regions of mainland Europe. In the UK, although climbing shops suffice for many things, caving shops may be a better source for more canyon-specific items such as semi-static ropes, robust wetsuits and tackle-sacs. A list of UK caving shops that may be useful is included in Appendix B. They may also be able to order things if they don't have them in store.

There is a greater selection of canyoning equipment available on the continent. A good place to start is www.expe.fr or www.resurgence.fr, both online shops in France. Canyoning equipment is also available from smaller shops locally. Details of known suppliers are given in each chapter.

Personal kit

Clothing
For the canyon Rivers in the Alps are cold. Some are glacial melt-water. A full wetsuit is therefore required, as close fitting as possible without being too restrictive of movement. Thickness is important, but a snug 3mm wetsuit with no air pockets is infinitely better than a baggy 5mm one. Surfing wetsuits are fine and readily available, but vulnerable to wear and tear. A tough pair of shorts (or a specialised harness – see below) will prolong the life of the seat, while neoprene pads (available from caving or skateboarding shops) are useful for knees and elbows. Caving oversuits can give excellent protection (and additional warmth), but at the expense of freedom of movement.

Specialist wetsuits are available that have zip-up fronts, fitted hoods and reinforced areas, but these are hard to find in the UK (although you may find something similar in caving shops). Neoprene socks are advised – and the thicker the better. Gloves and neoprene hoods are by no means vital, and the decision to use them will depend on personal preference. Hoods dramatically reduce hearing.

For the approach walk In general, the less worn the better; you will only end up having to carry it down the canyon. Shorts worn for the walk-in can be used to protect the seat of the wetsuit in the canyon.

Footwear
Footwear needs to be light, well made and well draining. Trainers are fine but offer little ankle support, while heavy walking boots provide little grip on account of their inflexibility. Rubber wellingtons are tough, cheap and provide fantastic grip, but don't drain at all and impede swimming. Specialist canyoning shoes (such as those by Five-Ten, Adidas or Etche) are available in the UK, but most shops normally need to order them in specially.

Harness
Any caving or climbing harness is suitable. Caving harnesses are more efficient if you need to prusik and are more durable. A few specialised canyoning harnesses are available in the UK, but again may need to be ordered in. These have a built-in seat protector to help prolong the life of the seat of the wetsuit. Seat protectors compatible with caving

INTRODUCTION

harnesses may also be available to buy separately. Check harnesses routinely for signs of wear and tear.

Descender

A number of types are available, but none is perfect (see 'Choosing your descender', below). Whichever device you choose, know how to lock it off and add friction mid-descent.

Helmet

Head injuries may result from slipping on wet rock, rockfall and from being tossed about by the river's current. Always wear a helmet in alpine canyons.

Flotation device

A flotation device, such as those used for whitewater kayaking, can provide peace of mind in very wet canyons, although they impede swimming performance.

Self-rescue and rigging equipment

How much of this is carried as personal kit and how much is shared between the group as a whole depends on personal preference. Everybody should have some means of ascending the rope, whether prusik loops, lightweight jumaring devices, or full-size jumars used by cavers. A figure-of-8 can be useful for rigging releasable belays (see 'Canyoning rope techniques', above) and will double as a spare descender in case one is lost.

Knife

Use this for cutting rope or freeing companions should they get trapped under the flow of water. Folding knives are available that clip safely to a karabiner, such as that made by Petzl.

Cow's tails (or lanyards)

These are useful for clipping into the anchors at the top of pitches or traverse lines. A 3m length of

Descending into Giumaglio's more vertical second half (Route 19 in the Ticino region)

9 or 10mm dynamic rope is sufficient to tie two long cow's tails. A short cow's tail is also useful – a quick-draw or similar is recommended.

Whistle
A loud whistle may be useful for communicating over the din of a large waterfall, but it is very annoying for everybody else in the canyon. Use sparingly!

Group kit

Rope
The choice of rope for canyoning is a tricky one. All caving and climbing ropes are safe, but certain types are better suited to canyoning. There are numerous points to consider (see 'Choosing ropes', below).

Security rope
This is an optional throw-rope, useful in high water conditions for assisting team mates out of whitewater hazards. Have it ready to hand rather than stuffed at the bottom of a tackle-sac.

Tackle-sac with flotation
A sturdy PVC tackle-sac with many drainage holes (or mesh sides) is essential. In general, standard caving tackle-sacs are not suitable. Without drainage holes bags will be excessively heavy and straps will break under the strain. Tackle-sacs should be big enough to accommodate rope and a flotation device, such as an empty bottle or waterproof drum, which should be secured to the bag by some means.

Waterproof drums and dry bags
These are needed to provide flotation to the tackle-sac and to store food, first aid kit (see below), dry clothes, headlamp and so forth. A separate key carrier (for car keys, mobile phone, money, etc) is useful just in case the drum leaks. Dry bags should not be relied upon for flotation – they usually deflate.

Emergency rigging equipment
Carry a length of cord for making anchors. A 'lightweight' bolting kit, such as those used for expedition caving, is useful for less popular or flood-prone canyons (most alpine canyons!).

Diving mask or goggles
These can be useful for assessing pool depth and searching for sunken equipment.

Camera
A waterproof digital camera is useful for recording guidebook information, so that the book need not be damaged by taking it canyoning. However, they don't always take the best photos (see 'Cameras and photography', below).

First-aid kit (and mobile phone)
A first-aid kit should include pain-relief medication, gaffer tape and a survival bag as a minimum. A small splint such as a SAM splint is highly recommended. If going to north-east Italy, take fine-tipped tweezers or a specialist tick-removing tool (see the introduction to 'The Belluno and Friuli Dolomites' for details). Mobile phones may work in some canyons.

Choosing ropes
There are a number of points to consider.

Number and length
The route summary table (Appendix A) will help in choosing the length of rope needed.

Note that with repeated wet–dry cycles a rope can shrink by ten per cent of its original length, sometimes more. It is advisable to soak and dry the rope a few times, then measure it again before using it. Bear in mind that pitch lengths quoted in this guide assume a pre-shrunk rope. Best practice is to carry a spare rope, so that the canyon can be completed safely if a rope is lost.

Dynamic versus static/semi-static
Semi-static ropes are most suited to canyoning, offering far greater control when abseiling and prusiking. They are dangerous for lead-climbing, but if this need arises (for example, if a rope gets stuck) tying three or more knots next to the harness will increase the dynamic nature of the rope a little.

Colour
Ropes of differing colours would be an advantage to aid with untwisting them before pulling through.

INTRODUCTION

The final encased section in Fogarè Inferiore (Route 62 in the Belluno Dolomites)

Diameter
The diameter affects the weight and durability of the rope. Thick ropes (>10mm) have a longer life span, but are heavy when wet and take up more space in bags. On the other hand, the bounce on thin ropes is greater, thus increasing the sawing action over sharp edges – beware!

Flotability
A few manufacturers produce special canyoning ropes that float, with obvious advantages. However, they are made of polypropylene rather than polyamide, which takes less punishment before breaking. Polypropylene melts at about 160°C and must therefore be used wet.

Choosing your descender
For the lack of a perfect device, the figure-of-8 is most often used by our European neighbours. It is cheap, lightweight, provides a smooth abseil and can be used with single or double ropes. For canyoning a figure-of-8 is better threaded differently to the usual method (see photo). This alternative method enables the device to be kept on the karabiner at all times and therefore reduces the very real risk of it being dropped while loading or unloading ropes.

The figure-of-8: extra braking

The figure-of-8: canyoning set-up

The Petzl Pirana (see photo), designed especially for canyoning, eliminates this risk altogether. It also prevents cross-loading an open screw-gate, a potentially fatal side effect of normal figure-of-8 usage. The rope runs quicker in the canyoning set-up, although there are several methods for increasing friction, such as putting in an extra twist or running a loop back through a karabiner clipped to the harness.

The most significant drawback of figure-of-8 use is that it twists the rope. At the least this can cause problems with rope retrieval, particularly if double-rope technique is used. On longer abseils it can cause a great nest of rope to bunch up beneath the device, making further descent impossible if not noticed in time.

Common alternatives to a figure-of-8 are a rack, a bobbin device and a standard belay device. None of these cause rope twisting, but all have their own drawbacks.

Racks
A rack is heavy and pendulous, time-consuming to rig and very difficult to release in turbulent water.

INTRODUCTION

Double ropes can be used, but may jam if previously twisted by figure-of-8 use. **Racks are not recommended for aquatic canyons.**

Bobbin devices
Bobbin devices give a horrible jerky descent in inexperienced hands (bounce = sawing action) and can't be used with double ropes. Bobbin devices with an automatic brake (such as the Petzl Stop) provide the most control over any device, but require two hands to operate – not always easy in high water.

Belay devices
Standard belay devices are cheap, lightweight and can be used with double ropes, but controlling speed is difficult and they are easily lost when unloading them in turbulent pools. **Belay devices are not recommended for canyoning at all.**

In addition to these is the Kong Hydrobot, another specialist canyoning descender, currently unavailable in UK high streets. It is essentially a single-barred rack – much less cumbersome than a standard rack and certainly much easier to rig and release. A central bar keeps double ropes separate, reducing the chances of jamming if twisted. However, it is dangerously slick when used with new or small-diameter single ropes, and applying extra friction or stopping mid-descent is not at all easy or reliable. **Use the Hydrobot with caution.**

The Petzl Stop, Kong Hydrobot and Petzl Pirana (photo: Simon Flower)

CANYON SAFETY – PRECAUTIONS AND PRE-TRIP PREPARATIONS

To help prevent accidents, and prepare for their eventuality, consider the following points.

Before leaving home
- Take out rescue insurance and know how to summon a rescue if needed.
- Learn some first aid, ideally with a wilderness slant – rescue can be a long way off.
- Get a European Health Insurance Card.
- Soak, dry, then remeasure your rope – it could shrink by 10 per cent of its original length.
- Familiarise yourself with canyoning risks and techniques, and have the correct equipment.
- Keep an eye on the weather a couple of weeks prior to your trip.

Before going canyoning
- Familiarise yourself with the route, making a note of specific hazards and escape points. Take a photo of the route in the guidebook, if taking a digital camera into the canyon.
- Know where the nearest hospital is.
- Leave a call-out, and make sure the person with your call-out knows what to do if you are overdue.
- Know your team well and limit party size on long or technical trips. Consider hiring a guide if uncertain.
- Assess water levels in the canyon.
- Determine flood risk (check the weather forecast, assess for snow-melt and, if possible, phone any upstream dams).
- Check equipment for signs of wear and tear, especially harnesses and ropes.

A phone call can save lives (photo: Simon Flower)

CANYONING IN THE ALPS

Capturing moving targets in poor light is one of the major challenges of canyon photography (Route 33, Ticino)

INTRODUCTION

CAMERAS AND PHOTOGRAPHY

Canyoning presents unique challenges for the photographer, and no camera is ideally suited to the task. While waterproof compact cameras are perfectly adequate for sunny scenes (and are great for getting close to the action), they fall short in low light conditions. Digital SLRs (DSLRs) are capable of far superior photos and perform much better in low light, but are expensive and bulky (especially with the sturdy waterproof box required). The newer mirrorless interchangeable-lens cameras are lighter than DSLRs, but lack some of their functionality. (The photographs in this book by Andrew Atkinson were taken with a Pentax K100D digital SLR with an SMC Pentax-DA 14mm f2.8 lens.)

The problem with low light

In low light, a camera set to auto may do one or more of the following.
- **Increase the aperture** This reduces the depth of field, which could result in unwanted blur or 'bokeh' (more likely with telephoto lenses).
- **Decrease the shutter speed** This could result in blurred subjects or scenes.
- **Increase the ISO** This makes the sensor more sensitive to light, but images tend to be grainier and less detailed. The large sensors in DSLRs cope far better with high ISOs than the tiny sensors of compact cameras. At ISO 800 (frequently required when canyoning), shots taken with a compact camera often look terrible.
- **Fire the flash**. In-built flashes are not usually powerful enough and often create a snowstorm scene as their light reflects off airborne water droplets. Better to turn the flash off.

Tips to improve photos in low light

- Take control over aperture, ISO or shutter speed. This is usually easy with DSLRs, impossible with compacts and long-winded (via fiddly on-screen menus) with mirrorless interchangeable-lens cameras.
- Buy a camera with good low-light/high-ISO performance, a good image stabiliser and a 'fast' lens (ie one with a low f number). Telephoto lenses are best for close-up action, but wide-angle lenses (ideally 28mm equivalent or less) are far more versatile, generally 'faster', and retain a good depth of field at wider apertures.
- Shoot in RAW (rarely possible with compact cameras). Difficult lighting means photos are rarely perfect straight out of the camera. RAW

Some welcome sunshine towards the end of Osogna Intermedio (Route 35, Ticino) (photo: Simon Flower)

CANYONING IN THE ALPS

files can be adjusted later. If your camera lacks RAW, avoid combining a dark canyon interior and bright skies in the same shot.
- Deliberately underexposing by 0.5–1.5 stops helps to keep ISOs down and shutter speeds up. Bright areas are less likely to be blown out, while darker areas can usually be recovered later (if shot in RAW).

Carrying and protecting the camera

Waterproof cameras can be attached (via the wrist-strap) to the chin-strap of a helmet, then tucked down the front of a wetsuit. As well as being secure and quick to hand, the neoprene will protect the seals from excessive water pressure (waterfalls and jumps can cause unprotected cameras to leak).

DSLRs obviously need more sturdy protection. The most convenient is a Peli Case or similar. Plastic sandwich bags are a cheap and effective way of keeping the spray off the camera while in use, and travel towels are a good way to dry hands and lenses. Always use a clear filter to protect the lens (look out for ones with a waterproof coating – others deteriorate quickly).

MOUNTAIN RESCUE, LOCAL HEALTHCARE AND INSURANCE

All the countries in this guide provide an excellent mountain rescue service, but in most of continental Europe mountain rescue is not free. If a rescue is called, you will be charged, usually a considerable sum. Therefore, it is important to be adequately insured. Suitable insurance can be obtained through (for example) the British Mountaineering Council or the UK branch of the Austrian Alpine Club. Other insurers may also cover canyoning, but it would be well worth a detailed check of the terms and conditions as the sport is not well known in the UK.

Canyoning injuries are reasonably commonplace, and (with a lack of mobile phone reception in canyons) rescue is often a long way off. First-aid knowledge (and a first-aid kit) is therefore invaluable. There are many excellent courses available that have a specific slant on wilderness medicine. It is important for teams to be adequately equipped and resourceful, and to have sufficient skills to deal

> **Emergencies**
>
> **If in doubt dial the International Rescue Number: 112**
>
> **Switzerland**
> Police 117
> Fire 118
> Ambulance 144
> Air Rescue. . . . . . . 1414 (Swiss SIM cards)
> . . . . . . +41 333 333 333 (other SIM cards)
>
> **Italy**
> Carabinieri 112
> (calls to this number can be directed to other emergency services, in line with other European countries)
> State police 113
> Fire 115
> Ambulance and mountain rescue
> 118
>
> **Austria**
> Police 133
> Fire 122
> Ambulance 144
> Mountain rescue 140
>
> **Slovenia**
> Police 113
> All other emergencies,
> including mountain rescue 112

with lesser emergencies themselves. Mountain rescue should be considered only as a last resort for major emergencies.

All areas described in this guide are well served by hospitals with emergency departments (detailed in their respective chapters). Italy, Switzerland, Austria and Slovenia offer excellent standards of healthcare.

UK residents should apply for a European Health Insurance Card (EHIC), which gives the holder a reciprocal right to healthcare when visiting countries of the European Economic Area and Switzerland. However, this does not mean that health care abroad is free. The expected fees are detailed in the table below (travel insurance can help offset some of these costs). This information is subject to change, and updates can be found at www.travelinsuranceguide.org.uk.

INTRODUCTION

Helicopter rescue

Before phoning, think whether helicopter rescue is feasible.
- Is it possible to land or will a winch be needed?
- Are there obstacles near the accident site (such as cables)?

When a helicopter approaches:
- signal whether rescue is required, and
- do not approach the helicopter until the rotor has come to a standstill.

Help required
Raise both arms above head to form a 'Y'

Help not required
Raise one arm above head and extend the other downward, to form the diagonal of an 'N'

EXPECTED COSTS WITH A EUROPEAN HEALTH INSURANCE CARD

Italy
Prescriptions – free or non-refundable fixed charge (depending on drug)
Doctors – no charge
Hospital – treatment free. Possible drug and ambulance fees (depending on area), which may or may not be refundable.

Switzerland
Prescriptions and doctors – fee charged but can be reclaimed
Hospital – refundable fees plus non-refundable fixed charge (the 'excess') and a non-refundable daily contribution towards bed and board. Also a charge for 50 per cent of the cost of ambulance transport, including air ambulance.

Austria
Prescriptions – non-refundable fixed fee
Doctors – fee charged (may be entitled to a partial refund)
Hospital – non-refundable fee for first 28 days. Refund may be possible in private hospitals.

Slovenia
Prescriptions – non-refundable fees. Charge depends on drug.
Doctors – non-refundable fee
Hospital – free apart from a non-refundable fixed daily fee

CANYON ETIQUETTE

Some of the most highly prized canyons in Europe are out of bounds to canyoners. Many more are at risk of going the same way. Canyons in national parks or other protected areas are particularly susceptible to legislation, but so too are those whose course or access routes pass through private property. The canyoning community lacks the political swing of its mountaineering or speleological counterparts, so once a canyon has been prohibited from use it generally remains so. It is important, therefore, to be responsible and avoid treading on any toes.
- Do not park on private land.
- Choose your changing areas well. Nobody wants a group of rowdy foreigners parading naked around their village.
- Be courteous to locals and other canyon users alike (see 'A note on guided groups', below).
- Restrict party size. While large groups are safer in the event of an accident, they are slower (risking hypothermia or benightment) and antisocial for others groups present in the canyon.
- Pay heed to local bye-laws and do not trespass. Information presented in this guide may change; seek local advice if there is any doubt.

CANYONING IN THE ALPS

Take care not to disturb the wildlife

- Respect the environment. With a climate that differs markedly from the world above, canyons are unique ecosystems, populated by plants and animals seldom found elsewhere. Follow the old adage 'Leave nothing but footprints', and go quietly so as not to disturb the wildlife. Birds, for instance, are easily disturbed by groups of canyoners whooping and hollering their way down waterfalls.

A note on guided groups
Canyoning in the more popular areas of southern Europe generally entails meeting long lines of identically clad adventure tourists, usually waiting around at pitch-heads as others in the group get ceremoniously lowered over on a rope. Thankfully, owing to the length and more technical nature of the canyoning in the Alps, this situation seldom arises here. Guided groups do exist, but are fewer in number and generally smaller in size. Outside the peak holiday season in August you may well meet none at all.

If you do happen across a group, be courteous. Remember that the guides with them may have installed the nice shiny anchors that you're using, and most will let you pass as soon as is safe. It is bad form to loiter behind in order to find out where all the good jumps and toboggans are!

Finally, if a canyon seems too daunting consider hiring a guide. Local tourist information offices (see Appendix D) usually have details.

USING THIS GUIDE

Canyon nomenclature
The naming of canyons is by no means consistent. One canyon may have several aliases, even within the canyoning community. Canyons may be named after the river itself or the valley the river runs in, which are not always the same. They may take the name of a nearby village or a nickname given by locals or canyoners. In this guidebook, the name given is that most commonly used by canyoners, but alternatives are supplied where necessary.

Many canyons are divisible into two or three separate parts. Where each part is a distinct trip in its own right, with a well-defined access route of its own, it is named according to local convention, for example Superiore, Intermedio and Inferiore (upper, middle and lower) or 1, 2, 3.

Divided up in this way, there are 101 canyoning trips described in this guidebook. Ninety of these are worthy of specific mention and are numbered 1 to 90 accordingly. Eleven of these routes have an additional canyon nearby described – one not worth visiting on its own, but worth doing if you're in the area. These additional canyons have 'a' in the route number.

Quality rating
This book contains a select group of canyons, chosen from a multitude of others available in the area. While all are celebrated in one way or another, some are more memorable than others. The five-star quality-rating system used in the guide (shown in the box at the start of each route) takes account of both beauty of the canyon and level of sport it offers.

Although the ratings reflect the opinions of many, they are still only a guide. They are subject to personal taste and depend to a great extent on water levels in the canyon at the time of descent. In general though, five-star canyons are unforgettable experiences, providing continual entertainment (particularly jumps, toboggans and atmospheric abseils) in a setting of immense geological grandeur and scenic beauty. They should not be missed. Those with fewer stars have similar appeal but may lack the edge of five-star canyons; the canyon may be less continuous, less aquatic, less scenic or have fewer pools for jumping.

Difficulty and grading of canyons
The canyons in this guide are graded by difficulty using the system employed by the Fédération Français de la Montagne et de l'Escalade (FFME), the Fédération Francais de Spéléologie (FFS) and

INTRODUCTION

the Associazione Italiana Canyoning (AIC), which has been adopted by guides and guidebook authors throughout Europe. See below for a full breakdown of the grading system.

Although this grading system is useful in describing the most technically challenging aspect of the canyon, it does not give an idea of how physically demanding the route is or how sustained

Grade	Vertical character (v)	Aquatic character (a)
1	Rope not normally needed; no climbs.	Walk in calm water; brief swims.
2	Easy abseils of up to 10m or simple, unexposed climbs.	Swims no longer than 10m in calm water; jumps up to 3m and short toboggans.
3	Simple abseils up to 30m in a weak current into calm water; simple hand-lines; some slippery, unstable or exposed passages; some tricky down-climbs (up to French 3c).	Swims no longer than 30m in calm water; progression in a weak current; simple jumps of 3–5m; longer toboggans on moderate slopes.
4	Abseils in a weak to moderate current, in excess of 30m or with difficult access. The base of the abseil may not be visible from above or the landing may be in turbulent water; sequence of rappels with comfortable relay stations; good technique required to avoid rope getting stuck; use of exposed hand-lines or down-climbs of up to French 4c/A0, exposed and/or needing protection.	Prolonged immersion in water, medium current. Jumps of 5–8m, or shorter jumps with a difficult take-off, trajectory or landing. Roomy sumps less than 1m in depth/length. Long or steep toboggans.
5	Technically difficult abseils in medium–strong current; series of rappels with hanging re-belay stations; rope recovery difficult (eg if swimming); difficult and/or exposed climbs (up to French 5c/A1).	Prolonged immersion in cold water; progression in reasonably fast-flowing water (enough to make swimming quite difficult); water hazards such as siphons and hydraulics likely; simple jumps of 8–10m or more difficult jumps of 5–8m (eg problematic take-off, trajectory or landing); roomy sumps of up to 2m length or depth.
6	Technically very difficult abseils, under very strong current; awkward relay stations, natural anchors, etc; difficult access to pitch-heads (eg a delicate hand-line needed); exposed and difficult climbs up to French 6a/A2; landing into very turbulent or white-water pools.	Progression in fast-flowing water (enough to make swimming difficult); pronounced currents and movements of water (waves, siphons, hydraulics, etc), with danger of submersion or entrapment; simple jumps of 10–14m or jumps of 8–10m with an awkward take-off, trajectory or landing; technical sumps of up to 1m length or depth.
7	Frequent difficult abseils in a very strong current; landings in pools with a powerful current; possibility of having to hold one's breath while abseiling; difficult and exposed climbs in excess of French 6a.	Progression in very strong current, rendering swims and pools very difficult to negotiate; violent movements of water, with a danger of prolonged submersion or entrapment; simple jumps over 14m or jumps over 10m with an awkward take-off, trajectory or landing; sumps more than 3m long or deep; technical sumps over 1m, with a current or poor visibility.

CANYONING IN THE ALPS

Engagement	Time to safe ground	Time to escape	Total time (approach, descent and return)*
I	Immediate	Easy to escape at all times	2hrs
II	15mins	30mins	2–4hrs
III	30mins	1hr	4–8hrs
IV	1hr	2hrs	8hrs–1 day
V	2hrs	4hrs	1–2 days
VI	2hrs+	4hrs+	2 days+

* Note that in this guidebook total time is not included as a criterion for rating engagement; this information is easily discernible from the canyon description.

the difficulties are. The canyons in this guide are therefore also given a basic overall grade (shown in the box at the start of each route), based on the colours used to grade ski-runs. From easiest to hardest, these are green, blue, red and black.

Grading of canyons is not an exact science and the difficulty of any canyon will change depending on the levels of water. Water levels can vary somewhat from year to year, and an 'easy' canyon may well become incredibly dangerous after a storm or prolonged rain. However, the grading gives an idea of what to expect in average conditions.

The **Route Planner** at the back of the book shows the star rating and difficulty rating for each route to help you plan your trip.

Canyon grading system
The grading is calibrated for a party of five people who have no knowledge of the canyon but who have a level of experience and fitness appropriate for it. It is comprised of three parts – vertical character (v), aquatic character (a), and the level of engagement, indicated by a Roman numeral. The letters v and a are followed by a numerical value from 1 (easiest) to 7 (hardest), although the grading is open-ended. Both components may change over time as the quality of rigging (which safeguards climbs as well as aquatic abseils) improves or deteriorates. Engagement is rated from I (frequent escapes) to VI and beyond (few, if any, escapes). The result is a grade in the form v4.a3.IV, meaning the canyon has a vertical rating of 4, an aquatic rating of 3 and an engagement level of IV.

Rope length
With repeated wet–dry cycles a rope can shrink by as much as 10 per cent of its original length, which means that a factory-stamped 50m rope may well turn out to be a few metres short on a 50m pitch. All pitch lengths and rope lengths quoted assume the use of a pre-shrunk rope. It is therefore essential to soak and dry the rope a few times, then remeasure it, before canyoning with it for the first time. The topo should not be relied upon too heavily for individual pitch lengths, given the difficulty of measuring pitches accurately while canyoning.

Descent times
Descent times are only a guide. They are based on a party of four canyoners with a level of experience appropriate for the descent, and assume normal summer conditions.

AIC rigging
The Associazione Italiano Canyoning (AIC) has equipped a number of canyons across Italy. The rigging is generally of a very high standard on double P-hangars and chains in well thought-out positions.

INTRODUCTION

Low water levels makes Chiadola (Route 69 in the Friuli Dolomites) great for beginners

The list of canyons equipped is growing – check the 'Progetto pro canyon' link on the AIC website.

Tick rating
Tick bites are a particular risk in Carnia and the Julian Alps and in the Dolomites. In these chapters the canyons are given a tick rating, dependent on the chance of encountering ticks during approach walks. Walks are graded 1 = small risk to legs only, 2 = bites to legs guaranteed without protection, or 3 = bites everywhere a possibility (ie a proper thrash in the undergrowth!). Risk is greatly reduced by taking simple precautions (see the introduction to 'The Belluno and Friuli Dolomites' for details).

Left or right?
In describing directions on the approach walk or in the canyon, the 'true' (or 'orographic') direction is given if there could otherwise be confusion. For example the 'true' right of a river is the right side of the river when facing in the direction of flow.

TIP
If you are taking a digital camera along, take a photo of the canyon description, topo and access details to refer to if needed, rather than taking this book down the canyon.

KEY FACTS

Time zone GMT +1

Language Italy and Ticino – Italian; Austria and Swiss Valais – German; Slovenia – Slovenian

Currency Euro (€) in Italy, Austria and Slovenia; Swiss Franc (CHF) in Switzerland

Visas Not required for citizens of the EU, US, Canada, Australia or New Zealand if staying less than three months. South Africans require a 'Shengen' Visa, allowing travel across the borderless states of mainland Europe.

International dialling code Italy +39 (for landlines, the zero of the area code must be included in the number dialled; for mobile phones it must be excluded); Switzerland +41; Austria +43; Slovenia +386

Electricity Switzerland has a three-pin plug system, while Italy has two-pin plugs with two different diameters. Take a universal plug to be certain.

CANYONING IN THE ALPS

The spectacular pitch-head at the end of the second encased section of Lodrino Inferiore (Route 33, Ticino)

Sunny, open canyoning typical of Val d'Ossola (Route 5)

Val d'Ossola

CANYONING IN THE ALPS

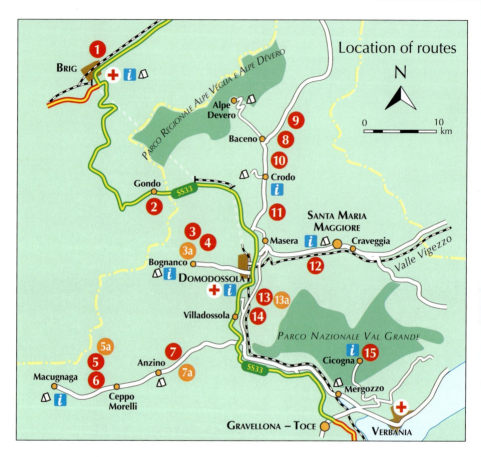

On first arriving in Val d'Ossola, you would be forgiven for feeling a bit apprehensive. The valley itself is a busy trunk route to Switzerland, lined with commerce and light industry. It is fairly nondescript on account of its steep, forested sides, and – worse still – there's not a canyon in sight! But delve into the side-valleys and the region starts to reveal its charm. Higher up, the forested foothills give rise to grassy clearings and mountain vistas. Seldom-trodden footpaths wind between tumbledown hamlets, while to the north and east two protected areas lend rugged beauty and isolation. Yet this is a region overlooked by foreign tourists. Most remain on the periphery, lured south to the sunny shores of Lake Maggiore or west to the mountaineering peaks along the Swiss border.

Canyoning here began in the early 1990s following the work of visiting French speleologists. Given the wealth of sporting routes in the area, it remained surprisingly little known outside Italy until just a few years ago. The region is gaining popularity, though, and justifiably so. The canyons here range from tall and spectacularly eroded gneiss chasms to high mountain waterparks, with abundant water and deep, sunny pools. A good selection of easier

Rasiga Superiore (Route 3) – endless deep pools and sunshine

CANYONING IN THE ALPS

The final pitch in Mondelli 1 (Route 5a)

routes caters for less experienced parties, but – like everywhere else in the Italian Alps – those with more experience will get the most out of the region.

WHERE TO STAY

Domodossola's central position makes it an ideal base. Shops and services are plentiful and the centre itself is surprisingly pleasant. Unfortunately, there is little suitable accommodation nearby. Most campsites are about a 30min drive away in different directions, and self-catering accommodation is surprisingly hard to find. Whether camping or self-catering, make sure that you are happy with the driving times to the canyons you plan to do. Note that the lakeside campsites are likely to be full in peak season. See Appendix C for details of campsites in the area.

The most useful websites for self-catering accommodation are that of the Comunità Montana Valli dell'Ossola (www.cmvo.it/UnDormire.asp), Ossolaland (www.ossolaland.com) and the Lake District tourist information (www.distrettolaghi.it). Local tourist offices (see Appendix D) may also be able to help.

PRACTICALITIES

Shops and services

While most settlements along principal roads have at least basic amenities, the major shops, banks and supermarkets can be found in and around Domodossola. The biggest supermarket is just off the SS33, near the Bognanco turn-off.

Gear shops
There are a few gear shops in the area. Surprisingly, given the popularity of canyoning in the area, none have much in the way of canyoning equipment. The options (at the time of writing) are
- Mosoni Sport on the northern fringes of Domodossola, on the main road that runs through town (Via Giovanni XXIII 74, tel +39 0324 242879, www.mosonisport.it).
- Sport Extreme in Domodossola, en route to Bognanco from the SS33 (Via Nosera, tel +39 0324 248390, www.sportextrem.it)
- Decontecno in Crodo (tel +39 0324 618888, www.decontecno.it)
- Sportway, in Parco Commerciali Laghi, just outside Gravellona-Toce (tel +39 0323 865206, www.sportway.net).

Hospitals
The only hospitals in the area are in Domodossola, Verbania and Brig.

Weather forecast
The weather forecast for the area can be found on the Italian-language ARPA website (www.arpa.piemonte.it), but many people use the Meteo Swiss website (www.meteoswiss.ch) because of the reliability of Swiss weather forecasting. Longer range forecasts can be obtained from 3B Meteo (www.3bmeteo.com) and Il Meteo (www.ilmeteo.it).

Maps
Both IGC and IGM (official Italian mapping), as well as Kompass, produce maps that cover the whole area at 1:50,000. The Swiss Survey 1:50,000 maps cover the area in just two sheets and are more detailed and reliable. Some 1:25,000 maps are available from IGM and Edizioni Multigraphic, but coverage and availability are currently limited.

Practicalities in Switzerland (Routes 1 and 2)
There is a simple campsite, Camping Tropic, just off the road into Brig (between Termen and Ried-Brig). A larger campsite with swimming pool (Camping Geschina) can be found a little closer to Brig. Brig itself is a large town with a range of facilities, including banks, hotels, train station, tourist information and a hospital.

TRAVEL AND TRANSPORT

Rail
The train line from Milan traverses Val d'Ossola on its way to Brig in Switzerland. The slower 'Regionale' trains stop in a number of small towns en route, including Mergozzo and Varzo. A small scenic train connects Domodossola and Locarno via Val Vigezzo, stopping at numerous places along the way, including Santa Maria Maggiore and Craveggia (where there are campsites). Details from www.centovalli.ch. Car hire is not available in the area.

CANYONING IN THE ALPS

The clear green waters of Variola Superiore (Route 4) (photo: Simon Flower)

Driving

Val d'Ossola is linked to Milan by the A26 motorway. North of Gravellona-Toce it becomes the SS33, a dual carriageway free of toll booths, which in turn becomes a single-lane highway at Domodossola. Junctions off the SS33 are not always straightforward. An exit possible in one direction is not always possible in the other. Describing directions is therefore not always easy.

OTHER ACTIVITIES

Although Val d'Ossola lacks the crowd-pulling scenery found elsewhere in the Alps, there is still plenty here to attract walkers. The region is home to two surprisingly little-visited protected parks which have a wild, rugged beauty. Visitors could also venture onto the lofty peaks along the Swiss border. A stroll in the forested hillsides has a charm, the slopes strewn with tumbledown hamlets, or *baite*, usually miles from any road and only sparsely inhabited at best. Some houses are used as summer retreats, while others are falling into disrepair. Many appear to be getting a new lease of life as ambitious building projects of wealthy city dwellers.

PROTECTED AREAS

Parco Regionale Alpe Véglia e Alpe Dévero (www.parcovegliadevero.it)
Parco Nazionale Val Grande (www.parcovalgrande.it)

For those looking for more action, try the Schmugglerweg near Gondo or the pricey Via Ferrata Gabi-Simplon a little further west (see Appendix B). Alternatively, head for the local crags. The main climbing guidebook to the area is *Ossola e Valesia – Sportive e Moderne* (available from the publishers direct at www.versantesud.it or through local gear shops). Some route information is also available online – try www.ossolaclimbing.org, www.planetmountain.com or the 'logbooks' page of www.UKclimbing.com.

Finally, it's worth wandering down to the tourist information office to find out about the frequent festivals that spring up all over the valley throughout the summer months.

VAL D'OSSOLA

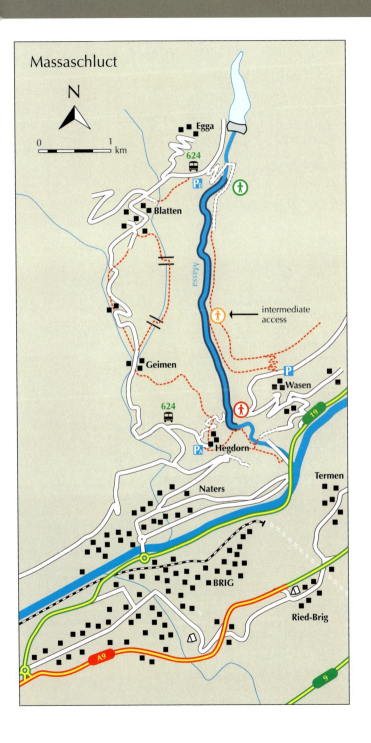

ROUTE 1: MASSASCHLUCT

MASSASCHLUCT ★★★↲  V4.A2.V

Rock	Gneiss
Dimensions	Depth 480m (1290m–810m); length 3500m
Ideal season	Early summer to autumn
Location	Switzerland
Time	Approach 20mins (Parking B); descent 4–6hrs; return 25mins (Parking A)
	Intermediate access 40mins approach and 3–4hrs descent
Shuttle	(Parking A to Parking B) 6.2km (1hr 40mins walk; regular bus service available)
Gear	2x35m ropes; head-torch useful (essential for intermediate access)
Technical notes	Current is splashy and pleasant in summer. Rigging is sturdy but often hard to find among boulders (2011). Two pitches awkward to rig.
Escapes	One, via the intermediate approach path

Massaschluct is the most spectacular and celebrated canyon of the Swiss Valais region. Being a 1½hr drive from Domodossola, it is also the most convenient for those canyoning in Val d'Ossola. However, it sits beneath a dam holding back the melt-waters of Europe's largest glacier. On warm days the reservoir fills, causing the dam to purge. If you can overcome this psychological barrier and the inevitable hassle of travel and dam checking, the sculpted, beautifully banded rock and the spectacular finale shouldn't disappoint. The remainder is rather bouldery and discontinuous, which may taint your overall experience.

 Dangerous dam upstream. Tel +41 (0) 27 921 65 25 to assess risk. The automated response is in Swiss-German and is refreshed at 7.30am daily. Advice from the local guiding outfits is to wait for cooler periods, and make sure that the water levels at the dam are 10m below the flood gates. A visit to the dam prior to descent is therefore essential.

PARKING A

Head into Switzerland, following signs for Sempione (don't forget passports). From Brig, head towards the Furka pass. Take the road signposted to Naters and Blatten. Above Naters, take an easily missed right turn to Hegdorn. Follow the road for 300m to a small car park on the right. There are further spaces where the road ends another 300m further on.

GETTING FROM PARKING A TO B

By car
Go back to the main road and climb to Blatten. Just above the village, take the turning to Egga and Rischinen. Continue straight on at the next junction (ignoring the second turning to Egga and Rischinen) and continue as far as a large car park with public toilets.

Before parking up, go and inspect the water levels at the dam. To do this, continue along the road for 150m to where it splits. Right descends steeply

VAL D'OSSOLA

to the base of the dam – ignore this for now (this is the way to the start of the canyon). Left leads to a vantage point above the dam. Just back from where this road terminates is a viewing platform. From here it is possible to descend to the dam on metal steps. A gauge at the base of the steps can be used to determine water levels in the reservoir.

On foot
A reasonably well-marked path climbs from the car park at the end of the road. Follow signs to Geimen (reached after 40mins), then Blatten (40mins) and finally Riederalp (20mins to Parking B).

Public transport and hitch-hiking
There is a bus stop at the turning to Hegdorn. Buses (service 12.624) go all the way to Parking B. They start at 7am and run every hour until 11pm. See the Postbus website (www.postbus.ch) for more details. With so many cars plying up and down the road, hitch-hiking is unlikely to be too difficult.

APPROACH FROM PARKING B
Follow the road that descends to the base of the dam. Cross the river (parking possible) and go right to where a flood-warning sign marks a faint path to the river bed.

ROUTE 1: MASSASCHLUCT

DESCENT

The descent begins with 30–45mins of boulder hopping in open streamway. The canyon narrows for a few short pitches with deep pools before the boulders begin again. Look out for the tunnel on the left (intermediate access point). There is more nondescript streamway, then things get more interesting again, with a string of three enclosed pitches. The third is awkward to rig, requiring acrobatic manoeuvres over the pitch-head to reach the main anchors. A more open section then follows, where the striped gneiss gives way to white granite. The canyon then closes down for the most spectacular section, the 'Cathedral', where all the water is funnelled through a 1m-wide gap before plunging into an airy 25m-deep abyss. An enormous boulder field is the final obstacle, where route-finding can be difficult. The canyon ends at an old water conduit on the right.

RETURN

Follow the conduit around. Pass through a tunnel (head-torch useful but not essential). For those who have accessed the canyon at the intermediate point, take a left and follow the ridge down to where it is possible to cross the river,

A serene moment mid-descent

VAL D'OSSOLA

The 'Cathedral' (photo: Simon Flower)

then make your way back to the Ried-Mörel road. Otherwise contour along the line of the conduit to a track. This joins the Hegdorn road – turn left for Parking A.

INTERMEDIATE ACCESS

This access shaves a third off the descent time. On the main road to the Furka pass, cross over the Massa stream and take a left turn for Ried-Mörel and Ebnet. Continue up the hill, following signs for Ried-Mörel at all junctions. Park 1.6km past the Wasen junction, in an exposed lay-by on the right. From here take the path marked Oberried. Just around the corner the path splits – go right. A brief climb leads to another split. Take a left, along the line of a water conduit. Follow the water conduit all the way to its end, skirting one small area of private property. A head-torch is needed to negotiate a string of lengthy tunnels.

ROUTE 2: GONDO

GONDO ★★★★ V4.A4.II

Rock	Gneiss
Dimensions	Depth 140m (1020m–880m); length 500m
Ideal season	Summer
Location	Switzerland
Time	Approach 0mins (Parking B); descent 1hr 30mins–2hrs; return 3mins (Parking A)
Shuttle	(Parking A to Parking B) 1.75km (20mins road-walk)
Gear	2x30m ropes (2x35m ropes if doing the slabs at the end)
Technical notes	Rigging sufficient; usually double anchors +/– chains (2011). Second pitch must be jumped or tobogganed (intimidating from above). In summer the current causes problems only on the final encased section, where the river is faced head on.
Escapes	After nearly every obstacle

The lower reaches of the Grosswasser stream offer a short sequence of well-sculpted waterfalls and plunge-pools, perfect for jumps and atmospheric abseiling. The main problem at present is the dam upstream. Since being modified in 2010, it is unclear how much danger it presents. Seek advice locally or through internet forums before making the trip. The canyon is north facing and the water cold, so it's better to arrive after midday.

⚠ **Dam upstream (no information currently available)**

A little reminder of how much water should be running through this canyon

VAL D'OSSOLA

PARKING A

Head up the SS33 into Switzerland. Once in Gondo, take the first left after the bell tower. Descend the hill and park in the large parking area. Don't forget passports if coming from Italy!

GETTING TO PARKING A FROM PARKING B

By car
Climb the hill on hairpins. Where the road levels out and flanks the river, a track heads off left. Park here.

On foot
Follow the road up, cutting the corners where possible on a well-defined path.

APPROACH FROM PARKING B

Just after the track leaves the road, follow a path down to the river. If feeling inclined, you could wander a bit further up the road to a path signposted to Bällega (alternative start). This path leads to the river in a couple of minutes. Aside from the first pool (possible jump), there is nothing else of interest.

ROUTE 2: GONDO

Certain pools lend themselves well to big jumps

DESCENT

The canyon is a sequence of waterfalls and beautiful plunge-pools, quite open in nature. The exception is the final pitch, two pitches after the rock arch. This is an aquatic, twisting tube, whose base cannot be seen from above. It can be rigged dry around to the left (or even avoided altogether), but it is much more fun to rig in the water. This is done in two stages – a 10m pitch to a set of P-hangars around to the right (not visible from above), followed by a 27m pitch to a spray-lashed shelf. From here a slippery and awkward 6m downclimb gains safe ground. The remainder of the canyon is walking and scrambling alongside the river. On reaching the slabs above the last waterfall, a path around left heads back to the main road. The slabs can be abseiled (two 35m pitches), but the single anchor was damaged at the time of descent.

ROUTE 3: RASIGA SUPERIORE

RASIGA SUPERIORE ★★★★⯪  V4–5.A4–5.III–IV

Alternative name	Arabianca Superiore
Rock	Gneiss
Dimensions	Depth 591m (1211m–620m); length 3500m
Ideal season	Summer
Time	Approach 30mins (Parking B); descent 6hrs; return 15mins (Parking A)
Shuttle	(Parking A to Parking B) 8.3km (1hr–1hr 30mins walk)
Gear	2x30m ropes (2x50m ropes needed for Rasiga Inferiore)
Technical notes	Excellent rigging on double P-hangars +/– chains (2010). Current considerable above dam – beware of certain pools. Current less below dam, but can still cause problems in the narrower parts.
Escapes	Many possibilities for improvised escapes above the dam; none below.

Rasiga is a regional classic. It offers a long and sporting outing, divisible into a number of distinct parts. Rasiga Superiore is the longest. Its first half consists of dozens of well-lit pools and small waterfalls that provide endless possibilities for jumps and toboggans. The river here is of a considerable size, but only occasionally troubles on account of its open nature. The canyon changes entirely at a dam part-way down. From here, the river sinks deeper into the rock, which becomes wonderfully sculpted and polished smooth. The obstacles become more continuous and vertical as the valley dips towards the Bognanco valley, and more technical on account of the closer proximity of the stream. The third and final part (Rasiga Inferiore) is less attractive, with a loose 70m pitch on questionable anchors, and cannot be wholly recommended. This part is described separately as Route 3a.

 Dams upstream and mid-descent (low risk)

The 23m pitch

ROUTE 3: RASIGA SUPERIORE

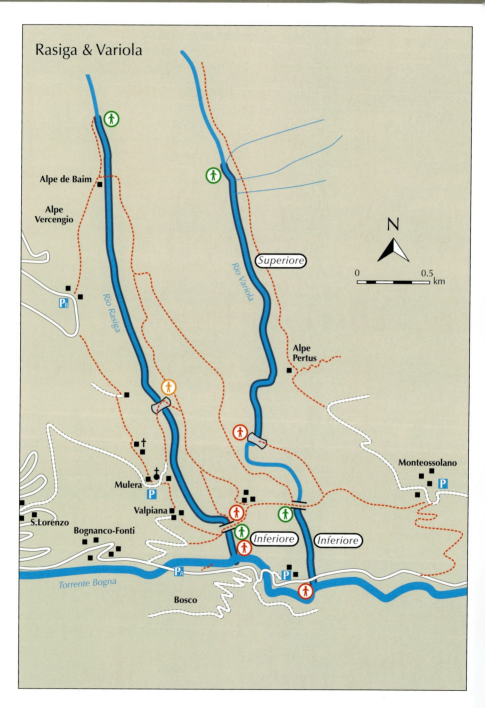

VAL D'OSSOLA

PARKING A

From the SS33, follow signs for Bognanco. Park a little beyond the turning to Poio/Bosco in a wide parking area on the right, just before the road crosses back over the river into Bognanco-Fonti.

Rasiga Superiore

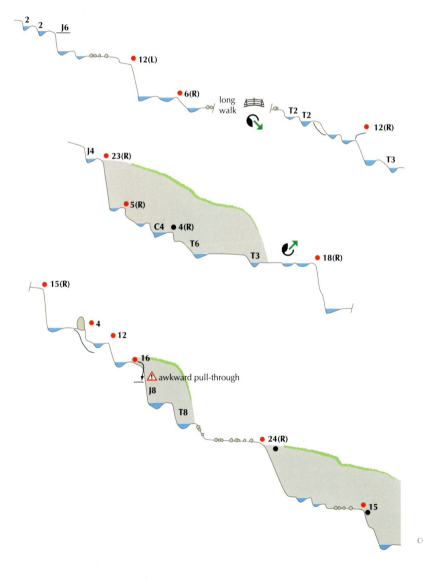

topo continued overleaf

ROUTE 3: RASIGA SUPERIORE

GETTING FROM PARKING A TO B

By car
Follow the road up from Bognanco, ignoring all turn-offs. It eventually levels out at a grassy plateau (Alpe Vercengio). Just after the road swings 90 degrees to the left, park in a narrow lay-by on the left by a sign indicating 'Fiume Arabianca'.

On foot
Cross the road bridge over Torrente Bogna and take the first road on the right. Follow this up to Valpiana, a little mountain village with a spring, passing a marked footpath on the right (this is the path to Rasiga Inferiore, 5mins). Climb through Valpiana following red and orange spots, and follow signs to Mulera. The path continues to climb, via another little hamlet (which also has a spring), emerging by the church in Mulera. Take the path which climbs just by the church, signposted to Vercengio. Follow the path steeply uphill to a hamlet, ignoring any paths branching off. At the hamlet, take a left, past a shrine, to a derelict building just inside the tree-line. Go around this and take a left up into the woods. Follow the path up to a vehicle track. Turn right along this for 30m to where it ends, then take a very faint trail up into the woods again. The path keeps on climbing, roughly along the line of a ridge, emerging on the road just downhill of Parking B. It meets the water pipe, a pylon and a house along the way.

APPROACH FROM PARKING B
Follow the path to the cluster of houses seen from the parking area. From here, take the path to Alpe de Baim. The path enters the trees and descends gently to almost river level by a couple of derelict buildings. A faint path heads up left here, which then skirts the river bank for 5mins. Descend to the river when easy to do so.

DESCENT
The canyon begins with a few playful little cascades, all of which can be jumped, tobogganed or bypassed. Past the bridge, a 23m pitch marks the beginning of a small enclosed section of small climbs, swims and toboggans. The waterfalls continue, a little discontinuous at times, all the way to the dam. Beware of the current in the enclosed sections, particularly towards the end. At the dam it is possible to escape right to Mulera (follow the tube back, accessible at a point about 100m beyond the dam) or left to the main path which descends the valley down to Fonti. Beyond the dam a 40m pitch, best split just over halfway down on the left, commits you to the descent. A series of aquatic pitches, down-climbs and toboggans follows (including one obligatory toboggan of 10m). Some walking in narrow meandering passages allows you a few moments to take in the scenery. The crux of the descent is a narrow descending passage, which must be down-climbed using opposition climbing technique (a slippery traverse and abseil exists right).

VAL D'OSSOLA

Rasiga Superiore (continued)

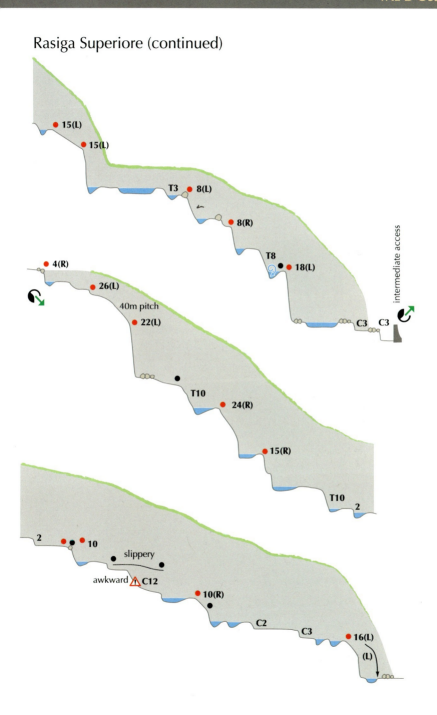

ROUTE 3: RASIGA SUPERIORE

RETURN
Where the canyon opens out, look for a path on the left which takes you in a few moments to a bridge. Cross the bridge and follow the path back to an asphalted road. Descend this to the main road and Parking A. Alternatively, descend Rasiga Inferiore.

INTERMEDIATE ACCESS
The descent can be reduced to 2hrs by entering at the dam (50min approach from Parking A, reduced to 20mins by parking in Mulera). From the church in Mulera, take the vehicle track down to the hydroelectric substation. From here, it is possible to follow the tube along the valley (exposed in places). Descend the bank to the river just before the second short tunnel.

In the more enclosed section beneath the dam in Rasiga Superiore

ROUTE 3A: RASIGA (OR ARABIANCA) INFERIORE

| RASIGA (OR ARABIANCA) INFERIORE | ★★  | V5.A4.III |

Rasiga's grand finale, but be prepared for a sharp decline in interest and rigging standards.

Allow 1hr 30mins for the final three pitches, including a 70m pitch with poor intermediate anchors (2x50m sufficient, but 2x70m ropes preferable). To exit, follow Torrente Bogna upstream for 100m or so to where it is possible to enter the woods on the left. Follow a very faint trail up to the road. If you miss Torrente Bogna entering on the right, the flood defences underneath the main road will bar your way.

Rasiga Inferiore

69

ROUTE 4: VARIOLA SUPERIORE

VARIOLA SUPERIORE  V4–5.A4–5.IV

Alternative name	Dagliano Superiore
Rock	Gneiss
Dimensions	Depth 400m (1200m–800m); length 3500m
Ideal season	Summer
Time	Approach 1hr; descent 4–5hrs; return 30mins
Shuttle info	N/A
Gear	2x30m ropes
Technical notes	Rigging improves with descent (generally double 10mm thru-bolts +/– chains in 2010). Some waterfalls and plunge-pools can be very problematic earlier in the season. Plenty of water even in summer.
Escapes	Improvised escapes are possible at the beginning, before the canyon becomes enclosed
Note	For map see Route 3

Rio Variola offers a varied mixture of jumps, toboggans and short abseils. Although rather open and discontinuous in its upper reaches, it becomes more enclosed with descent, rather like its sister canyon Rasiga. It lacks some of the character of Rasiga, however, being overall less continuous and spectacular. At the time of writing the section below the dam (Variola Inferiore) was forbidden to canyoners (it currently takes all the water from the Rasiga and Variola streams).

 Dam upstream (low risk, although in case of storms the inlet can block, returning the river to its natural state)

PARKING

From the SS33, follow signs for Bognanco, then Monteossolano. Park in the large car park at the foot of Monteossolano village.

APPROACH

Walk through the village, following the track signposted to Alpe Pertus. Ignore the marked path on the right just outside the village. Zigzag up through forest, emerging onto a long straight section that climbs steadily in the open. At the next hairpin right, take a good footpath on the left (no signpost), which soon arrives at Alpe Pertus (water fountain and abandoned house). The path continues, contouring the hillside past shrines, small tributaries and abandoned buildings. After 25mins the path crosses a wide bouldery gully. It is possible to descend this to the river, which avoids the canyon's rather lacklustre beginnings and shaves 1hr–1hr 30mins off the descent time. The main path continues to climb but nears the river about 15mins further on – strike left where easy to do so.

VAL D'OSSOLA

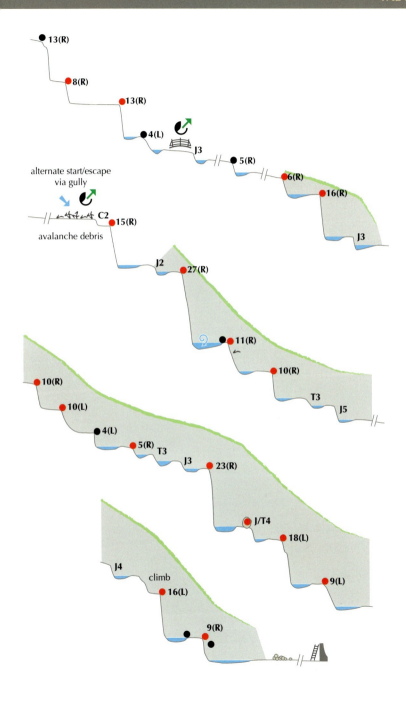

ROUTE 4: VARIOLA SUPERIORE

One of the sunny little pitches that characterise Variola Superiore

DESCENT

The canyon begins with a few open pots and short cascades. A pretty but brief enclosed section is the first test of the current. If it is too wet here an escape can be made up a watery gully on the left shortly after. Following an extensive stretch of strewn trees and logs, things begin in earnest. The canyon becomes steadily more enclosed as it cuts into the hillside, offering an almost constant stream of toboggans, jumps and little pitches.

RETURN

At the dam, follow the path left to a group of houses on the outskirts of Monteossolano. Pass through these to intercept the D0 footpath. Take a left to the village, or right to access Variola Inferiore.

VARIOLA INFERIORE

The situation in Variola Inferiore has changed in recent years. It used to be that the dam above removed much of the stream, rendering it far less technical than Variola Superiore. Now it takes not only the Variola water, but also the water removed from the Rasiga stream, rendering certain passages very technical (two deaths in 2010). Should the situation change, 2x40m ropes will be needed for the descent (not verified). Allow 30mins walk-in from the main road (or a long shuttle-run to Monteossolano) and 2hrs for the descent.

MONDELLI

Rio Mondelli is a wonderfully clean mountain river, etched into the granite of Monte Rosa's southern flank. An open nature and a sunny, south-facing aspect do much to temper its icy waters, which are as abundant as they are clear and inviting. The descent, a pearl of north-west Italy, is divisible into three parts. Done together, the two lowermost parts (Mondelli 2 and 3) are a classic trip, full of sport and variety. The second part is a beautiful canyon, full of superb jumps and toboggans, while Mondelli 3 is a more serious and technical prospect. Once revered for its aquatic and dangerous abseils, newer, more cautious rigging has made Mondelli 3 considerably safer. The older rigging, which throws you into the full flow of water, (sadly) appears to be falling into disrepair. Mondelli 1 is short and much less well formed, but a few aquatic abseils and two excellent toboggans make it a worthy addition to the day. It is described in brief here.

PARKING A (1 AND 2)

From the SS33, take the exit signed 'Piedimulera/Vogogna/Pallanzeno', then follow signs for Macugnaga at the next turning. Follow the road up the Macugnaga valley, past Ceppo Morelli and the turning to Mondelli. Either park on the bridge over the canyon 800m further on (Parking A1) – care required – or in a lay-by 500m before it (Parking A2). Here, there is a solitary building and, opposite, a walkers' sign indicating the path to Mondelli.

ROUTE 4: MONDELLI

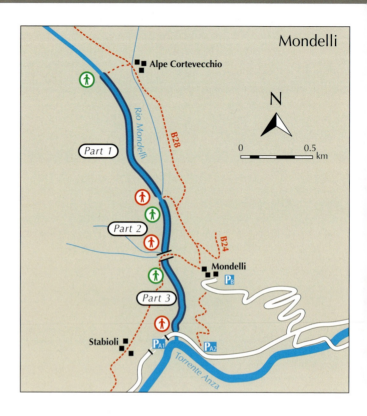

GETTING FROM PARKING A TO B

By car
Drive to the large car park outside Mondelli village (limited spaces).

On foot (Parking A2 to Parking B)
Follow the path signposted to Mondelli. It climbs to a cluster of tumbledown buildings. Pick your way through these to a little clearing. Keep on climbing on faint tracks until you emerge from the trees in Mondelli.

APPROACH FROM PARKING B

Walk into Mondelli village, following the marked path to 'Passo Mondelli/Alpe Cortenero' (red and white stripes). The path splits by the house with murals. Left (signposted 'Macugnaga/Stabioli') goes quickly to the bridge at the start of Mondelli 3. For Mondelli 1 and 2, take the upper (right-hand) path, following the red and white stripes. Ignore a right turning 200m past the village (Path B24 to Alpe Colla/Alpe Cortenero). Five minutes further on the path splits again. A left here (signposted 'Cascata/Rio Mondelli') leads quickly to the start of Mondelli 2.

ROUTE 5: MONDELLI 2

MONDELLI 2		★★★★✦ V4.A4.II
Alternative name	Mondelli Superiore	
Rock	Monte Rosa granite	
Dimensions	Depth 129m (1280m–1151m); length 400m	
Ideal season	Summer	
Time	Approach 10mins (Parking B); descent 2hrs; return 10mins (Parking B)	
Shuttle info	N/A	
Gear	1x35m and 1x40m ropes	
Technical notes	Current considerable, even in summer. Most abseils trouble-free due to excellent AIC rigging (2011), although some pools are quite turbulent.	
Escapes	Improvised escapes may be possible	

This is the most straightforward and spectacular of Mondelli's routes.

The canyon begins with an aquatic 32m pitch into a turbulent plunge-pool (40m rope recommended for pulling through). A couple of climbs and toboggans lead to the second pitch, 27m, rigged clear of the water from anchors up on the right (accessed by hand-line). A series of excellent jumps and toboggans leads to the end (care required on take-offs and in the often turbulent plunge-pools). Don't miss out on the toboggan just after the bridge. Climb out immediately after, unless doing Mondelli 3. It is 5mins back to the village from here.

The abseils in Mondelli 2 steer canyoners clear of the worst

ROUTE 5: MONDELLI 2

One good reason to add Mondelli 1 to your itinerary (photo: Simon Flower)

Mondelli 2

ROUTE 5A: MONDELLI 1

MONDELLI 1 ★★★ ■ V4.A4.II

A short, but very worthwhile addition to Mondelli 2.

Start as for Mondelli 2. Rather than turn off to Cascata/Rio Mondelli, keep climbing on path B28 (signposted 'Alpe Corte Vecchio/Passo Mondelli'). The path emerges from the trees about 200m higher up, at a cluster of houses commanding fine views over the valley (Alpe Cortevecchio, 1520m). At the level of the highest house, where the path crosses over a small side-stream, strike left across the hillside on a very faint path. Aim for the river, at a point just underneath a prominent rocky bluff. Allow 30mins for the approach from Mondelli village and 1hr for the descent (2x25m rope needed; rigging on double 8mm thru-bolts).

The last pitch (or jump) before the final toboggan section

ROUTE 6: MONDELLI 3

MONDELLI 3 ★★★♩ ■ V4–5.A4–5.IV

Alternative name	Mondelli Inferiore
Rock	Monte Rosa granite
Dimensions	Depth 231m (1151m–920m); length 700m
Ideal season	Well-established/late summer
Time	Approach 10mins (Parking B); descent 4hrs; return 0mins (Parking A1)
Shuttle info	Parking A2 to Parking B – 2.4km (30mins walk)
Gear	2x40m ropes; 1x15m escape rope; prusiking kit; sling or foot-loop
Technical notes	Very powerful flow after the tributary; plunge-pools very turbulent and waterfalls potentially lethal places. AIC rigging steers you clear of much of the danger, although some non-critical P-hangars were damaged in 2010.
Escapes	Outside enclosed sections
Note	For map and topo see Route 5

Mondelli's technical lower part is not for inexperienced groups.

⚠ **Do not descend into the Anza river! You must rig a 15m rope at the end of the canyon to prusik out on (from the bridge or from a tree on the true left).**

The hostilities begin with a 27m pitch, rigged with a very awkward traverse line (foot-loop recommended). Two uncomplicated 10m drops lead to a short but intimidating pitch in the full flow of water. An energetic hanging traverse line on the right avoids the worst of it, but many of the P-hangars were damaged in

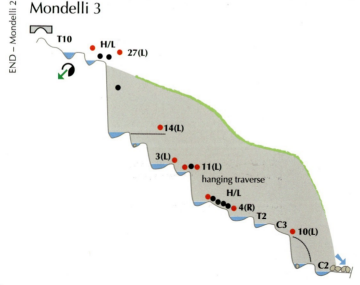

topo continued overleaf

The final pitch in Mondelli 3 before the prusik out

2010. A couple of minor obstacles later, the canyon opens out. Escape is possible on the right after the entrance to an old mine. A tributary enters left, then things begin again with a 10m pitch, bypassable on the right. The pool at the base of the following 20m pitch is difficult to exit, particularly if you are not of tall stature (the anchors are high, the current strong and the rock slippery). The 60m waterfall that follows, split halfway at a ledge on the right, is the crux of the descent. The first half can either be done in the flow of water (P-hangers damaged and loose in 2010) or well out of the water via shiny new anchors way up on the right. The aquatic route is not for the inexperienced, requiring four deviations to avoid the worst of the current. Escape appears possible to the right at the base of this pitch (not verified). The canyon then closes down for four largely trouble-free pitches.

ROUTE 6: MONDELLI 3

Mondelli 3 (continued)

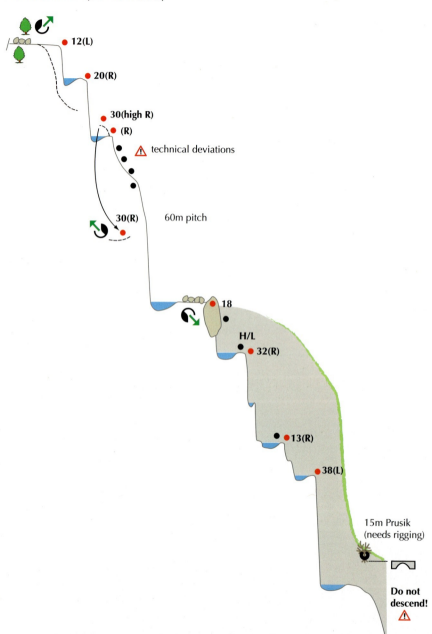

ROUTE 7: BIANCA

BIANCA ★★★☆ V4.A3.II

Rock	Gneiss
Dimensions	Depth 160m (660m–500m); length 450m
Ideal season	Early to late summer
Time	Approach 0mins (Parking B); descent 2hrs; return 0mins (Parking A)
Shuttle info	Parking A to Parking B – 3km (30mins walk)
Gear	2x50m ropes; foot-loop useful
Technical notes	Current unlikely to cause problems in the pools, but is reasonably forceful on the big cascade. AIC rigging.
Escapes	Two – after each enclosed section

Val Bianca is a superb little outing, perfect for an easy day or in combination with another short descent. An enclosed and playful part, full of jumps and toboggans, precedes an atmospheric 90m pitch overlooking the Anzasca valley.

⚠ **Dam upstream (low risk). It may stop working in times of very low or very high water levels**

One of Bianca's superb little toboggans

ROUTE 7: BIANCA

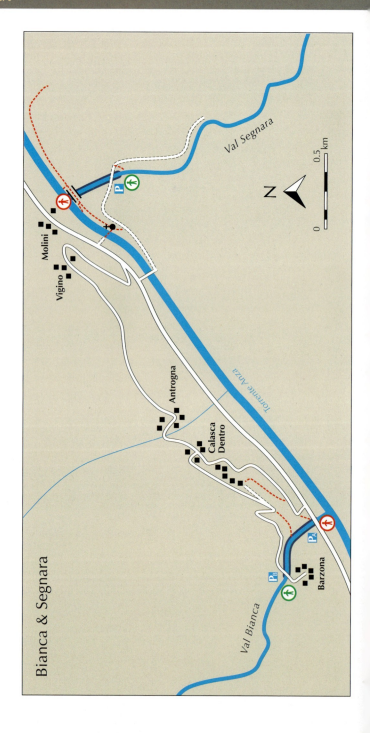

VAL D'OSSOLA

RETURN
Prusik out to the road at the bridge – do not descend into the Anza river (see above).

PARKING A
From the SS33, take the exit signed 'Piedimulera/ Vogogna/Pallanzeno', then follow signs for Macugnaga at the next turning. Follow the road up the Macugnaga valley. Pass through Molini, and 4km further on pass signs for Calsasca. The parking is just beyond this, next to a little hydroelectricity station. If there is no space here, park 200m further on in a large lay-by on the left. If Pontegrande is reached, you have gone too far.

GETTING FROM PARKING A TO B

By car
Take the road towards Calasca, then a left to Barzona at the top of the hill. Park by the bridge over the canyon, 300m further on.

On foot
From the bridge at the end of the canyon, take a wide track that climbs the hillside. This rejoins the road after the first hairpin of the shuttle-run. About 200m further on, take a path left into the trees. This climbs to a pretty cluster of homes among narrow cobbled streets. At the water fountain, take a left up an asphalted track to meet the main road again. A grassy path here leads to the canyon after the first encasement. To get to the top of the canyon, keep following the road up.

DESCENT
The canyon is divisible into three – an initial horizontal section (one 5m toboggan, the remainder is walking); a playful intermediate part (four cascades with deep pools, highest 21m); and a vertical final part. This is one 90m cascade, divisible into three pitches. The main anchors of the first pitch are difficult to access owing to the nature of the rigging (a foot-loop and long cow's tails useful). The plunge-pool of the first pitch is also awkward to exit (hand-line and anchors in situ – a foot-loop may be useful).

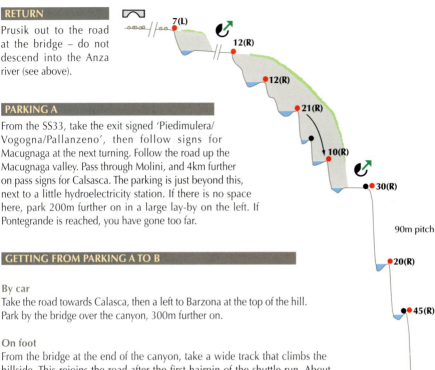

ROUTE 7A: SEGNARA

SEGNARA ★★   V3.A3.II

Segnara's brevity and position next to Val Bianca warrants its inclusion for a second canyon. Unfortunately, there is little else to recommend it; the river is mostly open in nature with no notable sections of canyon passage.

From the main road, take an unsigned turn over the Anza river (look out for the walkers' sign-post 'Alpe Lago/Campello Monte' if approaching from the west). Follow the road up and park just before the bridge over the canyon. Do not obstruct the access to the field. Take a descending path to right on the far side of the bridge. The descent takes 2hrs and consists of seven pitches into pleasant pools (2x40m ropes required). Rigging is on double anchors, but beware of slippery rock, especially on traverses. The last pitch is into the Anza river. From here, either scramble up a watery gully 50m to the right (steep and loose) or follow the Anza upstream for 300m or so and take a path by a flood-warning sign. Both routes climb to an aqueduct. Follow this west to a church. From here take a path marked with red and white stripes which climbs up to the road, then follow the road back to the car (20mins in total).

Segnara's pitches are pleasant, but lack character

ROUTE 8: TOCE

TOCE  V3.A5.IV

Alternative name	Orrido di Avera
Rock	Gneiss
Dimensions	Depth 120m (680m–560m); length 2400m
Ideal season	Summer/late summer
Time	Approach 30mins; descent 3–4hrs; return 20–30mins
Shuttle info	Possible (2.8km) but of little value
Gear	2x20m ropes
Technical notes	Rigging just about sufficient (2010) – a mixture of tree belays, double 8mm thru-bolts and pitons, sensibly placed to avoid worst of the current. Very large flow – a good knowledge of white-water hazards is essential. Long swims required. Questionable water quality.
Escapes	Three, outside enclosed sections (see descent description)

Fiume Toce is Val d'Ossola's most aquatic canyon, but only for brief spurts. The descent is characterised by a handful of ferocious waterfalls and aerosol plunge-pools, separated by (uncomfortably) long sections of swimming in perfectly calm water. The section around the first two pitches is the most critical, after which the going is much more straightforward. The second part is less interesting overall, and the descent can be cut short if so desired. Nevertheless, you'd be missing out on a couple of little challenges and some unusual little pools (or 'marmites') at the end.

 In 2010 the upstream dam was reported to be very dangerous, with automatic release a possibility. Descent is strongly discouraged!

PARKING

Go to Premia on the SS659 north of Domodossola, passing Crodo and Baceno en route. In Premia, take a right off the main road, signposted to Crego/Uriezzo (just after the 17km signpost). The road descends between two rocky buttresses, after which the road splits. Take a left to Crego. Pass over the Toce river and climb on the other side. Park on the first left-hand hairpin bend, just after the point at which the road meets the concrete-covered aqueduct (note that the parking by the church, marked on the map, is for Route 9).

APPROACH

Follow the aqueduct, then the path that follows. Continue on the path to the bridge over the Toce. The path splits on the far side. Take the right-hand path for 50m or so. Look out for a faint path that branches off this and heads towards the river. Pick your way down to the river on assorted faint trails.

OPTIONAL SHUTTLE-RUN

To reduce the walk-in by 15mins, park in Premia. On foot, follow the road signed to Crego. Take a left turn down a tarmacked farm road on the first

ROUTE 8: TOCE

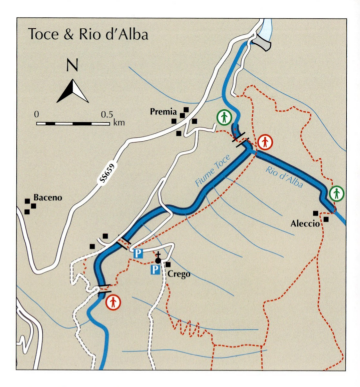

right-hand hairpin bend. At the end of the farm road, take the path which heads left. This leads to the bridge described above in 5mins.

DESCENT

The first gorge section begins immediately with a 2m jump (beware of boulders). A long swim follows, taking you back underneath the bridge. There is now 10–15mins of bouldery streamway, at which point Rio d'Alba enters on the left (escape possible). The canyon begins properly at the first pitch. You are likely to have to backtrack to find the belay, which is on a tree way up on the right. The 16m abseil lands clear of any danger. A number of down-climbs, jumps and swims in the current precede the second pitch. This is perhaps the most critical point. Two pitons provide a reasonably safe abseil to a ledge just above a very turbulent plunge-pool, which must then be crossed to gain safe ground. A number of long swims ensue (one is several hundred metres long). These take you beneath two bridges to where the canyon opens out, where it is possible to escape right to the road.

An 8m-deep pot marks the beginning of the next section of canyon. This can be jumped, but the current from the waterfall may well bar your exit from the pool – be careful! It is probably better to traverse around to the right, where there are anchors. The going is now much easier. Another escape is possible to the left just after passing beneath a footbridge. The final pitch follows shortly

VAL D'OSSOLA

after. More walking and down-climbing brings you to the beautiful final pools, or 'marmites'. Some can be jumped, while some are best avoided. Exit at the footbridge over the river.

RETURN

Take a right over the bridge and follow the gravel track up the hill to where it meets the tarmac road. You can take a short-cut through Orrido di Uriezzo Sud, an interesting fossil canyon rigged with ladders and walkways. Once on the tarmac road, keep walking up the valley past a church and car park. A little further on, take a path branching off right, signposted to Rifugio Monte Zeus. This crosses the river and heads steeply up the forested hillside, emerging by the car.

The final 'marmites'

ROUTE 9: RIO D'ALBA

RIO D'ALBA  V5.A2.V

Rock	Gneiss
Dimensions	Depth 600m (1300m–700m); length 850m
Ideal season	Early to late summer
Time	Approach 1hr 30mins; descent 5–7hrs; return 30mins
Shuttle info	Possible but of little value
Gear	2x65m ropes; jammers are useful for rope retrieval
Technical notes	Rigged on double 8mm thru-bolts (2010). Pulling through ropes of 10mm diameter or more is very awkward. Abseils could be problematic in high water (most are in the full flow of water).
Escapes	Improvised escapes only
Note	For map see Route 8

Rio d'Alba is a very steep canyon, losing around 600m of height in under 1km. The majority of time is spent on the final few pitches, particularly the impressive 250m cascade visible from the valley. The rock is nicely banded and sculpted in the lower reaches of the canyon, but the shallow encasement never really inspires. Expeditious rigging means that it can't yet be recommended to the masses, but competent parties fond of big pitches may get something out of it. Because of the tiny re-belay ledges on the final cascade, the descent is not recommended to parties of greater than three unless they are carrying a substantial quantity of rope. The canyon is probably better done earlier in the season or after a little rain (when its rating gains a star), as it is virtually dry in the height of summer.

PARKING

As for Toce (see Route 8), except continue all the way into Crego. Park by the large church.

OPTIONAL SHUTTLE-RUN

It is possible, in theory, to park a car in Premia to reduce the walk-out to 10mins.

APPROACH

Walk up the road for a couple of hundred metres and take a well-defined path on the left (signposted to Aleccio, marked with red and white paint). The path climbs steeply in the forest. After 30mins come to crossroads with a good path. Go straight over. Another 15mins of climbing brings you, via a clearing and a house, to a vehicle track. Go left and follow the track all the way to its end at Aleccio (water fountain with drinking water). From here, take a path signposted to Bee, which descends to the canyon.

VAL D'OSSOLA

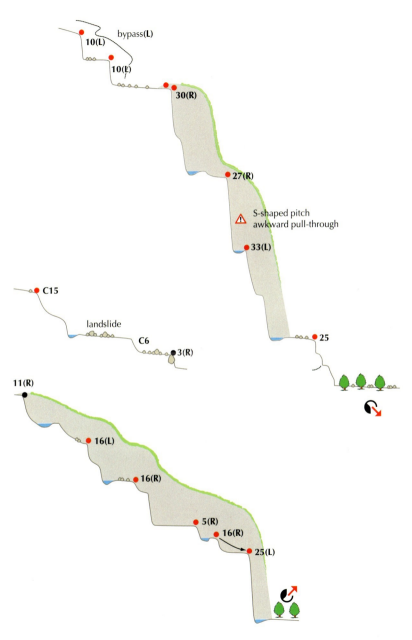

topo
continued
overleaf

ROUTE 9: RIO D'ALBA

Rio d'Alba (continued)

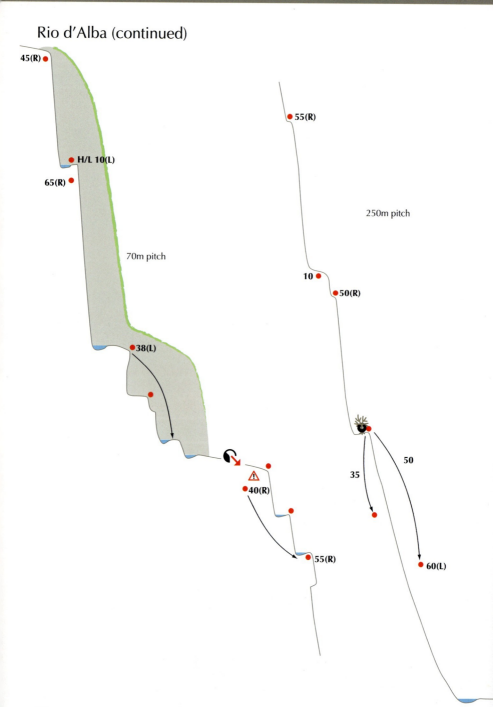

VAL D'OSSOLA

Rio d'Alba's vertical nature ensures frequent views over the valley

DESCENT

The canyon begins with two open abseils, which can be bypassed left. A 30m pitch commits you to the descent. A 60m S-shaped pitch follows, split at 27m (very difficult to pull through). A 25m pitch leads to a more open section (possible escape right – not verified). A few climbs and short abseils and the canyon closes down.

The section following, all the way to the final pitch, is perhaps the prettiest, with beautifully banded rock, sculpted waterfalls and pleasant little pools. An escape may be possible left after the 25m pitch (faint path left, unverified). The

ROUTE 9: RIO D'ALBA

The first tentative steps on the final 250m cascade

next pitch is 45m, followed immediately by a 70m cascade. The main hangars for the 70m waterfall are 5m down on the right, providing a 65m hang. One more pitch and you are upon the final cascade.

Being a climbing route, there are now plenty of rigging options here. Begin either with two short abseils in the flow of water or a 40m abseil from a good set of anchors on the far right – exposed access. From the lip, a 55m pitch leads to a two-bolt re-belay at a tiny grassy ledge (space for three maximum). Another 55m abseil leads to much safer ground at a roomy shelf. The best positioned anchors here are found 10m further down (exposed climb). From here things are far less vertical. A 50m abseil arrives at a large promontory, from where two or three pitches reach the floor (there are a number of possibilities from here, some more direct than others – maximum 60m pitch).

RETURN

At the dam at the base of the final pitch, take a path down by the grill, which then swings left. After a few minutes' walking the path picks up a concrete-covered aqueduct. Follow this all the way back to the road that climbs to Crego. If you have left a car in Premia, take a right at the dam rather than left, then cross the bridge over the Toce. The path climbs in a few minutes to Premia.

ROUTE 10: ANTOLINA

ANTOLINA		★★★✯  V4.A2–3.IV
Rock	Gneiss	
Dimensions	320m (870m–550m); length 1000m	
Ideal season	Early to mid-summer	
Time	Approach 30mins (Parking B); descent 3–4hrs; return 5mins (Parking A)	
Shuttle info	Parking A to Parking B – 2km (20mins walk)	
Gear	2x55m ropes	
Technical notes	Every sizeable pitch is rigged on double anchors and chains (2010), although some are hard to reach. The canyon carries a small stream in the summer.	
Escapes	Before the enclosed section and possibly at the bridge (not verified)	

A short and accessible canyon – ideal for an afternoon, given its westerly aspect. Its beginnings, which are a little ordinary, are soon forgotten as the river begins to cut deeper into the rock. A continual string of encased and sculpted pitches culminates in a superb 50m free-hanging abseil into a cathedral-like defile. A lack of deep pools and a feeble current in the summer mean that the descent lacks something of its neighbours', but the atmospheric finale leaves a lasting impression.

⚠ **Dam upstream (low risk). It can in theory become blocked, resulting in the water levels in the canyon returning to their natural state.**

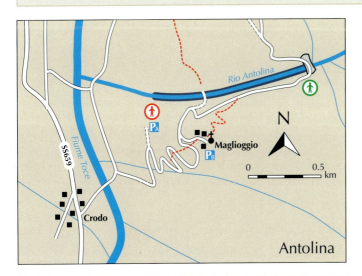

PARKING A

Go through Crodo on the SS659 north of Domodossola and take a right for Maglioggio. Cross the Toce river. After 300m, take a right signposted to Maglioggio. About 150m further on, the road swings back right on a hairpin bend. Take a left onto a gravel track here and follow it for 100m to its end.

ROUTE 10: ANTOLINA

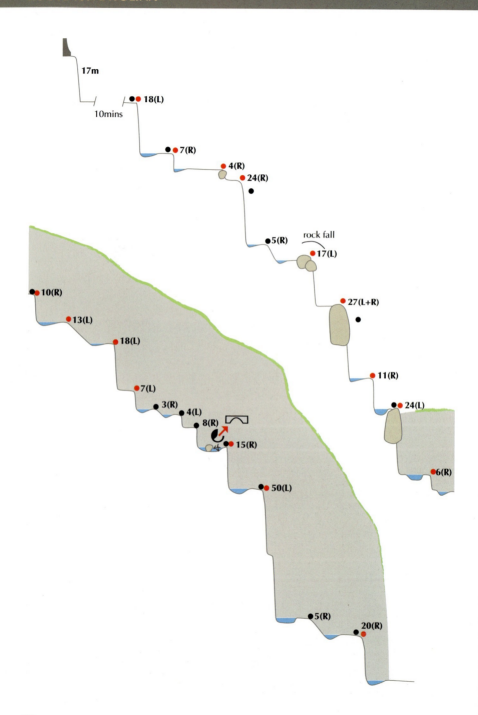

VAL D'OSSOLA

Antolina's impressive 50m pitch

ROUTE 10: ANTOLINA

GETTING FROM PARKING A TO B

By car
Continue up the main road to Maglioggio and park in the large parking area.

On foot
Walk up to Maglioggio on the main road, cutting corners where possible.

APPROACH FROM PARKING B

Take a mule track signposted to Alpe d'Aleccio. Keep following this, past the church, to a road closed to traffic. Follow this road, cutting corners where possible, all the way to the dam.

DESCENT

Abseil off railings by the dam. A 10min march in open stream precedes seven fairly open abseils. There has been a boulder collapse complicating the sixth pitch – the remaining rock looks unstable. Shortly after this, the canyon becomes more and more enclosed and continuous. Things get a little grim under the bridge, where all manner of household items have collected (escape may be possible here, if desperate), but the impressive pitches that follow more than compensate.

RETURN

Follow the stream down and head left, when possible, back to Parking A.

ROUTE 11: ISORNO FINALE

ISORNO FINALE ★★★★↘  V3.A3.IV

Rock	Gneiss
Dimensions	Depth 148m (608m–460m); length 550m
Time	Approach 20mins (Parking B); descent 1hr 30mins; return 2mins (Parking A)
Ideal season	Early to late summer
Shuttle info	Parking A to Parking B – 9.1km (path difficult to find – walk not recommended)
Gear	2x35m ropes
Technical notes	Rigging excellent (2010) on double P-hangars and chains. All pitches rigged clear of danger bar the final pitch, which is more open and less threatening. The current could quickly become problematic with rain.
Escapes	None

Isorno Finale, although short, is an absolute must-do. It has some of the most imposing canyon scenery anywhere in north-west Italy – a rare testament to the once powerful erosive forces that formed it. You could be forgiven for thinking that you were wandering between limestone walls, rather than those of ultra-hard granitic gneiss. The river is now tamed by upstream hydroelectric installations, without which canyoning would not be feasible, but the remaining current is still splashy and entertaining. The canyon is south-east facing, so benefits from a morning start.

 Dam upstream. It releases automatically if it becomes too full (eg after heavy rain). Always ring the Società Idroelletricche Riunite Spa on +39 0324 35112, mobile: +39 (0) 335 8486640.

PARKING A

From Domodossola, cross the Toce and Isorno rivers, following signs to Masera and Montecrestese. On the far side of the bridges, just past the turning to Montecrestese, take a left up Via Isorno towards 'Centrale Pontetto'. Follow this road, initially tarmac then gravel track, for 3.5km and park by the little electricity station.

GETTING FROM PARKING A TO B

Go back to the main road and take the turning up to Montecrestese. The road climbs on hairpins. At the top, take a road on the right signposted 'Giosio/Naviledo/Altoggio'. Follow the road to its end at Altoggio and park in the marked parking places. Do not change in the village.

APPROACH FROM PARKING A

There is apparently an approach from Parking A, but is very difficult to find and cannot be recommended. A long road-walk (possible hitch-hiking) is the only alternative.

ROUTE 11: ISORNO FINALE

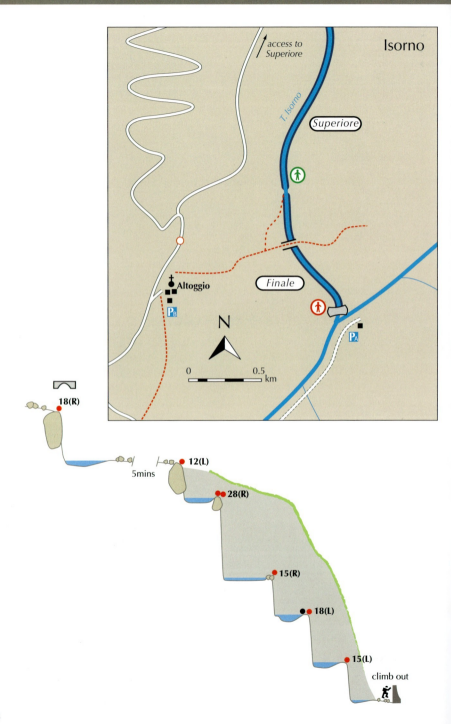

VAL D'OSSOLA

Emerging from Isorno's sombre interior

APPROACH FROM PARKING B

Make your way to the church in Altoggio, situated up and right (north-east) from the parking place. Take a path by the side of the church, then immediately follow it into a field by some vines. The path is not always obvious from here. It contours the hillside, initially following the line terracing and low-voltage power lines. Where this runs out, aim for a spot in the far left corner of the field, where there is a shrine and a better path, which then descends into the trees. After about 5mins of descent, take a faint cairned path on the left (beware: there is another, uncairned, left turn just before this), which arrives at a little crest before seemingly disappearing. Continue straight over the crest and descend a shallow valley on the other side, where the path eventually reappears. It passes a house and descends left to the river. The final 3–4m must be down-climbed (care).

DESCENT

Five minutes of bouldery streamway leads to a pleasant pitch into a pool, followed by another 5mins of bouldery streamway. Then the encasement begins. After the fifth pitch a short walk leads to the dam, which may or may not have water in it. Climb out left on iron stakes, avoiding the right side where the water intake is. Abseil from the dam. The ladders and walkways lead back to the road but are forbidden to the public.

ISORNO SUPERIORE

The canyon continues upstream. The descent has not been verified but is apparently mainly walking in bouldery streamway, punctuated by little jumps and toboggans. There are only two pitches over its long course (4–5hrs), maximum 20m. Access is from the dam road from Altoggio (forbidden to traffic).

ROUTE 12: ANTOLIVA

One of Antoliva's more sculpted sections

ROUTE 12: ANTOLIVA

ANTOLIVA ★★★ V3.A3.III

Rock	Gneiss
Dimensions	Depth 320m (1000m–680m); length 1500m
Ideal season	Early to late summer
Time	Approach 45mins; descent 3–4hrs; return 2mins
Shuttle info	N/A
Gear	2x25m ropes
Technical notes	Minimal flow after dam. Well rigged on double anchors (2011). Slippery rock in places. Cold water as north facing.
Escapes	Numerous, becoming less frequent with descent

This relatively recent addition to the Ossola line-up is hugely different from the big water descents elsewhere in the region. Antoliva is open, sunny and quite playful in places and, while truly encased canyon passage is rare, the rock is nicely sculpted and beautifully banded throughout. There are innumerable small drops, so climbing skills will help speed things up.

 Dam upstream (low risk)

PARKING
From the SS33, take the exit to Val Vigezzo and Malesco. At the '10 VII' marker post, just after Bar Alpi, take a right down towards the river (signposted 'La Bettola, Alpe Dallovio and Staz. Ferroviara Coimo'). Park on the far side of the Melezzo river. Parking beyond this is forbidden to non-residents.

APPROACH
Climb the road steeply, passing the hydroelectric plant and railway line. Pass through Dallovio (springs before and after). Five minutes further up the road splits. Take the gravel track on the left. Ten minutes further up it splits again. Take a left and contour around to the river, scrambling in when easy to do so.

DESCENT
The section above the dam is a series of open pots, mostly bypassable on the right. Only the final 4m drop before the dam is rigged. After the dam there are a number of encased sections, which become longer with descent. The final pitch is the longest and most technical, requiring a long hand-line to safeguard approach. A brief boulder-hop leads to the Melezzo river.

RETURN
Follow the Melezzo river left (downstream), beneath the road bridge, and exit left.

ROUTE 12: ANTOLIVA

Antoliva

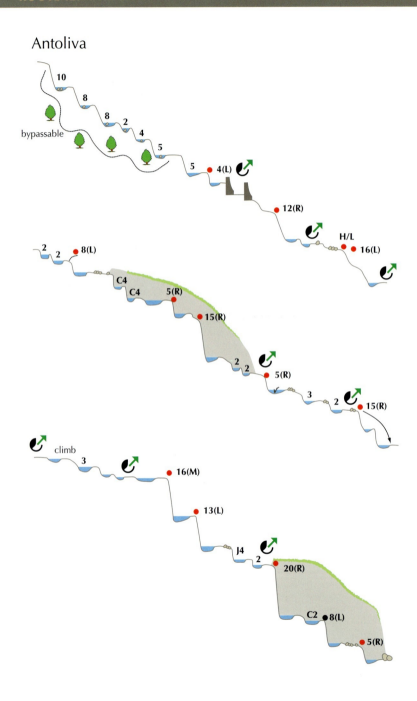

VAL D'OSSOLA

The gneiss is beautifully banded in places

ROUTE 13: OGLIANA DI QUARATA

OGLIANA DI QUARATA		 V5.A4.IV
Rock	Gneiss	
Dimensions	Depth 350m (600m–250m); length 1350m	
Ideal season	Summer	
Time	Approach 1hr 30mins; descent 4–5hrs; return 0mins	
Shuttle info	N/A	
Gear	2x35m ropes	
Technical notes	Rigging excellent on double P-hangars or 10mm thru-bolts +/− chains (2010). Flow always considerable; only those with sufficient experience should tackle this canyon outside the main summer months.	
Escapes	Only one evident, just before the 50m pitch. Scramble up right to the ridge, following a water pipe, where it is possible to pick up a path.	

The combination of abundant clean water and beautifully encased canyon scenery makes Ogliana di Quarata an important addition to any canyoner's itinerary. It is a superb descent, full of character and interest from start to finish. It is by no means straightforward – some passages are tight and aquatic, while others are more technical on account of awkward hand-lines and delicate abseils. However, the rigging is of reassuring quality and sensibly placed, without taking you too far from the action.

Ogliana di Quarata is just one part of the longest canyon in Val d'Ossola. The upstream canyon (called Rio di Menta) is largely open, with long walking sections, and the considerable effort of both walk-in and descent are difficult to justify. The final part (described in brief as Route 13a) is more continuous, but even then the approach walk is likely to provide more interest than the canyoning.

20m toboggan optional!

VAL D'OSSOLA

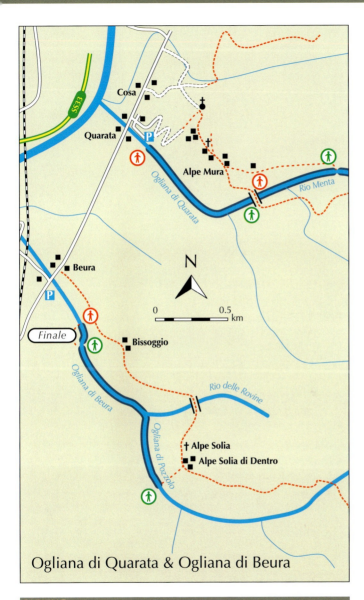

Ogliana di Quarata & Ogliana di Beura

PARKING

From the SS33, take the Villadossola exit and follow signs for Beura. Once in Beura, go north on the main road. After 1.5km the road crosses over the Ogliana di Quarata stream (canyon visible to the right). After another 250m take a right down Via 4 Novembre, then an immediate right onto a road leading to the river. Park on the road flanking the river (limited spaces). Do not change in the village.

ROUTE 13: OGLIANA DI QUARATA

Ogliana di Quarata

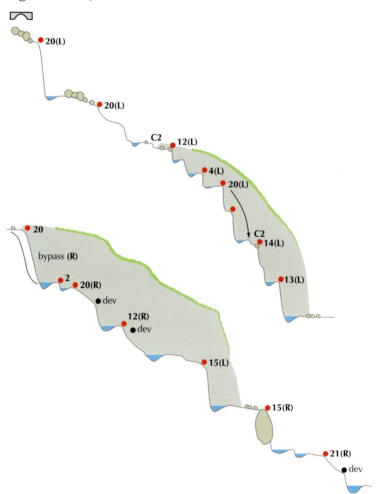

APPROACH

Walk back along the road to Via 4 Novembre. Take a right up the hill on a road closed to traffic. It soon turns into a gravel track. Follow this until the end. A path leads the rest of the way to a church overlooking the valley. From here take a mule track which climbs the hill directly. It passes a few isolated buildings before arriving at a pretty little hamlet with summer houses on the right. Do not enter the hamlet, but continue to climb. Keep on climbing on this path, ignoring all side-paths. The path soon arrives at another little hamlet (a mixture of derelict buildings and summer houses). Pick your way through this, up to a little shrine. Take a right and climb again on a good path. Finally arrive at a clearing and an abandoned, tumbledown hamlet (Alpe Mura). Two paths descend to the right; take the second from within the hamlet itself. This leads to a stone bridge at the head of Ogliana di Quarata in 15mins.

DESCENT

The canyon begins with a rather dull section of boulder-hopping and down-climbing in open streamway, punctuated by two pitches of 20m. The canyon closes down for five mostly uneventful pitches – the third can be split at a ledge halfway to ease pulling through. The next encased section begins soon after, when things start to get more interesting. Where the canyon opens out again an escape can be made right, following the line of a water pipe. The final encased section begins – the most technical part of the canyon. The first pitch (50m, split into two at a roomy shelf) requires an awkward hand-line to access the

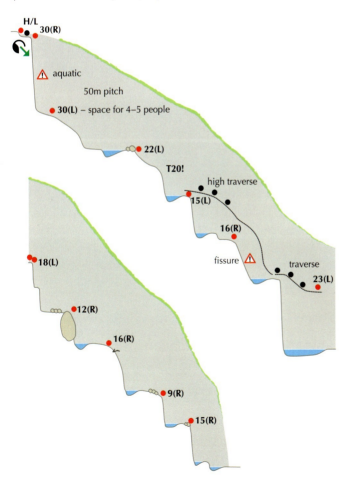

ROUTE 13: OGLIANA DI QUARATA

At the head of Ogliana di Quarata's more technical lower part

main anchors and careful abseiling to avoid a tight aquatic fissure. A 22m pitch (toboggan optional) is followed by a narrow section with two short aquatic pitches (avoidable by a bolt-traverse left). An impressive 30m-deep fissure is the last major obstacle. Anchors at the far end (accessed by a traverse line) provide a relatively safe abseil into a turbulent plunge-pool. After this, five largely uneventful pitches lead to the exit.

ROUTE 13A: MENTA INFERIORE

MENTA INFERIORE   ★★★   V4.A3.III

A short, open and verdant addition to Ogliana di Quarata.

From Alpe Mura, follow a faint path up the hillside. In 10mins it gains a grassy terrace overlooking the valley. Skirt around the outer edge of this and follow an ancient path that more or less contours the hillside, at times on ledges and steps cut into the rock. It is exposed in places, but ancient metal cables and the odd bit of rope are in place for the worst bits. The occasional red spot gives some reassurance that you're on the right track. It reaches the stream in another 30mins, arriving at two large flat rocks in the stream bed. Allow 1hr 30mins for 11 mostly bypassable pitches (maximum 41m). Rigging is on double anchors where needed.

The wild, open Rio di Menta

ROUTE 14: OGLIANA DI BEURA – PARTE FINALE

OGLIANA DI BEURA – PARTE FINALE  V4.A4.III

Alternative name	There is no firm consensus on the name of this river. Some guidebooks (and the Swisstopo map) refer to it as Rio delle Rovine, but apparently this is only the name of a tributary.
Rock	Gneiss
Dimensions	Depth 120m (400m–280m); length 400m
Ideal season	Summer
Time	Approach 20mins; descent 1hr–1hr 30mins; return 10mins
Shuttle info	N/A
Gear	2x25m ropes
Technical notes	Always very aquatic, but mainly rigged away from the flow of water or dangerous plunge-pools. Rigged on double anchors.
Escapes	One – after the first pitch (just before the crux)
Note	For map see Route 13

A short but intense canyon, very aquatic but relatively safe on account of sensible rigging. Perfect for a second canyon of the day.

PARKING

From the SS33, take the Villadossola exit and follow signs for Beura. Park in the *alimentari* (grocer's) car park on the true left of the river.

APPROACH

Gain the river by the *alimentari* and walk upstream for 10mins. Look out for a gravel bank on the right. If you go too far the final pitch will be seen in the distance. From the gravel bank, take a rising path which skirts the side of the canyon as far as the top of the first pitch (exposed in places).

DESCENT

Five pitches in quick succession. The second pitch is constricted and requires careful abseiling, but there is no plunge-pool at its base to create problems. It is possible to escape at the top of this pitch if needed.

RETURN

Walk back down the river bed.

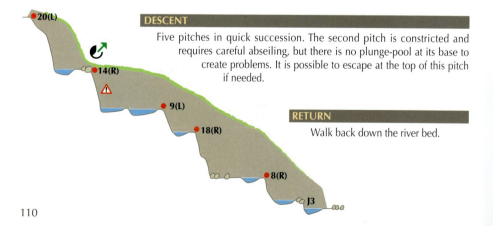

VAL D'OSSOLA

Sensible rigging means that Ogliana di Beura Finale is aquatic without being overly difficult

OGLIANA DI BEURA INTEGRALE

The full descent (which has not been verified) takes around 5hrs. It offers another half-dozen well-spaced pitches, which are aquatic and technical after the confluence with Rio delle Rovine (2x25m ropes needed). Access is complicated; allow 2h. After crossing Rio delle Rovine, it is 15mins to Alpe Solia (shrine). Another 15mins brings you to a cluster of houses at Alpe Solia di Dentro. At the penultimate house, take a little-seen path on the right, which improves as it descends (15mins to the river from here).

ROUTE 15: MARONA

MARONA		★★★✦ V4.A3.IV
Rock	Gneiss	
Dimensions	Depth 250m (750m–500m); length 1400m	
Ideal season	Summer	
Time	Approach 1hr 15mins; descent 3–4hrs; return 45mins	
Shuttle info	N/A	
Gear	2x30m (or 2x50m ropes – see descent description)	
Technical notes	Rigging sufficient on single or double 10mm thru-bolts (2010), although a number of jumps and toboggans seem obligatory. The river doubles in size after the confluence. Some toboggans, abseils and down-climbs could be problematic in higher than normal summer conditions.	
Escapes	None evident	

Rio Marona is a wild, clean river within the boundaries of the Val Grande National Park. While not being especially pretty or even canyon-like, its frequent deep pools are well exposed to the sun, providing excellent sport for those fond of jumps and toboggans. It is the furthest outlying canyon in the Ossola area, but well worth the journey for those who enjoy that sort of thing.

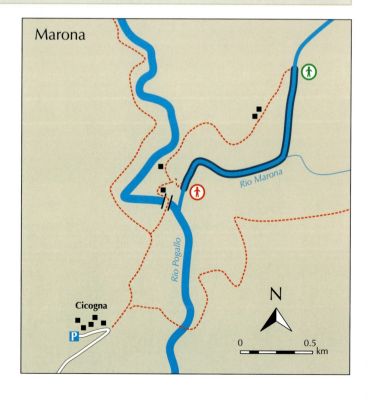

VAL D'OSSOLA

Pleasant, sunny canyoning in Marona (photo: Simon Flower)

PARKING

From the A26 south, take the exit for Verbania. Just before Fondo-Toce, take a left towards S.Bernadino. Look out for the turning signed 'Rovegro/Cicogna', 1.5km past Bieno. Continue through Rovegro onto the narrow, windy road up to Cicogna. Note that there are few passing places along its 3km length. Park in the designated parking in Cicogna.

APPROACH

On the final hairpin before Cicogna, take the good path signposted to Pogallo. Continue past the first junction right (signposted to Pian Cavallone) and take the second, also signposted to Pian Cavellona (as well as Tregugno and La Soliva). The path descends to the river, which is crossed on a narrow concrete bridge. The path takes a left and flanks the river for 100m or so before swinging back right (a turning that is easy to miss). Keep following the marked path up the hill, past a cluster of tumbledown houses to a shoulder. From here the path more or less contours around to the river.

DESCENT

The canyon begins with a 5m toboggan, followed by a 23m pitch into a deep pool. A few possible jumps and toboggans follow, then a 45m pitch, split after 20m on the left (space for two people). An open section follows, then a string of

ROUTE 15: MARONA

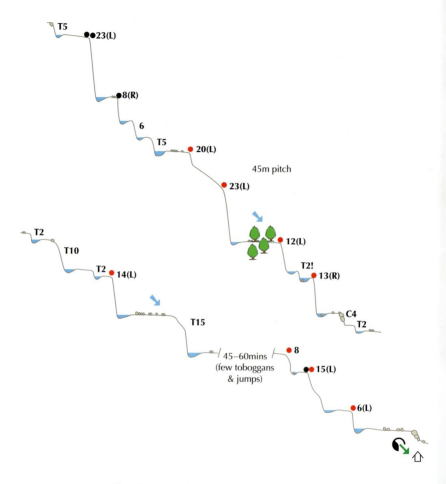

small pitches, most of which can be jumped or tobogganed after checking pool depth. A major inlet then comes in left, doubling the volume of water. Aside from an excellent 15m toboggan, the canyon then loses some of its character. Nearly an hour of more open streamway follows, punctuated by two or three short toboggans. Three cascades in quick succession are the final obstacles. After these, keep an eye out on the right for some old stone walls. If you miss them, the confluence with Rio Pogallo will be met about 100m further on.

RETURN

Take a path up the forested gully, just upstream from the stone walls. The path climbs to a house, from where the path is less evident. Keep on climbing to the ridge crest, where it is possible to pick up the approach path.

Salto's potentially problematic final section (Route 20)

Ticino

CANYONING IN THE ALPS

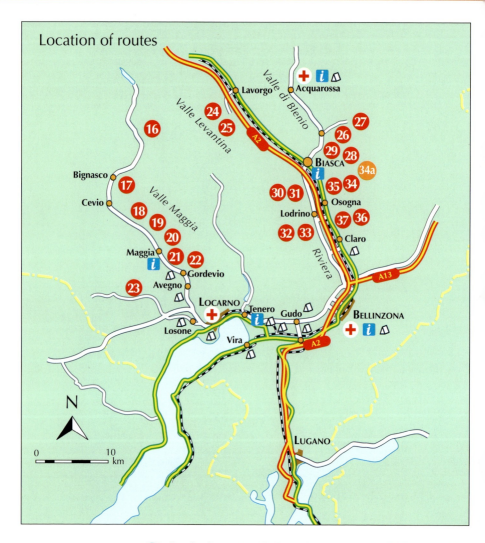

Switzerland's most southerly canton can seem decidedly out of place in a country famed for its lofty glaciated peaks. Its position south of the main alpine chain means that it has a Mediterranean rather than mountain feel, a mood enhanced by the fig trees and grape vines lining its valley floors. Along with the cuisine and the laissez-faire attitude of its Italian-speaking inhabitants you'd be forgiven for thinking you were in Italy rather than Switzerland (but don't be fooled – Ticino has been Swiss property for 500 years and its inhabitants remain loyal to the flag). Being largely off the mountaineering map, Ticino's uplands attract a fairly select group of visitors, from walkers seeking solitude among secret glens and ridge tops to canyoners drawn by its growing reputation as Europe's top canyoning destination.

TICINO

Bathers are not an uncommon sight in Ticino's canyons (Route 19)

The canyoning is clustered around two valleys snaking north from Lake Maggiore and the Magadino Plain – Valle Leventina and Valle Maggia. Valle Maggia is the quieter of the two. Its peaceful setting and more laid-back canyons provide an idyllic spot in which to while away a week's holiday. Valle Leventina, by contrast, is a major artery linking Milan and central Switzerland. The combination of road, rail, quarry and commerce ensures this is not the quietest valley in the Alps. Yet somehow it manages to retain a certain charm – noise reduction measures and the valley's considerable dimensions ensure that motorway traffic is seldom heard, while industry tends to be localised in certain areas. Pretty villages and hamlets are strewn across hillsides, linked by trails that wind their way among chestnut forests. Most importantly, however, is the canyoning. Valle Leventina has the highest concentration of memorable descents anywhere in Europe – virtually every side-stream has something sporting or spectacular to offer.

WHERE TO STAY

Most of the campsites in the region are of the holiday resort variety and consequently rather expensive, more so than comparable campsites in Italy. The campsites have a star rating, which gives some indication of price, but is not totally reliable. For example, the two- and three-star campsites in Losone are more expensive than the two nearby four-star establishments.

By far the cheapest option in the area is Camping La Serta in Gudo. Alternatives are Camping Bellavista, Camping Joghi e Bubu and Camping Acquarossa. The latter is very pleasant and quiet, but is perhaps a little far from

CANYONING IN THE ALPS

the action. See Appendix C for further details of campsites (there are a number of other campsites around the lake, but these are very expensive and are not listed).

If you don't fancy camping the tourist offices (see Appendix D) produce comprehensive lists of hotels and rental accommodation, available online. If there are enough people, the price may actually be comparable. Other useful websites are www.rustici.ch and www.agriturismo.ch.

Note that the Locarno International Film Festival (www.pardo.ch) runs for 10 days each year, starting the first Wednesday in August. During this time the campsites and other accommodation around Locarno can get fully booked up.

PRACTICALITIES

Shops and services
On the Valle Leventina side, banks and reasonably sized supermarkets are located in Bellinzona, Biasca and Claro. The largest supermarkets are in the commercial estate at the foot of the valley – follow signs for San Bernadino at the roundabout just south of Claro. There are no major towns in Valle Maggia, but a pharmacy, cash point and a reasonably sized supermarket can be found in Maggia and Cevio.

Gear shops
Surprisingly, given the popularity of canyoning in the area, there are very few shops selling canyoning kit. Belotti Sport in Locarno (Via Cittadella 22, tel +41 (0) 91 7516602, www.belottisport.ch) sells the odd items such as abseil devices and tackle bags. Intersport in Biasca (Via Parallela 1, tel +41 (0) 91 8621374, www.millenniumsport.ch) and Rockshop in Ponte Brolla (tel +41 (0) 91 7807565, www.rock-shop.ch) only sell climbing equipment.

Weather forecast
Good forecasts are available from the Locarno tourist information (www.ticino.ch) and Meteo Swiss (www.meteoswiss.ch). Alternatively, ring 162 if you have a Swiss SIM card.

Hospitals
There are hospitals with emergency departments in Bellinzona, Acquarossa and (most importantly) Locarno.

Maps
The best mapping is that produced by the Swiss Survey. A number of individual sheets are required to cover the whole area, both at 1:25,000 and 1:50,000 scales, so you may wish to opt for maps that cover the area in single sheet, such as the 1:50,000 Kompass map or the 1:60,000 Kümmerly & Frey map.

Guidebooks
An excellent English-language guidebook became available while this guide was being finalised, *Eldorado Ticino* (SwissCanyon) by Luca and Anna Nizzola. It is certainly worth getting hold of. As well as having many excellent

TICINO

Deep pools and a Mediterranean feel – welcome to Ticino (Route 37)

CANYONING IN THE ALPS

Lodrino Inferiore's imposing narrows (Route 33)

photographs and topos, it shows water-level check-points for just about every canyon in the region. It is available from a number of local campsites and tourist information offices – see www.swisscanyon.ch for details.

TICINO

TRAVEL AND TRANSPORT

Rail
Bellinzona is on the main train line between Milan and Zurich, and has links with Locarno (the best stop for the Maggia valley). Slower trains go to Biasca or Osogna-Cresciano (change in Bellinzona). A small scenic train connects Domodossola and Locarno via Val Vigezzo, stopping at numerous places along the way, including Santa Maria Maggiore (where there is a campsite) and Coimo (by Antoliva in the Val d'Ossola chapter). Details from www.centovalli.ch.

Driving
Driving times are less than anywhere else in this guide. Base yourself in the valley in which you intend to go canyoning and you'll hardly do any driving at all. Driving between Maggia and Biasca takes about an hour. A tunnel passing from one side of Locarno to the other substantially eases the journey between the two valleys. Car hire is available locally in Bellinzona and Locarno.

Public transport
Owing to the efficiency of Swiss public transport, and the proximity of the canyons to the main roads, canyoning by bus is a distinct possibility in Ticino. The most useful routes are shown below. (The canyon names are followed by their route numbers in this guide.)

Bus route	Destination	Via	Frequency	Canyon served
131	**Biasca** – Olivone	Lodeiro, Malvaglia, Acquarossa	Hourly (6am–midnight)	Pontirone (28, 29), Malvaglia (26)
193	**Bellinzona** – **Biasca**	Lodrino, Iragna	Hourly (6am–7pm)	Lodrino (32, 33), Iragna (30, 31)
191	**Bellinzona** – Airolo	Cresciano, Osogna, **Biasca**, **Lavorgo**	Hourly (5am–midnight)	Cresciano (36, 37), Osogna (34, 34a, 35)
123	**Lavorgo** – Chironico		1–2 per hour (6am–7pm)	Ticinetto (24), Barougia (25)
311	**Bellinzona** – **Locarno**	Gudo, Cugnasco	1–2 per hour (6am–midnight)	
315	**Locarno** – Cavergno	Avegno, Gordevio, Maggia, Giumaglio, Someo, Bignasco,	Hourly (6am–midnight)	Grande (22), Gei (21), Salto (20), Giumaglio (19), Sponde (18), Bignasco (17), Serenello (16)
324	**Locarno** – Spruga	Losone, Loco	6 per day (7am–6pm)	Loco (23)

Destinations for connecting services are shown in bold.

A good interactive map showing all services can be found at www.ti.ch (Italian only). The map provides links to all the various timetables, which are also available on the Postbus website (www.postbus.ch). An excellent journey planner (showing necessary changes) can be found on the Swiss Federal Railways website (www.sbb.ch).

CANYONING IN THE ALPS

Heli-canyoning
Cresciano Superiore (Route 36) and Osogna Superiore (Route 34a) are big days out, with lengthy walk-ins. Instead of toiling up the hill for 2–3 hours, why not take the chopper? It isn't as pricey as you may first think (€120 for four people and kit at the time of writing). Go on, treat yourself...

To find the heli-port, take the turning for Lodrino just south of Osogna. Just over the bridge take a left turn, signposted 'Centro Aeronautico – Restaurante Heli-TV'. The offices are situated at the far end of the airfield (tel +41 (0) 91 8734040, fax +41 (0) 91 8734044, info@heli-tv.ch).

OTHER ACTIVITIES

It is not only canyoners who have their eyes on the spectacular gneiss and granite in the area. Climbing is popular, and there are a number of guidebooks catering for climbers, including *Arrampicate Sportive E Moderne fra Varese e Canton Ticino* (available from the publishers at www.versantesud.it) and *Guida d'arrampicata Ticino e Moesano* (Club Alpino Svizzero), both in Italian. World-class bouldering can be found around Biasca. See either *Cresciano Boulder*, *Gottardo Boulder* or *Chironico Boulder*, which are available in the tourist information office in Biasca and in certain local eateries (see www.ticinoboulder.ch for details). Some information is available online at the logbook pages of www.UKclimbing.com.

There is also much to tempt the walker. *Walking in Ticino* (Cicerone Press) by Kev Reynolds is a useful guide to the area and certainly gets you off the beaten track (at least off any track beaten by a British tourist). A couple of via ferrata exist a little further afield (Ferrata Diovolo in Andermatt and Via Ferrata Salvador in Lugano) – see *Via Ferrata Switzerland* (Rother Press) by Iris Kürschner, available in UK bookshops.

There are a number of bathing opportunities to while away an afternoon or provide a pleasant few hours' repose after a hard day. The pools in Iragna, Osogna and Giumaglio villages, along with those on the walk-in to Cresciano, are spots favoured by locals. The most spectacular place for a spot of wild swimming is just south of Avegno in Valle Maggia, where the river cuts between 20m-deep canyon walls.

TICINO'S HYDROELECTRIC DAMS

Ticino's rivers are used extensively for hydroelectricity purposes, and more than half the rivers described in this chapter have been tamed to some degree by dams and water-intakes. In any other area of Europe this could introduce a level of risk many canyoners would be uncomfortable with. Not so in Ticino.

The canton has a well-organised system of river sharing, where it is possible to phone the various hydroelectric companies involved to determine the flood risk in affected rivers. If no dam movements are planned, an operator will take your name and party size and ask you to ring back once safely out of the canyon. While this system greatly reduces risk, it does not totally eliminate it. Although hydroelectric companies recognise canyoning, they officially discourage it and are careful to absolve themselves of any responsibility in case of accident or unforeseen increases in flow.

See individual canyon entries for details of numbers to ring. Note that the operators are Italian speaking, although some may speak English, French or German.

ROUTE 16: SERENELLO

SERENELLO ★★★ V4.A3.III

Alternative name	Ri da Sernel
Rock	Gneiss
Dimensions	Depth 160m (720m–560m); length 350m
Ideal season	Early to late summer
Time	Approach 20mins; descent 1–2hrs; return 5mins
Shuttle info	N/A
Bus number/stop	315 to 'Menzonio, Sentiero'
Gear	2x45m ropes
Technical notes	Rigging sufficient on single 10mm thru-bolts (2010). The two 18m pitches and the 22m pitch under the bridge can cause problems in high water.
Escapes	None evident

A continual, if short, string of pleasantly enclosed waterfalls, culminating in a beautiful deep pool and cave-like section. Although suitable for less experienced people during the summer, it becomes far more challenging in spring or after rain as many of the pitches must be abseiled in the full flow of water. Being largely west facing, it benefits from a later start.

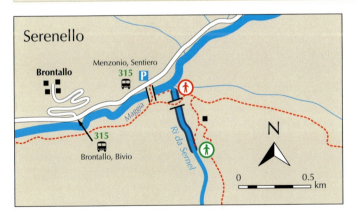

PARKING

Travelling north from Maggia, park in a large lay-by 800m north of the turning to Brontallo. Space here is limited. There are other small lay-bys nearby, but most are private. Further space can be found on the road to Brontallo.

APPROACH

From the parking place, follow a good path which crosses the river on a little stone bridge. Take a left off the main path about 50m further on, then a right before reaching some stables. The path passes over the canyon on a stone

ROUTE 16: SERENELLO

Relaxed canyoning in Serenello (photo: Simon Flower)

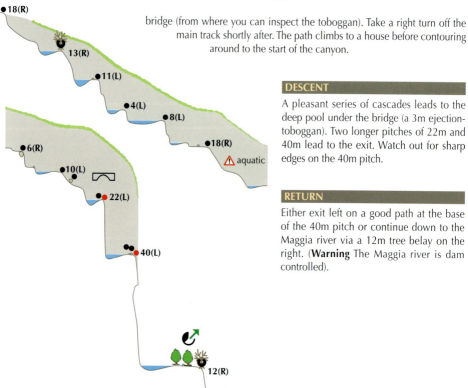

bridge (from where you can inspect the toboggan). Take a right turn off the main track shortly after. The path climbs to a house before contouring around to the start of the canyon.

DESCENT

A pleasant series of cascades leads to the deep pool under the bridge (a 3m ejection-toboggan). Two longer pitches of 22m and 40m lead to the exit. Watch out for sharp edges on the 40m pitch.

RETURN

Either exit left on a good path at the base of the 40m pitch or continue down to the Maggia river via a 12m tree belay on the right. (**Warning** The Maggia river is dam controlled).

ROUTE 17: BIGNASCO

BIGNASCO ★★★☆ V4–5.A3.III

Alternative name	Valle del Chignolasc
Rock	Gneiss
Dimensions	Depth 290m (740m–450m); length 700m
Ideal season	Early to late summer
Time	Approach 10mins (Parking B); descent 3–4hrs; return 2mins (Parking A)
Shuttle info	Parking A to Parking B – 4.2km (50mins walk)
Bus number/stop	315 to 'Bignasco Posta'
Gear	2x85m ropes (2x30m ropes also useful)
Technical notes	Longest pitches rigged with 10mm thru-bolts and chains (2010). Remainder single anchors or unequalised. Splashy and pleasant in high summer, but doesn't take much to make bigger pitches far more technical.
Escapes	Before and after the 60m pitch

Bignasco is a pleasantly enclosed canyon, well sculpted and encased for most of its length. Two long and technical abseils are the main feature, aquatic and potentially dangerous in high water, despite being well rigged. The latter half of the canyon, the section between these two waterfalls, is particularly continuous, with virtually all the time spent on rope or swimming across the deep pools between pitches. A very worthwhile addition to your itinerary.

PARKING A

When travelling north up the Maggia valley, the final waterfall is clearly visible from the road. Turn into Bignasco. Once over the bridge, take a right and follow the roads to the base of the waterfall. Park in a designated parking area by an outdoor swimming pool.

GETTING FROM PARKING A TO B

By car
Go back to the bridge. Without crossing the bridge, pass through the village to a road which flanks the river. This begins to climb. Where it splits, take the right branch, which climbs the hillside on tight hairpins. Park by a church where the tarmac ends. Note that the final few hairpins are very steep, but it is possible to leave your car a little further back if needed.

On foot
Go back towards the village on the road nearest the cliff. Once at the cliff, go right for a few metres to where a marked path climbs into the trees (at a point 200m or so north of the canyon). Follow this path for 15–20mins to where it meets the road. The path now cuts corners off the road as it climbs towards the church (Parking B).

ROUTE 17: BIGNASCO

The 83m final cascade (photo: Simon Flower)

TICINO

APPROACH FROM PARKING B

Follow the gravel track from the church. Scramble right to the river at the small goods cable-car station.

DESCENT

The first three cascades can be bypassed or climbed. A 20m pitch, accessed by a tree belay, marks the beginning of the canyon. The 60m pitch follows the next short pitch. The main hangars are on a ledge around to the right, not visible from above. A constricted 25m abseil is required to access them (**warning** strong current early in the season; 2x30m rope required). The canyon now becomes a little more continuous and technical. A number of pretty pitches precede the final 83m waterfall, which is accessed by a 20m abseil from a boulder. The exit from the pool at the top of the 83m pitch is awkward, so stay on the approach rope until clipped into the anchors.

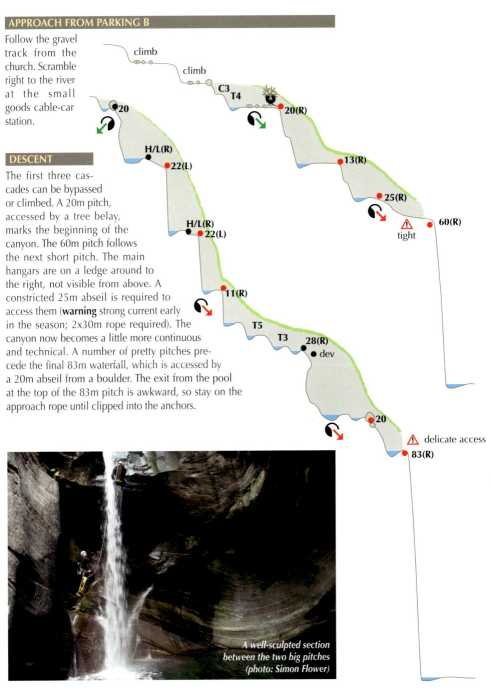

A well-sculpted section between the two big pitches (photo: Simon Flower)

ROUTE 18: SPONDE

SPONDE ★★★↙ ◨ V5.A3.IV

Rock	Gneiss
Dimensions	Depth 580m (960m–380m); length 1000m
Ideal season	Early to late summer
Time	Approach 1hr 30mins (Parking B); descent 6hrs; return 2mins (Parking A)
Shuttle info	Parking A to Parking B – 1.9km (20–25mins road-walk)
Bus number/stop	315 to 'Someo'
Gear	2x110m ropes
Technical notes	The three 100m pitches are well rigged with double anchors in sensible places (2011). There are intermediate anchors on the first and third, but they are not evident on the second. Although the flow is usually low in summer, it is best to check the water levels at the base of the final pitch. The approach abseils for the 100m pitches are in the flow of water on slippery rock.
Escapes	In the horizontal sections there are numerous opportunities to thrash out into the easy angled wooded slopes. A couple of more conventional escapes onto paths also exist.

One of Ticino's most celebrated canyons, famous for its dizzying 100m pitches. It is well exposed to the sun, and if you're comfortable with heights (and don't mind endlessly packing and unpacking huge amounts of rope) it makes a superb day out. The canyon unfortunately loses its charm after the final big pitch.

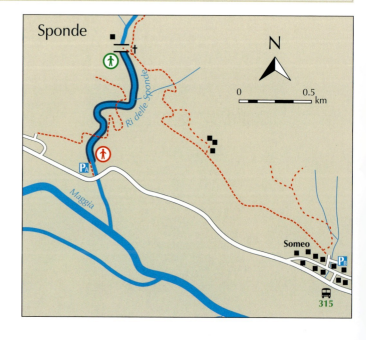

TICINO

PARKING A
Park the first car 1.6km beyond the last (third) turning into Someo, in the wide clearing on the right. Water levels can be inspected by a short walk through the trees to the base of the final pitch.

GETTING FROM PARKING A TO B
Go back and take the turning into Someo. Park in the designated parking area by the Alsasca restaurant.

APPROACH FROM PARKING B
Cross the bridge from the car park and take a right up the road. At its end follow the path left, through what seems like private property (but isn't). The path joins a couple of bigger paths coming in left. Keep on climbing steadily for 90mins, following the occasional red-and-white marker. A glimpse of the first 100m pitch is a sign that you are approaching the canyon. About 20mins further on, take a faint descending path on the left about 10m beyond a large shrine.

DESCENT
The canyon begins with a series of playful jumps and toboggans, which end abruptly in the first 100m pitch. Two short abseils take you to the main anchors on the right (invisible from above). The longest pitch (105m) follows immediately after – watch out for rope rub. There then follows another section of superb short toboggans, which would relieve the tension were it not for the impending third 100m pitch. This begins as a 35m abseil in the water to a set of anchors around to the right, just beneath a little perched pool (there is an intermediate set of anchors midway but the slippery rock makes them awkward to reach). After this the canyon loses its character somewhat, becoming bouldery and nondescript. A couple of climbs and abseils lead to the final ramp. The lower part can be down-climbed (care required – abseil from trees if needed).

RETURN
Follow the path through the trees back to the road and Parking A.

topo continued overleaf

ROUTE 18: SPONDE

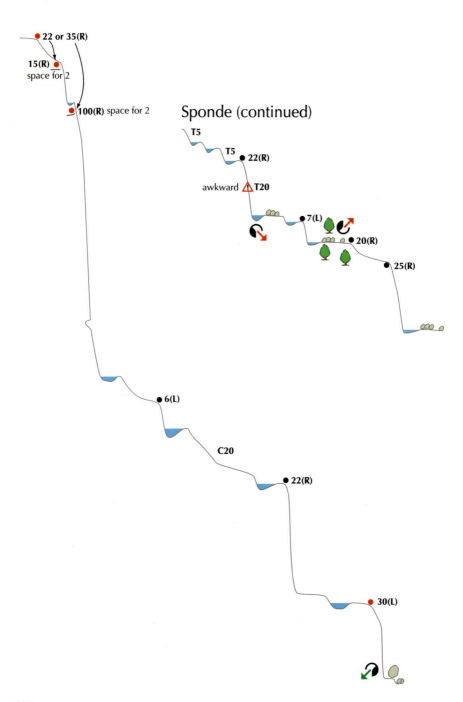

TICINO

The third 100m pitch

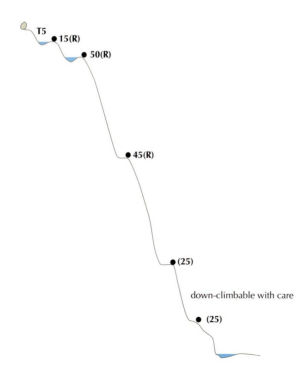

ROUTE 19: GIUMAGLIO

GIUMAGLIO		★★★↙  V3.A3–4.III
Rock	Gneiss	
Dimensions	Depth 150m (500m–350m); length 650m	
Ideal season	Early to late summer	
Time	Approach 30mins; descent 2–3hrs; return 5mins	
Shuttle info	N/A	
Bus number/stop	315 to 'Giumaglio'	
Gear	2x40m ropes	
Technical notes	Rigging mainly mono-points, except the 33m pitch, which is rigged double (2010). Current enough to entertain early in the season, without being threatening (but avoid during snow-melt). The most critical point is the 37m pitch.	
Escapes	None evident	

A very pretty and atmospheric half-day canyon, very varied for its short length, with big jumps into glowing green pools, aquatic pitches and narrow canal sections. Perfect for an afternoon.

⚠ Dam upstream – tel +41 (0) 91 7569301

A superb 15m jump

TICINO

PARKING

If coming from the south, turn right into Giumaglio immediately after crossing the Giumaglio stream. Park in the designated parking spaces. There is more parking in the village.

APPROACH

Go to the end of the road and take a path (marked with red and white stripes) to the church. At the church, take a left, then a right by the water fountain 50m further on. Follow this path past a bar with a pretty beer-garden to a tarmacked road. Take the path behind the bar, marked for Arnau and Berzona. This path climbs steeply on impressive granite steps. After 10–15mins arrive at a gate, then a house (spring with drinking water). Immediately after the house, descend the wooded slope for 10m to a faint track. This takes a gently descending course to the river.

To access the stream further up (not recommended) continue on the main path to a shrine, then skirt the hillside on the ruins of an old path. Follow this to its end. From here, an exposed descent (protected with rope) leads to a tree belay, from which a 25m pitch gains the river. About 30mins of uninspiring boulder-hopping in open streamway leads to the lower access point.

DESCENT

The first pitch descends off a large boulder, best done to the left. After that, the canyon becomes more enclosed. A series of beautiful swims follow, interspersed with short pitches (many jumpable if you're brave). Finally the canyon turns vertical, with two long, aquatic pitches. The second (37m) is protected by a hand-line on the left bank (not rigged). A final 25m pitch reaches the bathing pool in the village.

RETURN

Feel your way back to the church, which is clearly visible from here.

ROUTE 19: GIUMAGLIO

Descending into Giumaglio's more encased part

ROUTE 20: SALTO

SALTO	★★★★ V4.A4.IV
Rock	Gneiss
Dimensions	Depth 380m (740m–360m); length 3000m
Ideal season	Early to late summer
Time	Approach 1hr 20mins; descent 6hrs; return 5mins
Shuttle info	N/A
Bus number/stop	315 to 'Maggia Centro'
Gear	2x65m ropes (1x80m rope useful for pull-through); 2x20m ropes OK if avoiding final pitch
Technical notes	Rigged with single 10mm thru-bolts in 2009 (65m pitch rigged double). Some anchors hard to find and hard to reach (climbing skills and steady head required). Some jumps obligatory. Water levels sporty in early season, but only the section under bridge problematic (evaluate from approach walk). Water cold, with frequent immersions.
Escapes	At the top of the 65m pitch. Possibly up an inlet prior to the 20m toboggan (see topo).

Valle del Salto is a very pretty canyon. Open, wild and discontinuous at the beginning, it becomes steadily more enclosed and spectacular towards the end. Deep green pools are a feature, which provide innumerable jumping possibilities and are particularly stunning when the early afternoon sunlight catches them. Prolonged periods of immersion in cold water, sparse rigging and slippery rock means this is not a canyon for beginners.

 Dam upstream – tel +41 (0) 91 7569301

PARKING A

Turn right into Maggia opposite the supermarket/tourist information. Take an immediate left at a T-junction. Cross the bridge over the River Salto, and 400m further on take a right down a narrow unmarked lane. Park at the end of the road in a designated parking area.

PARKING B

Just before the bridge over the River Salto, take a right up Cassacia street. Follow this, past I Campioi, down some worryingly narrow streets to a church (a struggle in a wider car). Behind the church take In Campii street. Park about 200m further up in a designated parking area.

APPROACH FROM PARKING A

Follow the well-marked path. After 15mins climbing, cross the bridge over the canyon (assess the current here). Take a left at the chapel on the far side, signposted 'Rif Alpe Marnee' and marked with red and white stripes. This path leads all the way to the dam at the head of the canyon.

ROUTE 20: SALTO

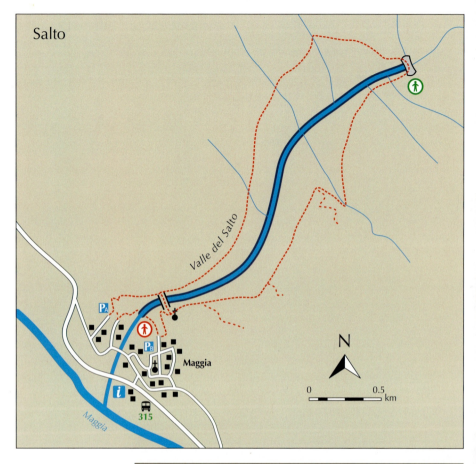

APPROACH FROM PARKING B

Follow In Campii for another 100m. Take a right at the spring on La Strada de la Mont (signposted to Capella de la Pioda), climb on historic granite steps as far as the chapel described above, then continue to the head of the canyon.

DESCENT

A succession of short pitches, many of which can be jumped. Initially the interesting obstacles are separated by a few hundred metres of walking in open stream or over boulders, but steadily the descent becomes more continuous. The final half is a series of short pitches in surrounds as spectacular as any in Ticino. The section under the bridge is the narrowest point, an S-shaped slot where the current can cause problems. It can be split into two, or done as one if the last section is jumped. A single anchor off a boulder protects the approach to the final 65m pitch just beyond (escape possible at the head of this).

TICINO

Salto

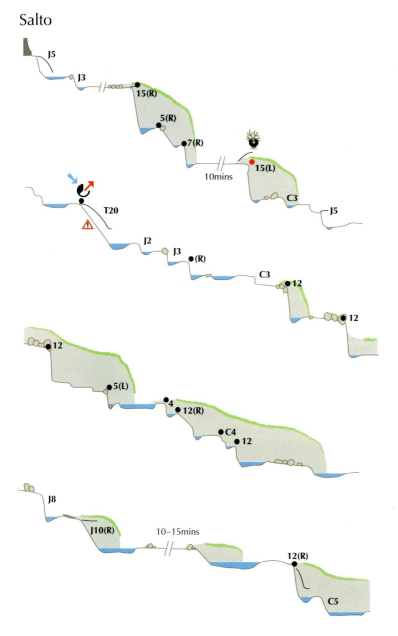

ROUTE 20: SALTO

One of Salto's many deep green pools

The final 65m pitch

Salto (continued)

RETURN TO PARKING A
Follow the path on the right, avoiding paths which descend back to stream level. Pass through a vineyard onto a paved road. Take a little-seen path on the right after 30m, then another right after 5m. This takes you back to the car.

RETURN TO PARKING B
Follow the concrete wall and trend up in the woods on a faint path. This leads to the far end of In Campii. It's a brief stroll down here to the car.

ROUTE 21: VAL DI GEI INFERIORE

VAL DI GEI INFERIORE	★★★✦	V4.A3.IV
Rock	Gneiss	
Dimensions	Depth 160m (500m–340m); length 400m	
Ideal season	Summer	
Time	Approach 30mins; descent 2–3hrs; return 0mins	
Shuttle info	N/A	
Bus number/stop	315 to 'Gordevio'	
Gear	2x50m ropes	
Technical notes	Only longer pitches on double anchors (2010). Water levels sporty in summer without causing any great problems. The two big pitches in particular would be awkward in high water.	
Escapes	None evident	

An excellent little canyon – very pretty and full of sporting interest. The first half is characterised by little sloping cascades and emerald pools perfect for tobogganing; the second by longer pitches to keep the technicians happy. The waterfalls follow one after the other, with barely any time spent walking. The only downside is that it's all over a bit too soon.

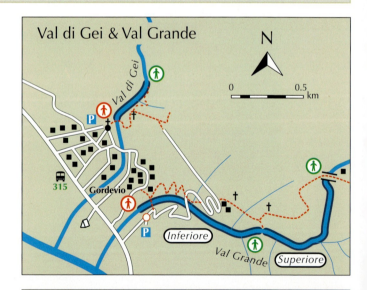

PARKING

If approaching from the south, take the second right after the turning to Camping Bella Riva (the turning is signposted 'Gordevio paese' if approaching from the north). Follow the road up to a T-junction at Ristorante Unione, then take a left up a narrow lane to the church, where the road ends. Park here (limited spaces).

TICINO

APPROACH

Cross the stone bridge and follow the path up the hill (marked with red and white stripes). After 15–20mins the path arrives at a little shrine. Take a faint track off left here, which first descends then ascends, then redescends to the river.

DESCENT

The canyon begins with a number of optional jumps and toboggans (some more straightforward than others) up to the 20m pitch, where the canyon turns more vertical. The following 60m pitch is a little awkward to rig, especially in high water. There is a deviation on the right about 40m down, which secures the final few metres to an obvious spacious ledge 15m above the pool. A 33m pitch follows, requiring a 10m handline to access the main anchors (difficult to see from above). It requires an abseil in the full flow of water. A couple of small drops lead back to the bridge.

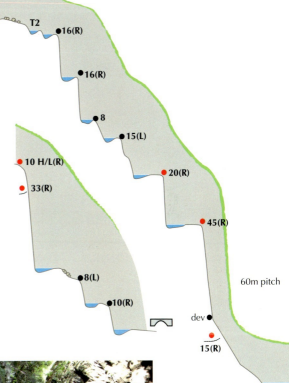

A characteristic scene in Val di Gei (photo: Simon Flower)

ROUTE 22: VAL GRANDE INFERIORE

VAL GRANDE INFERIORE	★★★⌒	V3–4.A4.III
Rock	Gneiss	
Dimensions	Depth 150m (480m–330m); length 750m	
Ideal season	Early to late summer	
Time	Approach 30mins; descent 2–3hrs; return 2mins	
Shuttle info	N/A	
Bus number/stop	315 to 'Gordevio'	
Gear	2x30m ropes (a longer rope would aid in pulling through)	
Technical notes	Rigging sufficient (some on single anchors). Flow minimal in summer, but creates problems early in season or after rain.	
Escapes	None possible until after the encased section	
Note	For map see Route 21	

Val Grande offers a varied, if short outing, very pretty on account of its beautifully banded rock. Although a worthwhile trip in its own right, the canyon will appeal mainly to less experienced groups (in the summer months) and to connoisseurs of gnarly toboggans.

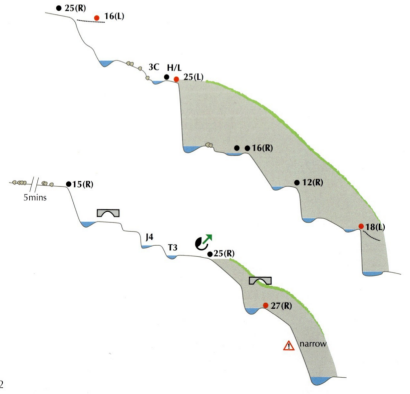

TICINO

A pleasant start to Val Grande (photo: Simon Flower)

PARKING

If coming from the south, pass through the tunnel north of Avegno. About 500m further on, take an unsigned turning on the right, just before crossing over the river into Gordevio. The road (or gravel track) flanks the river on its south side. Park where a barrier bars further progress.

APPROACH

Pass the barrier and continue up the road for 50m. Cross the stone bridge over the canyon (inspecting a possible toboggan on the right). A few metres further on, take a steep path on the right that climbs the hillside above the village. The path meets an asphalted road a little further up. Continuing straight over cuts out a short section of road-walking. On meeting the road again, follow it right (uphill) to where a path branches off right at a couple of stone buildings. Take this, passing a shrine after 100m. Look out for a well-trodden track off to the right on a sharp left-hand bend (if you reach another shrine you have gone too far). The path contours for a few metres before descending steeply to the canyon (a hand-line may be in place).

DESCENT

Don't miss the nice little toboggan just upstream from the start. The descent begins in earnest with a sloping 16m pitch (just about tobogganable!). The

ROUTE 22: VAL GRANDE INFERIORE

One of Val Grande's more nerve-racking toboggans! (photo: Simon Flower)

canyon then becomes more encased, with a 25m abseil into a deep pool (caution in high water). Three more short pitches follow (possible jumps or toboggans depending on desire and skill). The canyon then opens out. A 5min walk in open streamway (escape possible) precedes a 15m pitch, followed by a few little jumps and toboggans. Either escape to the bridge or continue down for the final two pitches. The pitch just before the bridge provides a nerve-racking ejection-style toboggan into a small area of deep water (verify first). Walk downstream until it is possible to scramble left to the road.

> ### VAL GRANDE SUPERIORE
>
> Descent not verified. Approach as for Val Grande Inferiore but continue climbing on the main path for another 30mins. A stone bridge marks the head of the canyon. Descend to the river on its near side. The canyon consists of around 16 quite open, mainly sub-horizontal pitches (double anchors on most; 2x40m ropes needed). The canyon becomes more aquatic in its lower reaches after meeting a tributary. The descent takes about 3–4hrs.

ROUTE 23: LOCO INFERIORE

LOCO INFERIORE		( final part)	V4.A3.III
Alternative name	Ri Bordione Inferiore		
Rock	Gneiss		
Dimensions	Depth 140m (700m–560m); length 250m		
Ideal season	Summer		
Time	Approach 5mins; descent 1h 30mins–2hrs; return 30mins		
	Allow an extra 1hr 30mins for the lower part, plus a 45mins return walk		
Shuttle info	N/A		
Bus number/stop	324 to 'Loco Paese' (stops in Loco itself) or 'Loco Salei' (further on)		
Gear	2x60m ropes		
Technical notes	Good equipment (2010); usually double anchors +/– chains. Low flow in high summer, but current still potentially problematic on two longest pitches. No problems in second part.		
Escapes	None in the first part		

Loco is a short, south-facing canyon, well exposed to the sun. It provides a continuous stream of sculpted pitches and deep pools, some rather technical in high water. The canyon unfortunately loses its character entirely in its second half, but this section can be avoided by an escape route halfway down.

PARKING

Take the road to Centovalli from Locarno, then the turning to Onserone. Follow the road up to Loco. Just as you leave Loco the road passes over the canyon. Park 100m or so beyond in the shaded lay-by (limited spaces) or back in the village.

APPROACH

Back at the bridge over the canyon, take the vehicle track on the true right of the river. Take the path on the right just before it reaches private property.

DESCENT

The canyon begins with a few jumps and toboggans. On the far side of the road bridge a short abseil leads to the first big pitch (50m). Stay on the rope here to access the anchors (exposed). A series of small cascades leads to the final obstacle, an aquatic 35m pitch in the full flow of water – difficult in high water. A 4m toboggan precedes it, but this is probably better abseiled in high water as the anchors for the 35m pitch following are difficult to access. At the base of this a rope dangling into the canyon signifies the end of the first part.

ROUTE 23: LOCO INFERIORE

The aquatic 35m pitch that marks the end of the recommended route (photo: Simon Flower)

TICINO

RETURN

Scramble up the slope (rope assisted) to a hydro-electric turbine and follow a faint path back to the village.

FINAL PART

This is really of interest only if water levels are high. A series of long slabby pitches (maximum 60m, split at a roomy shelf midway; 2x30m rope needed) lead to an old building above the Isorno river. A 45min back-breaking slog uphill punishes you for straying beyond the recommended route! It is possible to descend into the Isorno river, but this is not recommended owing to the unpredictability of the dam upstream.

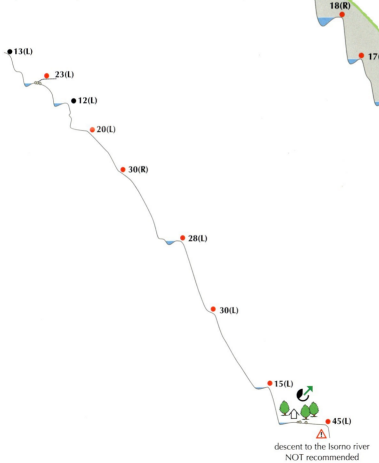

descent to the Isorno river
NOT recommended

147

ROUTE 24: TICINETTO INFERIORE

TICINETTO INFERIORE ★★★★ V4.A4.III

Rock	Gneiss
Dimensions	Depth 170m (770m–600m); length 250m
Ideal season	Early to late summer
Time	Approach 0mins; descent 1hr 30mins–2hrs 30mins; return 15mins
Shuttle info	N/A
Bus number/stop	123 to 'Chironico, Posta'
Gear	2x40m ropes
Technical notes	Mainly single anchors in the first half; double anchors in the second. Strong current to begin with. The flow of the current is mainly avoided in the second half, but the passage is rather intimidating and technical.
Escapes	One, before the second part

A stunning little canyon, composed of a sunny, playful first half and a more technical and atmospheric second. The flow rate in the canyon is considerable, but more or less constant thanks to the upstream dam regulating the flow. Not for inexperienced groups.

⚠ **Dangerous dam upstream – tel +41 (0) 91 7569301**

Descent into the wet and noisy second part

TICINO

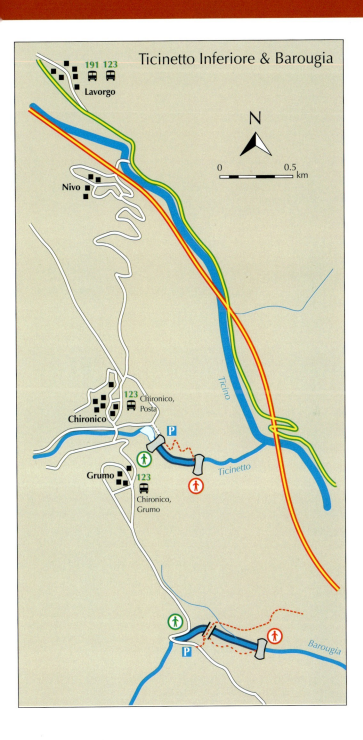

ROUTE 24: TICINETTO INFERIORE

PARKING
From Lavorgo take a road to Chironico. In Chironico, follow signs for 'Grumo/Centro Comunale'. Park on the rough ground to the left of the dam.

DESCENT
The canyon is accessed by a 6m jump. The following 7m pitch is also unrigged (jump, or toboggan after verification). The 40m pitch after is split in two half-way down (ledge for two to three people – two anchors). The second half can be tobogganed from whatever height you feel comfortable. An escape can be made here if you are not comfortable with the current. A 34m pitch to a small shelf (space for three to four people) precedes the crux – a 30m abseil into an aquatic spray-filled chasm. A spray-lashed traverse on the left protects another 30m pitch. It is then an 8m pitch or 5m jump to safer ground. Two large pyramids of rock precede a final bouldery section (two dry 8m pitches/climbs).

RETURN
Exit on the right at the dam. Cross back over the bridge and follow the path back up to the car.

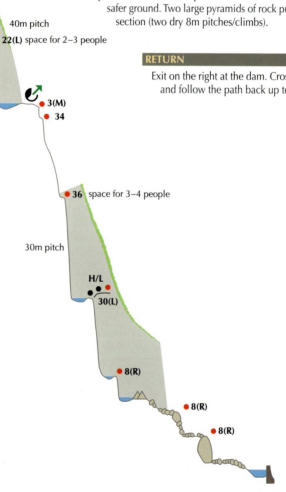

ROUTE 25: BAROUGIA

BAROUGIA ★★★ V3.A3–4.III

Rock	Gneiss
Dimensions	Depth 116m (776m–660m); length 500m
Ideal season	Early to late summer
Time	Approach 0mins; descent 1–2hrs; return 15mins
Shuttle info	N/A
Bus number/stop	123 to 'Chironico, Grumo'
Gear	2x35m ropes
Technical notes	All pitches rigged with single thru-bolts. Rigging mainly out of the water, but plunge-pools can be turbulent, especially the base of the 32m pitch.
Escapes	Numerous
Note	For map see Route 24

Barougia is often in condition when everything else is too wet. High water levels make an otherwise fairly ordinary canyon quite sporting. In normal summer conditions, the canyon is very much easier and suited to less experienced groups.

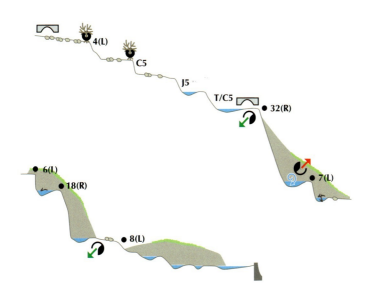

ROUTE 25: BAROUGIA

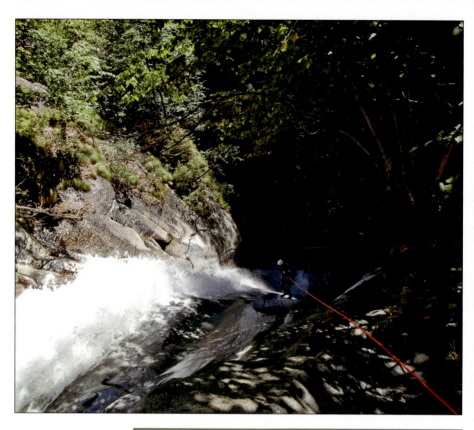

The base of the 32m pitch can be turbulent in high water

PARKING

From Lavorgo take a road to Chironico. Traverse through Chironico, and after about 1km park just after crossing the river.

DESCENT

The canyon begins as fairly open stream until an old footbridge over the canyon (escape possible). Four pitches follow. The canyon then narrows down briefly before the end (8m abseil required in high water).

RETURN

Exit at the dam and take a faint path on the right. This gains a more obvious path after 10mins. Take a left and follow the path back to the car.

ROUTE 26: MALVAGLIA INFERIORE

MALVAGLIA INFERIORE ★★★ V4.A3.III

Alternative name	Riale Orino Inferiore
Rock	Gneiss
Dimensions	Depth 210m (580m–370m); length 800m
Ideal season	Early to late summer
Time	Approach 10mins (Parking B); descent 2–3hrs; return 2mins (Parking A)
Shuttle info	Parking A to Parking B – 2.9km (45mins walk)
Bus number/stop	131 to 'Malvaglia, Chiesa'
Gear	2x45m ropes; short cow's tail useful
Technical notes	Rigging mostly on double 10mm thru-bolts and chains (2009). Flow causes few problems in 'normal' summer conditions.
Escapes	One – after the pitches beneath the bridge

Sombre and vegetated, Val Malvaglia has a different feel to other canyons in the valley. It is an open gorge for most of its length, and the more interesting sections tend to separated by slippery boulders. Despite lacking the 'wow factor' found in neighbouring canyons, the mixture of enclosed pitches, toboggans and a two-pitch waterfall provides sufficient amusement for an afternoon's canyoning.

⚠ Dam upstream – tel +41 (0) 91 7566615

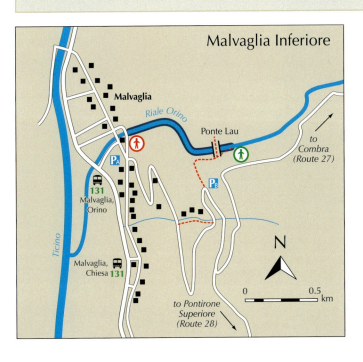

ROUTE 26: MALVAGLIA INFERIORE

Abseil beneath boulders in Malvaglia Inferiore

Midway down the 80m pitch

TICINO

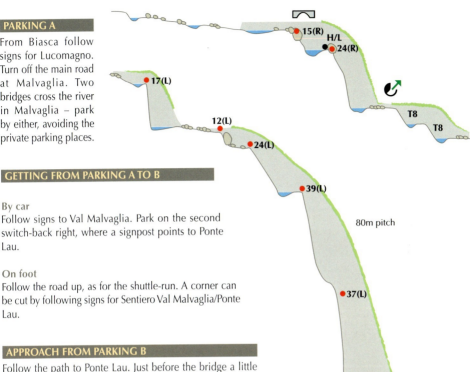

PARKING A

From Biasca follow signs for Lucomagno. Turn off the main road at Malvaglia. Two bridges cross the river in Malvaglia – park by either, avoiding the private parking places.

GETTING FROM PARKING A TO B

By car
Follow signs to Val Malvaglia. Park on the second switch-back right, where a signpost points to Ponte Lau.

On foot
Follow the road up, as for the shuttle-run. A corner can be cut by following signs for Sentiero Val Malvaglia/Ponte Lau.

APPROACH FROM PARKING B

Follow the path to Ponte Lau. Just before the bridge a little path on the right leads to the head of the canyon, slippery and exposed in places (ropes in situ). It is advisable to change at the bridge as there is little room at the river.

DESCENT

The canyon begins laboriously with a section of slippery streamway. Interest begins under the bridge with two beautifully sculpted pitches. The traverse line in situ for the second pitch is reasonably strenuous (short cow's tail advised). There are more boulders, then a tobogganing section, including a possible 18m toboggan into a giant pool (rope recommended to access the take-off). Boulders again, then the final vertical part is reached, consisting of 12, 24 and 80m pitches. The 80m pitch is split halfway down on the left (two-bolt hanging re-belay; room for two people only). A 3m down-climb/jump is the only obstacle remaining before the bouldery walk-out.

RETURN

Exit just past the bridge, on the left.

ROUTE 27: COMBRA

COMBRA		★★★↙ ◧ V4.A4.II
Rock	Gneiss	
Dimensions	Depth 150m (1140m–990m); length 500m	
Ideal season	Summer	
Time	Approach 25mins; descent 1hr 30mins–2hrs; return 5–10mins	
Shuttle info	N/A	
Bus number/stop	As for Malvaglia Inferiore (ie no convenient service)	
Gear	2x25m ropes	
Technical notes	Rigging is fairly rudimentary, on single anchors and naturals. Some jumps are not rigged at all. Certain pitch-heads would be hard to protect and dangerous in high water. Water levels are always sporting and surprisingly cold.	
Escapes	Several	

A virtually constant string of sporting jumps and toboggans means that this canyon would be a classic were it not let down by a boring, bouldery finale. Ideal in combination with Val Malvaglia (Route 26), as it is in the sun from late morning onwards.

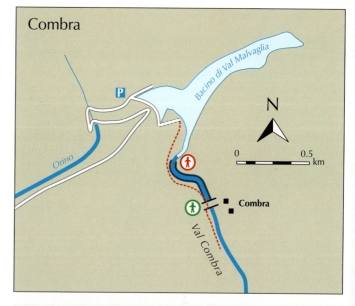

PARKING

Start as for Malvaglia Inferiore (Route 26). Follow the road to the dam at Bacino di Val Malvaglia, then climb again to the top of the dam on hairpins. Take the right to Val Combra where the road splits and park immediately. Parking places further on are for residents only.

TICINO

APPROACH
Cross the dam, pass through the tunnel and double back right onto a broad track. Follow this all the way to a bridge over the canyon.

Combra – aquatic and surprisingly cold

DESCENT
An 18m pitch precedes a string of (often obligatory) jumps and toboggans. An escape can be made left at a more horizontal section. Then comes the crux,

ROUTE 27: COMBRA

There's little need for a rope in Combra's first part

should you want it – a 20m toboggan (best accessed by a short length of rope) that throws you horizontally across the pool. After this a couple of slippery ramps precede a possible escape to the left. It is best to exit here, as the remainder of the canyon is bouldery and lacks character.

RETURN
Aim up left by the giant overflow pipe.

VAL PONTIRONE

A long descent, divisible into Superiore and Inferiore parts. Despite being very short, or perhaps because of this, Pontirone Inferiore should be high on everybody's tick-list. The encasement is severe and imposing, possibly more so than anywhere else in Ticino. The towering scalloped walls stand as a monument to powerful erosive forces, while high water levels and deep pools provide constant sporting interest. In the late afternoon, the sun finally creeps round to illuminate the moody colours of the interior, making Pontirone Inferiore the perfect finish to a day's canyoning.

Pontirone Superiore is less spectacular but makes a very worthwhile extension to Pontirone Inferiore. The canyon is rather discontinuous in nature – there are only a dozen cascades over its 2.6km length – but a couple of technical passages and numerous jumping opportunities make for plentiful entertainment. The canyon should not be underestimated – it is long, cold and committing, and (as in the lower canyon) the current can cause problems in places.

PARKING A
From Biasca follow the signs for Lucomagno. Park in the wide lay-by next to the canyon, about 2km out of Biasca (1km past the left turn to Lodeiro).

GETTING FROM PARKING A TO B

By car
Continue north on the main road. Turn into Malvaglia and weave up the hillside following signs for Val Malvaglia. Pass the parking place for Malvaglia Inferiore (Route 26). On the next (second) hairpin left, branch off right, following signs for Val Pontirone. Follow the road all the way to Pontirone. Just before entering the village, take a dirt track off right which leads over a bridge to the parking place.

On foot
Cross the old bridge and follow the old vehicle track which gently zigzags its way up the hillside to Pontironetto (1hr). From here it's horizontal going along the road to Pontirone (2km).

ROUTE 28: PONTIRONE SUPERIORE

PONTIRONE SUPERIORE

 V4.A4.IV

Alternative name	Riale Lesgiüna Superiore
Rock	Gneiss
Dimensions	Depth 360m (830m–470m); length 2600m
Ideal season	Summer
Time	Approach 0mins (Parking B); descent 3–4hrs; return 20mins (Parking A)
Shuttle info	Parking A to Parking B – 10km (1hr 30mins walk)
Bus number/stop	131 to 'Malvaglia, Brugaio'
Gear	2x35m ropes; a 40m rope is useful for pulling through
Technical notes	Rigged with single 10mm thru-bolts in 2010. Canyon very aquatic, even in summer. The second and 30m pitches are in the flow of water and require careful abseiling to negotiate. Cold water, and canyon in shade until the afternoon.
Escapes	None evident

Pontirone's long upper section maintains interest despite its discontinuous nature.

⚠ **Dam upstream – tel +41 (0) 91 7566615**

The 30m cascade (photo: Simon Flower)

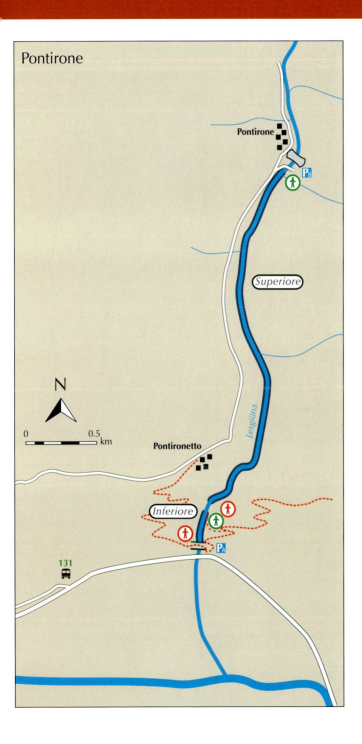

ROUTE 28: PONTIRONE SUPERIORE

An 8m jump commits you to Pontirone Superiore (photo: Simon Flower)

APPROACH FROM PARKING B

Cross back over the bridge and take a faint path down on the left.

DESCENT

The canyon begins with a long section of walking in open streamway, punctuated by little climbs and a nice 8m jump that commits you to the descent. Things liven up at the next pitch, where an anchor on the right bank provides an enclosed and aquatic abseil to a perched pool. An anchor on the left (barely visible from above) provides a 10m abseil to a turbulent pool (possible jump). A short walk followed by four pitches in reasonably quick succession brings you to the 30m cascade, where the canyon again closes down. This can be abseiled in one (40m rope recommended for pulling through) or split halfway down at a dry ledge on the right (single anchor; space for 3–4 people). A long walk in the stream leads to two short pitches (with deep pools), followed by a pretty section of canyon passage with several small jumps and down-climbs. The canyon then becomes increasingly bouldery and open. After an area of enormous boulders the main valley at last becomes visible.

TICINO

Pontirone Superiore

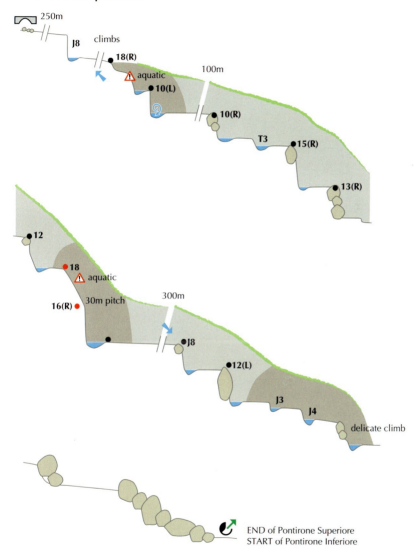

RETURN

Trees on the left bank mark the whereabouts of the exit path (the Pontirone Inferiore approach path). If you wish to exit here, scramble up to a broad sloping ledge. Follow the ledge, protected in places, to a promontory with a flood-warning sign. Follow a good path along the hillside for a couple of hundred metres to where it intercepts the main path. Follow this down to the road to Parking A.

ROUTE 29: PONTIRONE INFERIORE

Superb scenery and great sport make Pontirone Inferiore a regional classic

TICINO

PONTIRONE INFERIORE ★★★★★ V4.A4.IV

Alternative name	Riale Lesgiüna Inferiore
Rock	Gneiss
Dimensions	Depth 100m (470m–370m); length 250m
Ideal season	Summer
Time	Approach 30mins (Parking A); descent 1hr–1hr 30mins; return 0mins (Parking A)
Shuttle info	N/A
Bus number/stop	131 to 'Malvaglia, Brugaio'
Gear	2x45m ropes
Technical notes	Rigged with single 10mm thru-bolts in 2010 (40m pitch rigged double). Canyon very aquatic, even in summer. Only the 40m pitch is rigged clear of danger; the remainder must be approached with caution. Some may be safer jumped than abseiled.
Escapes	None
Note	For map see Route 28

Pontirone's short but intense lower section is one of Ticino's finest outings.

⚠ Dam upstream – tel +41 (0) 91 7566615. Frequent violent floods ensure that the canyon changes considerably each year – pools silt up, watercourses change and whole passages fill and empty of boulders.

Unusual shapes and colours in Pontirone Inferiore

ROUTE 29: PONTIRONE INFERIORE

APPROACH FROM PARKING A

Follow the track which rises from the lay-by. Zigzag up through the trees. After 10–15mins, take a track which branches off left. This more or less contours along the hillside towards the canyon. Once out of the trees (by a flood-warning sign), follow the path right, under the cliffs, to the start of the canyon.

DESCENT

Pick your way over and around the boulders to the head of the first (40m) pitch. This is either rigged from the left-hand wall or on the huge boulder perched against it (both are quite exposed). A number of small aquatic pitches follow, some of which can be jumped. The first few constitute the 'Terrible S', two pitches that intermittently fill with boulders, forming siphons and causing great problems for rope retrieval.

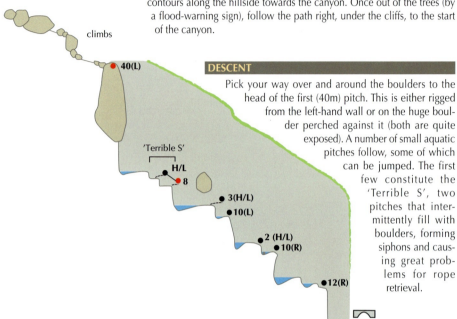

Descending into Iragna Superiore

ROUTE 30: IRAGNA SUPERIORE

IRAGNA

Iragna is a beautiful alpine canyon – long, wild and aquatic. In its entirety it constitutes a full and tiring day out. Timed correctly it is well sunlit along most of its length, but arrive after midday and you'll be shivering in the shadows for six hours. The full descent, which consists of numerous moderate-sized pitches and jumps, can be split into Superiore and Inferiore parts. Iragna Inferiore is accessible at two places, depending on time constraints and enthusiasm.

IRAGNA SUPERIORE	★★★★  V4–5.A4.III
Rock	Gneiss
Dimensions	Depth 229m (749m–520m); length 750m
Ideal season	Summer
Time	Approach 15mins (Parking B); descent 2–4hrs; return 20mins (Parking A)
Shuttle info	Parking A to Parking B – 8km (1hr walk)
Bus number/stop	193 to 'Iragna, Ponte dei Ladri'
Gear	2x35m ropes
Technical notes	Sensibly placed double 10mm thru-bolts. Some pitches in full flow of water – dangerous in medium to high water. Water levels cannot be assessed directly from Iragna village, as some water is removed further upstream.
Escapes	Possibly one (not verified)

Wild and committing, Iragna Superiore is the more technical of the two parts.

PARKING A

Coming from the south, pass the turning into Lodrino and enter Iragna village. Park in the little square just before the bridge.

PARKING B

Return towards Lodrino on the main road. After 1km take a little-seen turning on the right, disguised as a garage forecourt (Garage Carrozzeria). This road climbs on hairpins before levelling out. Take the next turning right (unmarked, 4.3km from turn-off). Follow this for a further 2.5km to Citt. Park on the edge of the village, where the road doubles back left.

APPROACH FROM PARKING A

Follow the road which climbs on the left (true right) of the river. Follow the footpath which leads off. After 5–10mins, reach a fork in the path. Take the left (signposted Citt). The path now winds its way up through deciduous woodland. After

ROUTE 30: IRAGNA SUPERIORE

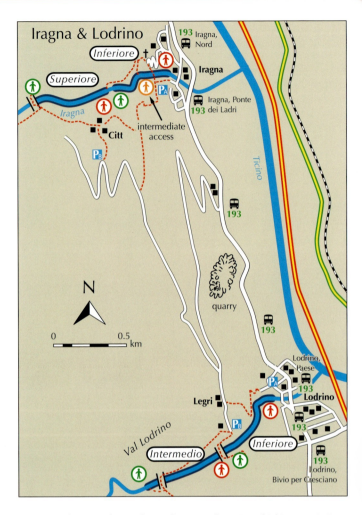

50mins reach Citt, a cluster of pretty houses and a spring (drinking water). From here follow the signs for Pön. The path contours the hillside above the canyon. Where the path splits take the right path, which descends to a stone bridge over the canyon. Get in here.

APPROACH FROM PARKING B

Walk horizontally through Citt. At the far end pick up signs for Pön and follow the description above.

TICINO

DESCENT

The crux of the descent is the 32m pitch. The anchors are accessed by descending the flume about 15m before stepping up right onto a thin ledge (20m of rope needed). The final 10m of the abseil and the plunge-pool, out of sight from the top, can cause problems in medium to high water conditions. The 25m and 22m pitches that follow will also cause problems in high water. After the 22m pitch the canyon opens out a little. It may be possible to escape right into the trees here (not verified). The canyon closes down for a further three pitches before opening out again. A long open walking section follows, after which an escape can be made up a gully on the left (Inferiore access point).

RETURN

Go right at the top of the gully, scrambling up over rocks. The path, faint at times, skirts the canyon then descends to a fenced enclosure. Pass beneath this, climb the low fence and follow the main path down to Iragna village.

ROUTE 30: IRAGNA SUPERIORE

Iragna Superiore: intermittently narrow and sporting

ROUTE 31: IRAGNA INFERIORE

IRAGNA INFERIORE		★★★★ V4.A4.III
Rock	Gneiss	
Dimensions	Depth 233m (520m–287m); length 750m	
Ideal season	Summer	
Time	Approach 30mins (Parking A); descent 3–4hrs; return 2mins (Parking A) Intermediate access 20mins approach and 2hrs descent	
Shuttle info	N/A	
Bus number/stop	193 to 'Iragna, Nord' (Inferiore)	
Gear	2x45m ropes	
Technical notes	Sensibly placed double 10mm thru-bolts. Some pitches in full flow of water – dangerous in medium to high water. Water levels cannot be assessed directly from Iragna village as some water is removed further upstream.	
Escapes	None until after the 40m pitch, then numerous	
Note	For map see Route 30	

The more popular lower canyon provides a succession of pretty pitches and deep pools.

APPROACH FROM PARKING A

Start as for the walk to Citt. Take a right at the first T-junction, signposted '77'. Cross the bridge over the canyon and gain the road again (parking a second car here saves only 10mins walking). From the end of the road take a path which climbs to a shrine. Just beyond the shrine the path splits. Take the left fork and keep climbing to a gate and low fence. Climb over and skirt beneath a fenced enclosure. Just beyond this, the path splits again. Take the left fork, which takes a gently rising line along the edge of the canyon. Ignore the faint paths which branch off it. The path eventually leads to a gully which is descended to the canyon.

DESCENT

The canyon begins as a pretty narrow section, which becomes increasingly encased. The 15m pitch is in the full flow of water, but can be avoided by traversing up left to a higher stance (fixed hand-line in situ). A more open section follows, followed by an enclosed 24m pitch (dangerous in high water). A little further downstream two short pitches gain the head of the 40m pitch. From the base of this, stay high on the left, which leads to two decent anchors for the following 22m pitch (escape possible; a single anchor also exists in the streamway and provides a very aquatic descent). Escape is also possible at the stone bridge described in the walk-in. Here, some of the water gets tapped off. A 5m drop is followed by a canal which precedes a 20m pitch (back-up anchors damaged in 2009). A few more straightforward drops lead to Iragna village.

ROUTE 31: IRAGNA INFERIORE

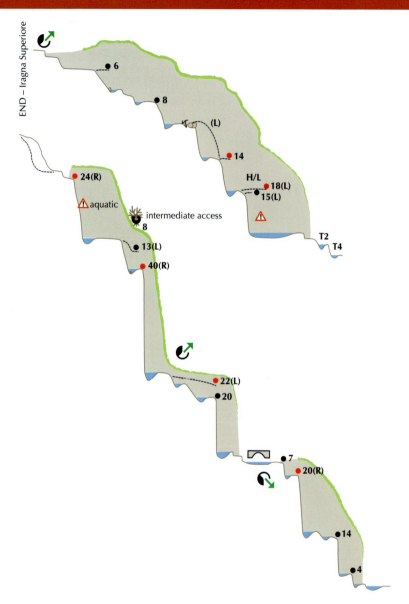

INTERMEDIATE ACCESS

If time is short, the trip length can be shortened to 2hrs. Above the shrine look out for a faint track leading off the main path (on a right-hand bend, after a few minutes' climbing). This descends a little way before contouring around to the canyon. Access to the canyon is by 8m abseil from a tree, just above the 40m pitch.

TICINO

The 40m pitch in Iragna Inferiore

LODRINO

Lodrino is one of the most aquatic canyons in Ticino – dangerous for the inexperienced but a canyon par excellence for competent canyoners. For the most part, the canyon is deeply and beautifully encased, with a mixture of abseils, jumps and (if you're brave enough) toboggans in spectacular surrounds. Unmissable, when conditions and experience allow.

The canyon is divisible into Superiore, Intermedio and Inferiore parts. Lodrino Superiore is long and discontinuous, with few rewards for a lengthy walk-in. Only the Intermedio and Inferiore parts are described here.

PARKING A
Park in Lodrino village. Do not change here.

GETTING FROM PARKING A TO B

By car
Continue along the main road towards Iragna. After 2km, beyond the large quarry and just after a bus stop on the right, take the turning to the left. The turn is difficult to see, disguised as a garage forecourt (Garage Carrozzeria). Follow the road for another 5km, ignoring a turning on the right, until the road ends at a wide turning area (Legri). Park here.

On foot
From the far end of Lodrino village, a street back from the river, take a path signposted to Legri, marked with red and white stripes. It climbs relentlessly for 20mins in the merciful shade of deciduous woodland. When it meets the road, go left. A 5–10min walk along the road brings you to Parking B.

ROUTE 32: LODRINO INTERMEDIO

LODRINO INTERMEDIO ★★★★ V4.A4.III

Rock	Gneiss
Dimensions	Depth 170m (650m–480m); length 900m
Ideal season	Summer
Time	Approach 30mins (Parking B); descent 1hr–1hr 30mins; return 15mins (Parking B)
Shuttle info	N/A
Bus number/stop	193 to 'Lodrino Paese'
Gear	2x50m ropes
Technical notes	Rigged with 10mm thru-bolts, sensibly placed. Only bigger pitches are rigged double (2009). Always aquatic, even in high summer. Avoid in early season and wait for settled weather.
Escapes	None
Note	For map see Route 30

An excellent addition to Lodrino Inferiore and a worthwhile trip in its own right.

An aquatic pitch in Lodrino Intermedio

TICINO

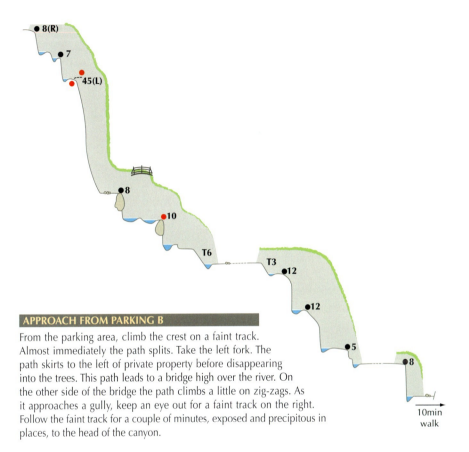

APPROACH FROM PARKING B

From the parking area, climb the crest on a faint track. Almost immediately the path splits. Take the left fork. The path skirts to the left of private property before disappearing into the trees. This path leads to a bridge high over the river. On the other side of the bridge the path climbs a little on zig-zags. As it approaches a gully, keep an eye out for a faint track on the right. Follow the faint track for a couple of minutes, exposed and precipitous in places, to the head of the canyon.

DESCENT

The canyon begins with a brief open section, culminating in an aquatic 45m pitch. This is followed by two stunning encased sections, each with a series of small pitches. Some of these may be jumped, depending on confidence. The canyon opens out again, with 5mins of boulder-hopping to a bridge (the access point for Lodrino Inferiore – exit possible left).

ROUTE 33: LODRINO INFERIORE

LODRINO INFERIORE   ★★★★★  V5.A5.IV

Rock	Gneiss
Dimensions	Depth 200m (480m–280m); length 900m
Ideal season	Summer to late summer
Time	Approach 10mins (Parking A); descent 3hrs–3hrs 30mins; return 2mins (Parking A)
Shuttle info	Parking A to Parking B – 7km (30mins walk)
Bus number/stop	193 to 'Lodrino Paese'
Gear	2x50m ropes (60m rope useful for pulling through)
Technical notes	Rigged with 10mm thru-bolts, sensibly placed. Only bigger pitches are rigged double (2009). Always very aquatic, even in high summer, and dangerous in high water. Avoid in early season and wait for settled weather. Some pitches in full flow of water. Water levels can be judged at the base of the final pitch.
Escapes	Two, between encased sections
Note	For map see Route 30; for topo see Route 32

Ticino's finest outing is for experienced parties only.

Deep pools mean that many pitches can be jumped or tobogganed

TICINO

APPROACH FROM PARKING B

Follow the track which descends from Parking B. Enter where a bridge crosses the river.

DESCENT

The imposing lower canyon now begins, consisting of a further three encased sections. The second encased section ends with a 45m pitch at the far end of a large pool. A single anchor protects a right-to-left traverse to the main belay. A 60m rope is advised to ease the pull-through. The canyon now opens out and an escape can be made at a small dam. Beyond this, some sketchy downclimbing among boulders gains the first pitch (35m) of the final section. Two anchors here provide an aquatic descent (rope difficult to retrieve). In wetter times this pitch is dangerous, when it is perhaps better to use anchors out left (accessible via traverse line). The following 21m pitch is the final obstacle. Exit left into Lodrino village to well-earned ice creams and beer (or a slog back uphill to the car for the unlucky).

VAL D'OSOGNA

Done in its entirety, Osogna constitutes one of the longest days out in Ticino. It can be divided into Superiore, Intermedio and Inferiore canyons, each with their individual character. Osogna Inferiore is one of the jewels of Ticino, a 'must' if you're in the area. It is short but continuous, one pitch after another with virtually no time spent walking. The entire canyon is distinguished by its sculpted, decorative walls and deep green pools. Osogna Intermedio and Superiore require much longer walk-ins. The former is well worth the extra effort, consisting of an open, playful first half and a more enclosed and technical second. An early start is recommended (particularly if wanting to combine it with Osogna Inferiore), but it will ensure that you spend the majority of the descent in the shade. Osogna Superiore offers a series of well-formed, but essentially dry waterfalls – very pretty, but lacking the sporting appeal of the rest of the canyon. A worthy addition to the day if you take the helicopter (see chapter introduction), but trickier to justify if approaching on foot.

PARKING

From the south, pass the first two turnings for Osogna. Turn off at the next junction, signposted 'Safe Driving'. Pass under the railway bridge into the northern end of Osogna. Park in the designated parking area by the first left-hand turning.

ROUTE 33: LODRINO INFERIORE

The penultimate pitch in Lodrino Inferiore

ROUTE 34: OSOGNA INTERMEDIO

OSOGNA INTERMEDIO

★★★↘  V4.A4.IV

Alternative name	Riale Nala Intermedio
Rock	Gneiss
Dimensions	Depth 360m (820m–460m); length 1600m
Season	Early to late summer
Time	Approach 1hr 30mins; descent 4–5hrs; return 15mins
Shuttle info	N/A
	Helicopter access available (reduces approach walk to 20mins – see chapter introduction)
Bus number/stop	191 to 'Osogna, Paese'
Gear	2x40m ropes
Technical notes	Rigging mainly off single 10mm thru-bolts; longest pitches rigged double (2009). Substantial stream – some pitches in second part in full flow of water.
Escapes	Only at the beginning (see descent description)

Osogna's longest part is sporting from beginning to end, and gathers aesthetic interest with descent.

⚠ **Dam upstream – tel +41 (0) 91 7566615. Note there is ordinarily no flow below the dam. The water in the canyon is from a tributary that is not dam controlled.**

APPROACH

Take the left-hand turning (passing behind the cemetery), then take an immediate left up to a little water fountain and shrine. Start towards the gate at the base of the hill and take a right down an alley to the river. Cross the bridge to the road on the other side. Take a left and follow the road for about 5mins until a signpost directs you to Pönt/Alpe d'Örz. Climb in the woods on a well-marked path (red and white stripes), ignoring all turnings off. After an hour's steady climbing reach a little cluster of houses and a clearing (Pönt). From here, the path more or less skirts the hillside to the river. There is a spring 5mins beyond Pönt (drinking water). Continue to the bridge over the river, where the canyon starts. The section of canyon just beneath the bridge is of little interest. It can be avoided by taking a faint path just before the granite steps leading up the bridge.

DESCENT

The canyon begins with a few modest-sized pitches, a number of which can be jumped or tobogganed depending on bravery levels. A more open section follows – beware of very loose rock looming over the base of the 25m pitch (escape possible to the left just after this). The 40m pitch marks the beginning of the more technical half. The first 21m of this are in the full flow of water, making the roomy re-belay halfway down awkward to access (an anchor exists near the stream to rig a hand-line if needed). After the next two pitches (34m, 15m),

ROUTE 34: OSOGNA INTERMEDIO

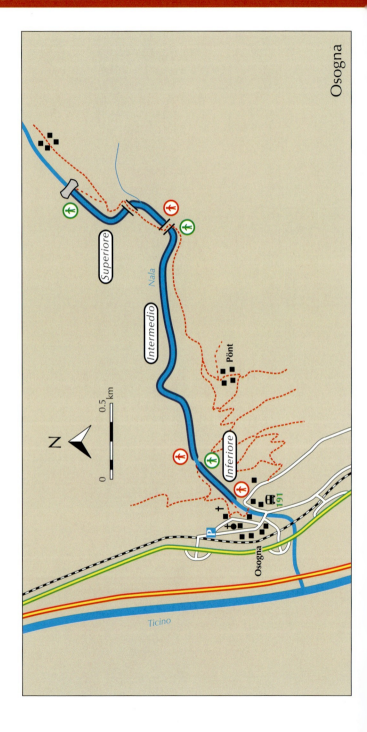

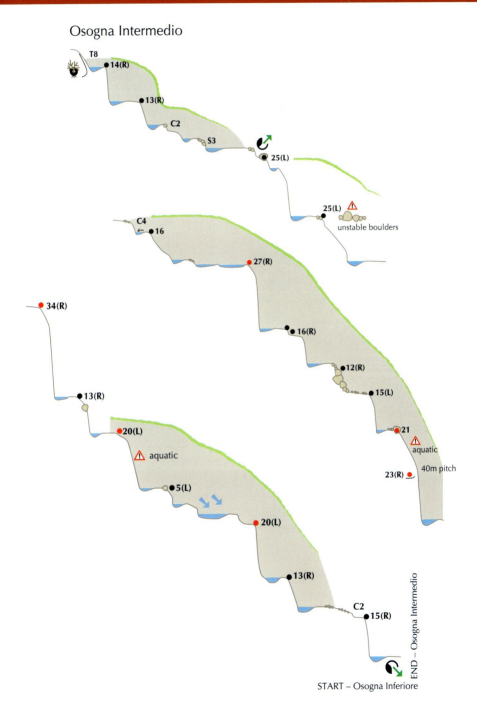

ROUTE 34: OSOGNA INTERMEDIO

The 40m pitch marks the start of the more technical half of the canyon (photo: Simon Flower)

a constricted 20m waterfall provides access to a narrow and well-sculpted section of canyon. This pitch would be difficult in high water. After three more pitches the canyon opens out. A 15m abseil is the last before Osogna Inferiore.

RETURN

The exit (which is the Osogna Inferiore approach path) is located by the first pitch of Osogna Inferiore. At a point where you first have views of the main valley, look out for a line of square holes spanning the canyon floor (abandoned dam workings). A faint and brambly track up right leads down to an old stone building (exposed in places). From here take a right to the main path leading up from Osogna village.

ROUTE 34A: OSOGNA (OR RIALE NALA) SUPERIORE

OSOGNA (OR RIALE NALA) SUPERIORE ★★↗ V4.A2.II

Osogna's uppermost part is recommended only to fast-moving groups who wish to do the whole descent of Osogna.

From the bridge at the head of Osogna Intermedio, climb again. After 15mins or so, the path crosses another bridge over the canyon (which is dry). Climb the impressive granite steps, then enter the woods, keeping a keen eye out for a very easily missed path on the left. Initially this path is faint, but steps are soon encountered. If you miss the turning a cluster of little buildings will be reached after about 5–10mins (the helicopter lands close by). Allow a further 30mins for the walk and 2hrs for the descent (highest pitch 34m; only longer pitches rigged with double anchors).

A tiny trickle is only just enough to keep Osogna Superiore's pools clean

ROUTE 35: OSOGNA INFERIORE

OSOGNA INFERIORE ★★★★↘ ◼ V4.A4.III

Alternative name	Riale Nala Inferiore
Rock	Gneiss
Dimensions	Depth 180m (460m–280m); length 400m
Ideal season	Early to late summer
Time	Approach 20mins; descent 2hrs; return 5mins
Shuttle info	N/A
Bus number/stop	191 to 'Osogna, Paese'
Gear	2x60m ropes
Technical notes	Rigging mainly off single 10mm thru-bolts; longest pitches rigged double (2009). Substantial stream – can cause problems on 50m pitch (in full flow of water).
Escapes	Two – before the 50m pitch and by the 14m toboggan
Note	For map see Route 34

Short, varied and spectacular, this is a descent not to miss!

⚠ **Dam upstream** – tel +41 (0) 91 7566615. Note there is no flow below the dam. The water in the canyon is from a tributary that is not dam controlled.

APPROACH

Start as for Osogna Intermedio (Route 34). Pass through the gate at the base of the hill, and start zigzagging up the hillside on a wide path. Where the path splits, take the right fork. Follow this, flanking a wall, into the trees. Head to a rustic farm building and follow a faint path up to the left. The path then levels off and skirts the canyon (often a bit overgrown), arriving at the head of the 26m pitch.

DESCENT

Five beautiful pitches in quick succession bring you to the aquatic 50m pitch. A further 23m pitch and the canyon opens out. The first 14m pitch of this second section can be tobogganed, but it is difficult to align yourself – sliding down sideways hurts from this height!

RETURN

Take a right through the village back the car, or stop for a beer in Grott al Pozzon on the left.

Nearing the end of the encased section

ROUTE 35: OSOGNA INFERIORE

Osogna Inferiore

VALLE DI CRESCIANO

Cresciano Superiore and Inferiore, if done together, make for a big day out. A lengthy walk-in and around 40 pitches means that the full descent demands an early start, although efficient parties shouldn't struggle too much with time (especially if they take the helicopter up the hill). Cresciano Superiore is most memorable for its first half, where sculpted white gneiss and deep pools mean that many pitches can be tobogganed or jumped. The main problems are the lack of running water (the majority of which has been tapped off for hydroelectrical purposes) and the lack of sunlight in the mornings, when most groups will want to arrive. Cresciano Inferiore is probably the most popular canyon in Ticino, and justifiably so. Although short and not especially encased, the pretty perched pools, stunning rock scenery and plentiful jumping opportunities make the canyon a regional classic. Its brevity and friendly nature make it a favourite of professional groups, which means it is better to turn up outside peak hours.

PARKING A

Driving north from Claro, pass the turning to Lodrino. Take the next turning on the right, 50m beyond a Honda garage (difficult to spot and not signposted). Pass under the railway and take a right at a T-junction. Park in the parking spot by the flood-warning sign.

GETTING FROM PARKING A TO B

Head south on the main road. Turn off at Cresciano village (a right turn by Ristorante degli Amici, just before a church on the right) then double back beneath the main road. Park at the back of the village in designated parking spots.

ALTERNATIVE PARKING

It is possible to park near Riale di Censo just to the south of Val Cresciano, which at 800m above sea level ensures a relatively pain-free approach walk (allow 50mins). Access is via a toll road above Claro (4 CHF at the time of writing) – remember the fee will need to be paid again when retrieving the second vehicle. The 1:25,000 Swisstopo map will be needed to navigate your way to Sotaregn.

ROUTE 36: CRESCIANO SUPERIORE

CRESCIANO SUPERIORE  V4.A3.IV

Alternative name	Riale Boggera Superiore
Rock	Gneiss
Dimensions	Depth 550m (1030m–480m); length 1500m
Ideal season	Early summer or after heavy rains
Time	Approach 1hr 45mins–2hrs (Parking A or B); descent 4–6hrs; return 15mins (Parking A)
Shuttle info	Parking A to Parking B – 3.5km (50mins road-walk)
	Helicopter access available – see 'Ticino' chapter introduction
Bus number/stop	191 to 'Cresciano, Paese'
Gear	2x40m ropes
Technical notes	Only pitches over 25m are rigged with double anchors (2009). Some small jumps, toboggans and awkward down-climbs are obligatory. A tiny trickle in summer, so some pools take on a decidedly seaside odour.
Escapes	Easy escapes only possible at the top of the canyon, between encasements. Much more difficult lower down.

A long, continuous descent, full of entertainment in spite of the lack of flowing water.

 Dam upstream – tel +41 (0) 91 7566615

APPROACH FROM PARKING A

Swiss 1:25,000 maps show a path snaking south from the Cresciano Inferiore walk-in, but in reality this is very difficult to follow. Climb on the steps at the rear of the car park. Cross over the river and continue up. About 70m before the main path crosses back over the river, take a faint path which trends horizontally to the south. The path is initially obvious but soon deteriorates – follow the yellow and red markers. Eventually even these become difficult to follow – just keep trending south on faint tracks. After 30–40mins and a couple of small river crossings the path intercepts a bigger track on the edge of the Cresciano bouldering area. Trend uphill slightly, always heading south, to intercept the main path from Cresciano village, marked with red and white stripes (ie the approach from Parking B – see below).

APPROACH FROM PARKING B/'CRESCIANO PAESE' BUS STOP

Climb the hill on the road marked 'Confinante Autorizzati', passing a large parking area on the first hairpin bend. It is possible to take the path marked with red and white stripes to cut the corners. From the end of this road, a path climbs on granite steps through the Cresciano bouldering area (the approach from Parking A joins here, although you probably won't see it). Above this the path splits. Take the right-hand turning to Cauri (a local spelling of Cavri), which is reached in another 10mins (spring with drinking water). Keep on the obvious path, following signs for Sotaregn. The path cuts across a gravel track a

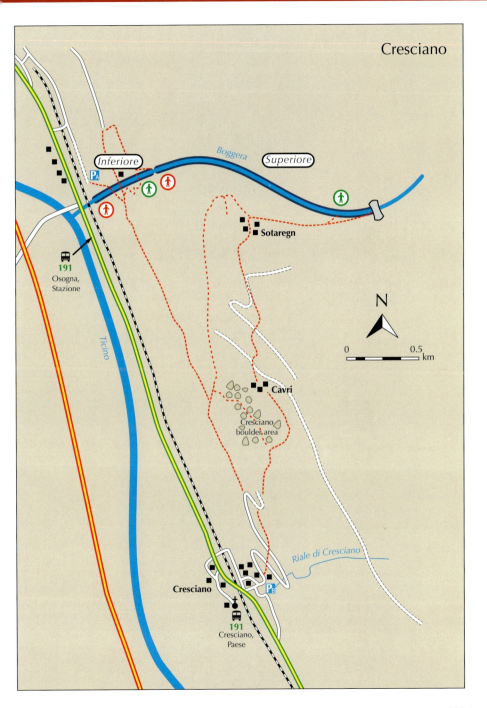

ROUTE 36: CRESCIANO SUPERIORE

Cresciano Superiore

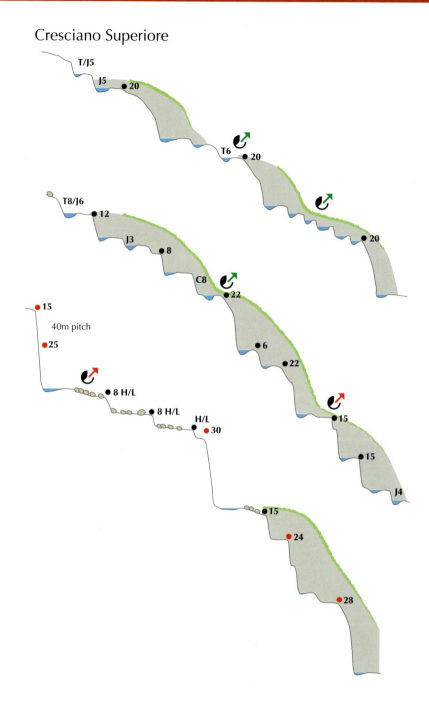

Cresciano Superiore (continued)

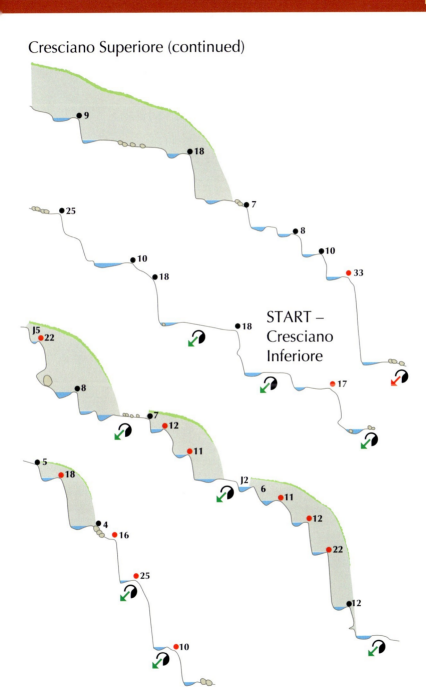

ROUTE 36: CRESCIANO SUPERIORE

The penultimate pitch of the long Cresciano Superiore

couple of times (not marked on Swiss topo maps) before climbing the last little bit to Sotaregn (a surprisingly well-kept cluster of houses and a spring). From here, following signs to Sasso Bianco, the path becomes more level as it skirts Valle di Cresciano. After about 5mins meet a flood-warning sign, where a small path left leads down to the river.

DESCENT

The canyon begins as a series of short, playful encased sections. The biggest pitch is 40m, split at −15m on double hangers (small ledge for two or three people). Beyond this (in summer) the water disappears into the gravel, and a drier section of bouldery stream bed follows. The water returns a couple of pitches further on, and the canyon continues down in a series of longer pitches (maximum 33m). There are 25–30 roped pitches in all. It is easy to miss the exit and continue into Cresciano Inferiore, but escapes from Cresciano Inferiore are frequent (if needed).

ROUTE 37: CRESCIANO INFERIORE

CRESCIANO INFERIORE

★★★★⯪ V3.A3.II

Alternative name	Riale Boggera Inferiore
Rock	Gneiss
Dimensions	Depth 210m (480m–270m); length 500m
Ideal season	Early to late summer
Time	Approach 30mins (Parking A); descent 1hr 30mins–3hrs; return 2mins (Parking A)
Shuttle info	N/A
Bus number/stop	191 to 'Osogna, Stazione' (Inferiore)
Gear	2x30m ropes
Technical notes	Excellent – double anchors on most pitches. Splashy in summer without ever being threatening.
Escapes	Frequent
Note	For map and topo see Route 36

The sunny, no-stress Cresciano Inferiore is Ticino's most popular canyon.

⚠ **Dam upstream – tel +41 (0) 91 7566615**

The final few pitches overlooking the main valley

ROUTE 37: CRESCIANO INFERIORE

The upstream dam ensures the narrow parts are pleasant and splashy

APPROACH FROM PARKING A

Climb the steps at the rear of the car park. Cross over the river and continue up. Some 50m before the path crosses the river for the second time, take a climbing path on the right. Follow this up to another river crossing. The path on the other side of the river quickly intersects with a much bigger path. Follow this rightwards to the canyon.

DESCENT

A series of jumps, slides, ejection-style toboggans and pleasant abseils. Careful not to splash the bathers!

RETURN

At the base of the final pitch, take a right back to the car at Parking A.

the gently sculpted granite of Ferro (Route 48)

Lake Como

CANYONING IN THE ALPS

LAKE COMO

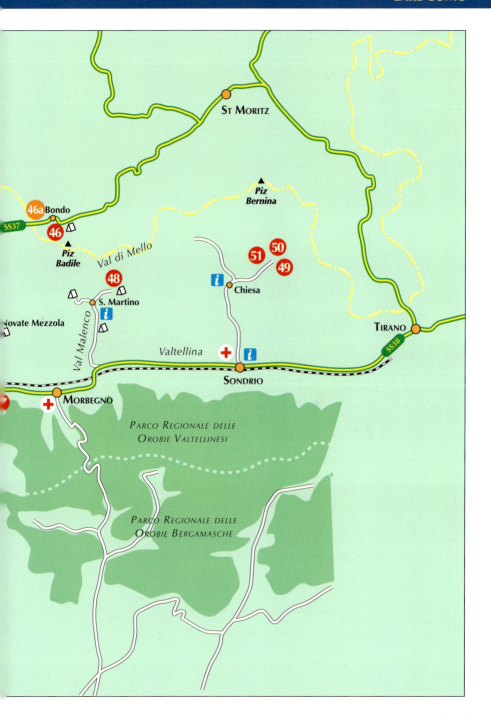

CANYONING IN THE ALPS

Late season in Lake Como

William Wordsworth once described Lake Como as 'a treasure the Earth keeps to itself'. Certainly the lake's beauty is legendary. It has inspired artists and musicians as well as poets, and has been a popular retreat for aristocrats and wealthy people since Roman times. However, a secret it is not. Today Lake Como is among Italy's most popular tourist attractions, and as such it can seem horribly overcrowded. Fortunately the canyons (and some campsites) are hidden away up quiet valleys around the lake and beyond.

The other good news is that the mountains around Lake Como are home to the some of the most spectacular canyoning in Italy. Four geologically distinct ranges encircle the lake, lending the area fantastic variety. To the north-west are the Lepontine Alps, where the gneiss canyons share much in common with the finest canyons of Val d'Ossola and Ticino. Further east is the Bernina group, the highest range in the eastern Alps. The mountains here are mainly granite, but the southern slopes of Piz Bernina itself are serpentinite, a rock which provides a canyoning experience unique in Europe. To the south are the limestone pre-Alps, where 'classic'-style canyons prevail, with deeply cut gorges and karstic features.

WHERE TO STAY

There are innumerable campsites dotted along the shores of Lake Como. The most central of these for canyoning purposes are situated around Sorico on the northern tip of the lake. Be warned, convenience comes at a price. In summer,

LAKE COMO

the idyllic shoreline seethes with tourists and biting mosquitoes, which renders camping here a costly and unpleasant option. Alternatives would be to hire an apartment or head for the quieter campsites at Lago di Mezzola (Camping El Ranchero), Taceno (Camping Le Rocce Rosse, a 20min drive east from Bellano) or Chiavenna. (See Appendix C for details of campsites away from the lake shore.) The campsite in Chiavenna (Camping Acquafraggia) is perhaps the best – cheap, quiet and no motor homes allowed. Self-catering accommodation should not be too difficult to find, but expect to pay a premium if staying anywhere near the lake. Tourist information offices (see Appendix D) have lists of flats and houses for rent.

PRACTICALITIES

Shops and services
Being a tourist destination, shops, banks, tourist offices and hotels can be found in most towns in the region.

Gear shops
The only real gear shop in the area is Effe 3 Sport in Chiavenna (10 Via Chiavennaschi, tel +39 0343 34619). It sells mostly climbing kit, but stocks a small selection of canyoning hardware. To get there, take a right at the second roundabout in Chiavenna, following signs for Centro Storico and the station.

Campsites in the Lake Como area aren't usually this tranquil (photo: Simon Flower)

One of a few rappels under the full flow of water in Bares (Route 43)

LAKE COMO

Hospitals
Emergency departments can be found at Sondrio, Morbegno, Chiavenna, Gravedona, Menaggio and (most importantly) Lecco, the largest hospital in the area.

Weather forecast
The forecast for the area can be found on the Italian-language ARPA website (www.arpalombardia.it), but many people use the Meteo Swiss website (www.meteoswiss.ch) because of the reliability of Swiss weather forecasting. Longer range forecasts can be obtained from 3B Meteo (www.3bmeteo.com) and Il Meteo (www.ilmeteo.it).

Maps
Both IGC and IGM (official Italian mapping), as well as Kompass, produce maps that cover the whole area at 1:50,000. The Swiss Survey 1:50,000 maps are more accurate and detailed, but sadly do not cover the southern aspect of Valtellina. Although 1:25,000 maps are available from IGM and Edizioni Multigraphic, coverage and availability are currently limited.

TRAVEL AND TRANSPORT

Rail
Trains run up the east coast of Lake Como from both Milan and Bergamo, before turning east along Valtellina bound for St Moritz in Switzerland. They stop at a number of towns en route, including Lecco, Colico and Sondrio. Smaller trains go north from Colico to Chiavenna. On the west coast, the Milan trains stop only at Como before moving on to Lugano.

Driving
The canyons in this area are well scattered and here, more than anywhere else in this guide, it is important to choose your base well. Cormor, for instance, is over an hour's drive from Sorico. A dual carriageway runs up the east side of Lake Como between Colico and Lecco, which means that traffic here is never too bad. On the other hand, the road down the western aspect of the lake gets very busy during the summer months, as does the road along Valtellina. Car hire is possible locally in Lecco, Como and Sondrio.

OTHER ACTIVITIES

There are plenty of opportunities for walking, via ferrata and climbing to cater for all tastes and abilities. The walking ranges from easy low-level day-walks among pretty valleys and hamlets to more involved higher-level hill-walking. (A useful guide for walkers is Gillian Price's *Walking the Italian Lakes*, Cicerone Press) Those wishing to get away from the crowds may want to aim for the Orobie Alps, which remain little known outside Italy. Climbing and via ferrata are prevalent around Lecco – see Appendix B for more details. There are a few climbing guides produced, including *Arrampicate Sportive Moderne Fra Lecco e Como*; *Arrampicate Sportive e Moderne in Valtellina, Valchiavenna, Engadina*; *Mello Bouldering*; and

Solo Granito. These are all Italian-language books, available online from the publisher's website (www.versantesud.it). An English-language guidebook is also available, *Swiss Rock – Granite Bregaglia* by Chris Mellor (Void), which details 110 climbs, from single-pitch crags to multi-pitch excursions along the Swiss-Italian border. Alpinism is also popular in the border region. The main English-language guide is the Alpine Club's Bernina and Bregaglia.

PROTECTED AREAS

Parco Regionale delle Orobie Valtellinesi (www.parcorobievalt.com)
Parco delle Orobie Bergamasche (www.parcorobie.it)

VAL BODENGO

Val Bodengo rates as one of Italy's most aesthetic and sporting canyons. Thundering waterfalls and deep pools provide innumerable opportunities for jumps and toboggans, and on a sunny day the beautifully sculpted white gneiss gives the whole place an ethereal quality. The canyon is divided into three distinct parts, all accessible separately. The combination of parts two and three offers one of the most complete and memorable descents in the Alps, an outing with all the key ingredients of a superb canyoning trip. Be warned, though, Bodengo 3 is long and technical, rendering it dangerous for inexperienced parties. Bodengo 1, while not worth a special trip, provides a pleasant introduction to the sport.

PARKING A

Take the SS36 north from Lake Como. About 4km before Chiavenna, cross the river to Gordona on the SP2. Just before the village take the left turn to Cascate Boggia. At the power station, take a left and park on a track opposite the mouth of the canyon.

GETTING FROM PARKING A TO B

By car
Following the SP2 through Gordona, take a left following brown signs to Val Bodengo. Follow the road up to Trattoria Dunadiv, a restaurant commanding fine vies of Valchiavenna. Park 1.6km further on in a lay-by on the left, shortly before the bridge over the first major tributary (Val Pilotera).

A permit is needed to use this road, which can be purchased from a number of bars in Gordona. The easiest is Bar Doc, just after the turning from the SP2. The cost was €5 at the time of writing.

Toboggan in Bodengo 2 (photo: Simon Flower)

On foot

Walk back to the power station. Head right (north) on a path by the perimeter fence. At the end of the first side, either follow the fence up the hill to the left (steep and miserable) or continue over a tiny stream a little further on, then take a left. Both climb in a few minutes to a good path which runs horizontally (north–south) across the hillside, marked with yellow paint. Follow this right (left leads in a couple of minutes to a bridge over the canyon from where the true water conditions can be properly assessed). In 10mins meet a T-junction by a house on the outskirts of Gordona. Take a right, then an immediate left up to a shrine. Take a left here onto an excellent but unmarked path, which climbs in a southerly direction all the way to the road beyond the *trattoria* (allow about 1hr). It is a 10–15min walk along the road from here to Parking B.

PARKING C1

Whether walking or driving, continue along the same road. Just before entering Prato Pincèe, take a left over the river following signs for parking and Bedolina. Park on the other side of the bridge. Access to the river is a little further along the main road.

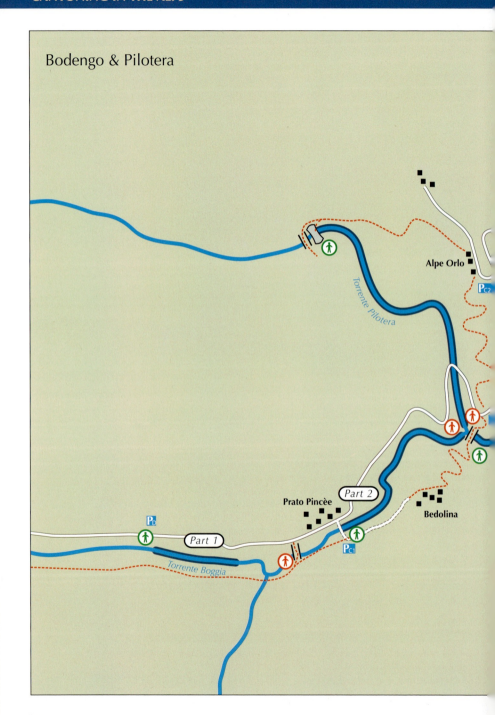

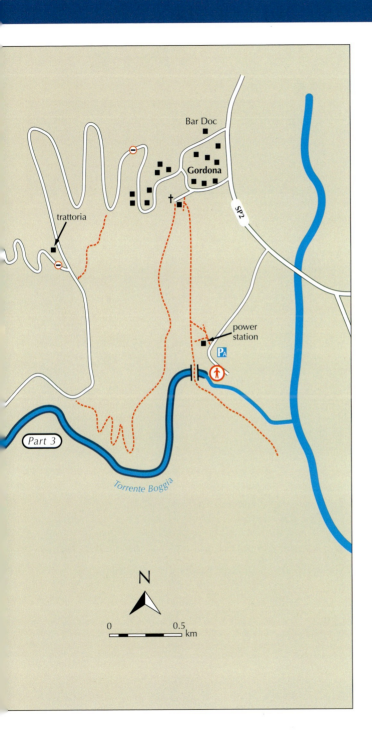

ROUTE 38: BODENGO 2

BODENGO 2: ★★★★ V3.A5.III

Alternative name	Torrente Boggia 2
Rock	Gneiss
Dimensions	Depth 195m (925m–730m); length 1400m
Ideal season	Summer
Time	Approach 0mins (Parking C1); descent 2–3hrs; return 10mins (Parking B)
Shuttle info	Parking B to Parking C1 – 1.8km (20mins road-walk)
Gear	2x20m ropes
Technical notes	Excellent rigging (double P-hangars and chains), generally out of the flow (which can be strong)
Escapes	Frequent, well marked

A short, sporting descent, full of jumps and toboggans.

⚠ Dam upstream. Low risk, but may open in case of heavy rainfall.

One of the numerous jumps possible in Bodengo 2 (photo: Simon Flower)

Bodengo 2

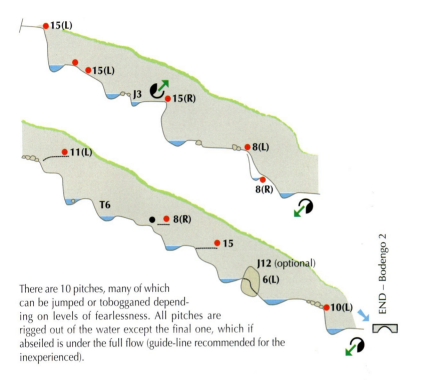

There are 10 pitches, many of which can be jumped or tobogganed depending on levels of fearlessness. All pitches are rigged out of the water except the final one, which if abseiled is under the full flow (guide-line recommended for the inexperienced).

RETURN

Exit on the right just before the stone bridge. Cross the bridge and follow the path back up to the road by Parking B, or continue on to Bodengo 3.

ROUTE 38A: BODENGO 1

BODENGO 1 ★★★  V2.A3.II

This no-stress introduction is difficult to justify without the other two sections of the canyon.

For an extra half-hour's easy canyoning, head up the road from Prato Pincèe for 1km. Parking D is in the large clearing on the left, where the canyon begins (highest pitch 15m; canyon over-rigged).

Ornamental gneiss patterns in Bodengo (photo: Simon Flower)

ROUTE 39: BODENGO 3

BODENGO 3 ★★★★↗ V5.A5.IV

Alternative name	Torrente Boggia 3
Rock	Gneiss
Dimensions	Depth 470m (730m–260m); length 2700m
Ideal season	Summer
Time	Approach 5mins (Parking B); descent 5–6hrs; return 0mins (Parking A)
Shuttle info	(toll road) Parking A to Parking B – 7.8km (1hr 30mins walk)
Gear	2x40m ropes
Technical notes	Rigging (usually double P-hangars) more discrete. Some down-climbing skills necessary. Requires good understanding of turbulent water and strong currents, although abseils usually clear of danger. Note water levels cannot be assessed from Parking A due to dam – better to walk 10mins to bridge (see approach walk description).
Escapes	Only at end of canyon, before the 60m and 40m pitches
Note	For map and topo see Route 38

This is Bodengo's long and aquatic final part, where even the fun bits are serious.

⚠ **Dam upstream in both Bodengo and Pilotera canyons. Low risk, but may open in case of heavy rainfall.**

The superb but risky ejection-toboggan in Bodengo 3

ROUTE 39: BODENGO 3

Bodengo 3

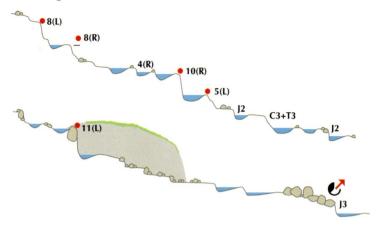

APPROACH FROM PARKING B

Walk down the well-made path to the old stone bridge (marked with red and white paint). Cross this and take a faint path right about 20m further on, which leads down to the river.

DESCENT

The first hour or so is spent in quite open streamway, with short cascades separated by periods of swimming and walking. An area of large boulders precedes the most sporting part of the canyon. One feature is worthy of a special mention – the 25m ejection-toboggan (the last 7m are spent in a helpless, twisting free-fall). Be warned that numerous injuries have occurred here, and the pool, which cannot be seen from above, must be verified by somebody beforehand. A few pitches further on a dangerous canal (strong current) can be avoided by climbing up to a high-level traverse on the left. After this the canyon opens out again. A long sunny area of large boulders marks the halfway point.

From here the canyon becomes more vertical, starting with a 60m waterfall. In order to prevent rope-rub it should be done in two or three stages. The final anchors are beneath a large roof 15m or 25m down (space for one or two people; rope retrieval awkward). Depending on the re-belay used, it is a 30m or 40m abseil to the ground. Traversing left leads to a further 20m pitch, then an exposed scramble down on the left of the stream to a final 8m jump or 10m pitch. The going is then more horizontal again before the final enclosed section. Two 12m pitches precede the last major obstacle – an impressive 40m pitch into a deep pool. Be warned that in the pool preceding it there are two dam intakes – one is obvious on the left (near the ladder); the other is on the right beneath the water.

RETURN

The canyon exits by Parking A.

LAKE COMO

211

ROUTE 40: PILOTERA

PILOTERA ★★★ V3.A3.III

Rock	Gneiss
Dimensions	Depth 290m (1020m–730m); length 2300m
Ideal season	Early to late summer
Time	Approach 30mins (Parking C2); descent 2–3hrs; return 5–10mins (Parking B)
Shuttle info	(toll road) Parking B to Parking C2 – 5km on toll road (1hr walk)
Gear	2x25m ropes sufficient – see descent description
Technical notes	AIC rigging, but some hand-lines awkward to rig. Very small stream in summer
Escapes	None evident
Note	For map see Route 38

Although there are a few pleasant sculpted pitches and pools along its 2.3km length, the ensemble is very discontinuous and the overriding impression is one of walking and boulder-hopping in open streamway. It has a sunny, south-facing aspect and provides a pleasant excursion for those not keen on jumps or high water. However, its main reason for inclusion here is that it's a good option after rain, when everything else is too wet.

 Dam upstream. Low risk but may open in case of heavy rainfall.

PARKING B

As for Val Bodengo Parking B. Note that a permit is needed to use this road, which can be purchased from a number of bars in Gordona. The easiest is Bar Doc, just after the turning from the SP2. The cost was €5 at the time of writing.

PARKING C2

Go back down the road and take a left just before the trattoria. The road climbs steeply on hairpins to Alpe Orlo. Park in the large parking spot on a sharp right-hand bend just before Alpe Orlo. Note that the road is private. You must purchase another ticket from the trattoria (€5 in 2010).

APPROACH FROM PARKING B

Take the path which climbs into the woods (marked with red and white stripes). The path climbs steadily to Alpe Orlo (and a water fountain) in 20–30mins. Turn left and pass through Alpe Orlo on the marked path. After the last house in the village take a left on path D7 (signposted to Val Pilotera). After 20mins take a good path down on the left, marked with AIC markers (blue spot on white background). Descend on this path to the dam.

APPROACH FROM PARKING C2

Take the track from the car park up into Alpe Orlo. After a short distance, it meets the water fountain. From here, follow the route described above.

LAKE COMO

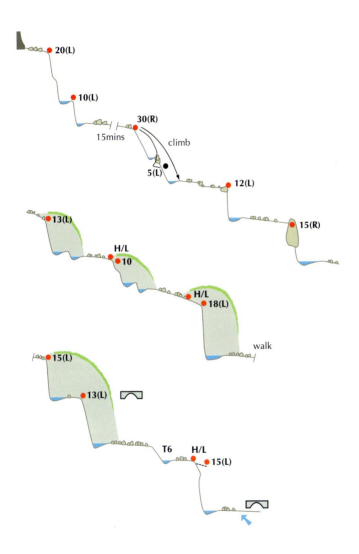

DESCENT

There are 11 pitches up to 20m in height, interspersed with long periods of walking and boulder-hopping. Note that the third pitch is a 30m abseil from the main anchors, but the pitch can be down-climbed easily to a point 5m from the floor, where a single anchor provides rigging for a hand-line. After the first hour, things become a little more continuous, with a few nice enclosed sections. After passing beneath the road bridge, there is a 6m toboggan and the final pitch.

ROUTE 40: PILOTERA

Pilotera's enclosed sections are pleasant but well spaced (photo: Simon Flower)

RETURN TO PARKING B

Look out for a path on the left by a flood-warning sign, a short distance beyond the final pitch. Climb on this back to the car park. If this cannot be found, continue as far as the stone bridge, where the Pilotera and Bodengo canyons meet. Exit here (a reasonable path exists on the true right of the river, just back from the bridge). Follow the path left back to the car.

ROUTE 41: MENGASCA

MENGASCA ★★★★ ⌐ ◼ V5.A4.III

Rock	Gneiss
Dimensions	Depth 300m (580m–280m); length 1200m
Ideal season	Summer
Time	Approach 1hr–1hr 30mins (Parking B); descent 3–4hrs; return 5mins (Parking A)
Shuttle info	Parking A to Parking B – 1.5km (25mins road-walk)
Gear	2x50m ropes +/– 2x15m ropes (or 2x60m ropes)
Technical notes	Sturdy-looking rigging on all pitches (2010), but not always in the best position to avoid water. Some pools turbulent. Assess the flow from the final pitch.
Escapes	One, after the 56m pitch

A wild, beautiful and unjustifiably overlooked canyon, being a more or less continuous string of sporting abseils and deep green pools. The crux of the descent is the 56m pitch, requiring good rope skills and a head for dizzying heights. Not to be underestimated, especially if water levels are higher than normal.

PARKING A
Drive to San Pietro on the SP2. Turn into the village down Via Tonaia at the 7km marker post. Park in the designated parking spots by the bridge over the river.

GETTING FROM PARKING A TO B
Follow Via ai Crotti up the hillside to the enclosed village of Monastero. Note that this is a private road – a ticket is needed, available from a number of bars in San Pietro (€5 in 2011). Bar Truck at the turning off the SP2 is probably the most convenient. The ticket is valid for three days and can be used in Val Casenda (Route 42).

APPROACH FROM PARKING B
Keep following the road around. Just before it heads downhill again, take a track on the right, which initially heads in a north-westerly direction. After 15–20mins the track levels off, where there are a few ruined buildings. Continue on the main track (marked with occasional red-and-white markers), which again climbs steeply for 15mins or so. Just before the path switches back left, take a path of similar size off to the right. This leads in a few minutes to a cluster of pretty houses and a spring overlooking the valley. Take a faint path diagonally up to the left. Cross over two adjacent gullys and pick up faint red spots on the far side. Just round the next bend descend into the trees, and trend right, back towards the gully, when things become less obvious. Scramble down a 2m climb (loose). The path crosses back over the gully and descends easily to the river.

ROUTE 41: MENGASCA

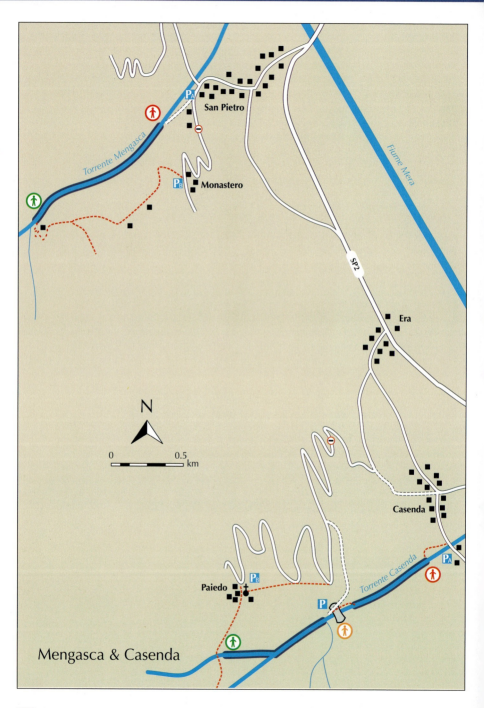

LAKE COMO

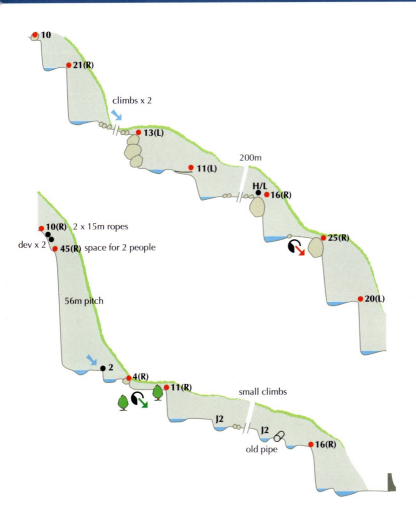

DESCENT

Six often aquatic pitches up to 25m precede the 56m grand cascade. This is probably best tackled via an intermediate belay 10m down to the right, accessed by using two deviations (space for two people only). After this a couple of short drops lead to a more open section – an escape is possible right (climb 100m or so to a good path, then go left to intercept the approach walk). After the next 11m pitch things become a lot more straightforward.

RETURN

Follow the vehicle track back to the car at Parking A.

ROUTE 41: MENGASCA

Easy going in Mengasca's upper reaches

The 56m pitch

ROUTE 42: CASENDA

CASENDA   ★★★ V4.A3.III

Rock	Gneiss
Dimensions	Depth 620m (870m–250m); length 1900m
Ideal season	Summer
Time	Approach 10mins (Parking B); descent 5hrs; return 5mins (Parking A)
Shuttle info	(toll road) Parking A to Parking B – 11.5km (1hr 30mins walk)
Gear	2x50m ropes
Technical notes	Excellent rigging; double P-hangars +/– chains (2010). Current considerable before the dam (and top of 48m pitch in full flow); minimal after, but canyon walls much narrower. Water levels may rise quickly due to steepness of the catchment area.
Escapes	Two – at the dam, then after the first encased section in the lower canyon
Note	For map see Route 41

Although by no means a classic, Val Casenda provides a few hours of varied and often dramatic canyoning. It is divisible into two parts, separated by a dam mid-descent. The upper canyon, open and well exposed to the morning sun, delivers a few aquatic and at times intimidating abseils, while the lower canyon is very much more enclosed but carries far less water. Aside from a long walking section between the two parts, the canyon is continuous from start to finish, and almost the entire time is spent on rope. An atmospheric outing, but one that misses the deep pools and grandeur of other descents in the area.

 Dam (low risk) mid-descent

PARKING A

From the SS36, turn onto the SP2 to Gordona. Take a left turning to Casenda/Giavere (not signposted if approaching from the north). Follow this road (ignoring all turnings) to a crossroads, then take a left along Via Casenda. Park on the other side of the bridge over the canyon.

GETTING FROM PARKING A TO B

Go back to the cross-roads and take a left. Follow this road up, where it eventually meets a much bigger road that climbs the hillside. Keep following the road up the hill, passing the track to the dam, and park in Paiedo (it can get rather crowded). This requires a permit (€5 in 2011, available from the Comune di Samolaco on Strada Trivulzia in Era or from the bars in San Pietro). It is valid for three days and can be used for Mengasca (Route 41). The section requiring the permit begins after 2.1km.

APPROACH FROM PARKING A

The path from Casenda village to the dam-access track, marked on maps, is very difficult to find and is not recommended. Follow the road up instead. Pass

ROUTE 42: CASENDA

the vehicle track to the dam. At the next hairpin bend a faint path heads up the hill by a pylon. Stay alert – the path is easy to lose. The quality of the path improves where it next meets the road, and eventually emerges by the church in Paiedo. Continue up to the water fountain (drinking water). From here, take a left and follow a path that skirts the hillside all the way to the canyon. Ignore turnings off to the right.

APPROACH FROM PARKING B

Cut through the Paiedo via a fountain (drinking water), and follow the path as described above.

DESCENT

The canyon begins with 5–10mins in open streamway. A couple of short drops precedes the first major obstacle, a 26m pitch accessed by a slippery traverse on the right. After this, an inlet on the right (Val Piccola) more or less doubles the current. An 8m drop precedes the most technical part of the descent, the 48m pitch (2x50m ropes needed). A hand-line gives access to a short but awkward pitch in the full flow of water. A difficult step left gains the main anchors (not visible from above), which provide a trouble-free descent. Two further pitches (the second down-climbable on the left with care) bring you to a series of flood defences and an obvious escape route. The lower canyon is accessed via a disused track on the left bank – follow it all the way to stream level. It begins with a 5m abseil from a concrete flood defence. A series of six very enclosed pitches precedes a more open 70m pitch, divisible into two or three parts. After this the river passes between a narrow and bouldery fissure, which provides the final few abseils.

topo continued overleaf

LAKE COMO

Using single rope technique to negotiate Casenda's open first half

ROUTE 42: CASENDA

The atmospheric lower canyon

Casenda (continued)

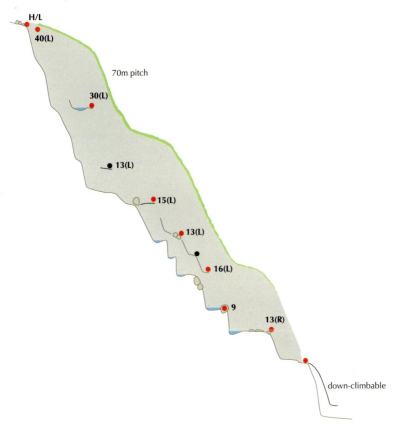

INTERMEDIATE ACCESS

The descent can be reduced to 3hrs (and the walk-in to 1hr) by starting at the dam. The descent is technically easier overall (v4.a2.III), and may be suitable when everything else is too wet.

ROUTE 43: BARES

BARES ★★★★⌐ ◨ V5.A5.V

Rock	Gneiss
Dimensions	Depth 700m (1300m–600m); length 3000m
Ideal season	Summer
Time	Approach 2hrs; descent 6–8hrs; return 30mins
Shuttle info	N/A
Gear	2x30m ropes
Technical notes	Rigging mainly on double P-hangars. The first half is rigged for high water, but some abseils are under the flow of water into very turbulent pools. After the second escape point rigging is less suited to high water, and the more enclosed nature means that things could get very dangerous. If you have problems on the first half, don't commit to the second. Avoid after heavy rain or if rain threatens.
Escapes	Two – at the hamlet of Bares (obvious) and another midway down, which is difficult to see; look for it on the approach walk

Beautifully encased and highly aquatic, Val di Bares is one of the finest canyons in the Alps. Located at the head of a remote valley, it has a true alpine feel. It is long and committing, and an accident here could have serious implications, yet the rewards of the descent are considerable. The water is abundant, crystal clear and perfectly clean, and the gneiss is ornamental, patterned with bands of grey and ruby browns. The jumps and abseils are continuous, virtually without respite from beginning to end.

PARKING

From Gravedona on the northern shores of Lake Como, take the tarmac road that climbs to Peglio and Livo. From Livo a narrow gravel track winds its way along the valley to Crotto Dangri. Park in the large car park by the restaurant at the end of the track (very busy at weekends – turn up early). A ticket is now required to park here, available from either a machine outside the town hall in Livo or from the restaurant itself (€1 in 2012)

APPROACH

Cross the stone bridge and take an immediate right. After about 30m take the left fork, which climbs the hill on hairpins. Pass through the pretty hamlet of Provego and continue as far as another, more tumbledown hamlet, Pianezzola (no signpost). Traverse horizontally through the hamlet, passing a spring (drinking water). At the far side, take a rising path out into the woods. The path, faint at first, rounds the corner into Val di Bares. A short climb out in the open leads to a promontory overlooking the valley. After a few minutes on the next horizontal section, look out for evidence of a faint path to the right. This is the second escape route – it is worth descending to the river to check it out, as the escape is not obvious from within the canyon. Continue up the valley as far as the ruins of Bares (no signpost). The river here is 50m away, so both access and escape are possible. To access the top of the canyon, continue along the path, now very faint, for a further 10–15mins. It crosses a tributary and passes through a small patch of woods just prior to the entry point.

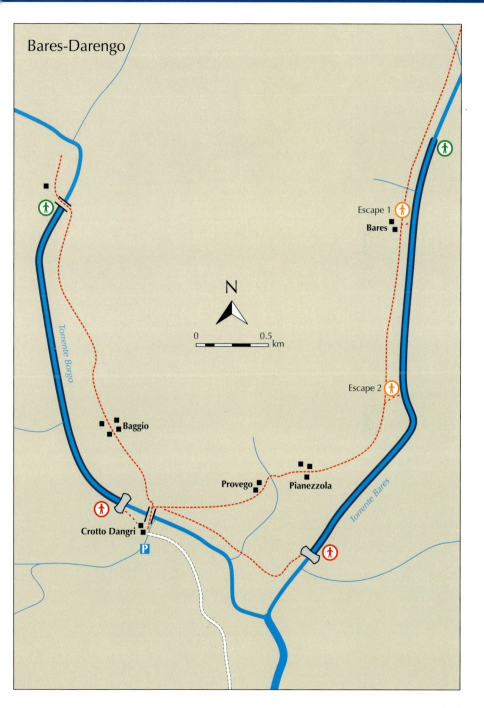

In the beautiful lower canyon

LAKE COMO

Bares

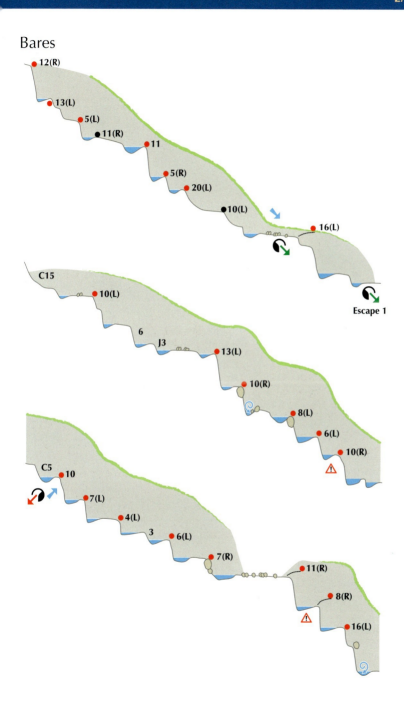

topo continued overleaf

ROUTE 43: BARES

Bares (continued)

DESCENT

The top section consists of a dozen small pitches which give an opportunity to test the current. Escape to the ruins of Bares (Escape 1) or continue into the lower canyon. This is much more committing. The encasement begins immediately and continues more or less unabated. After Escape 2, things get much narrower and potentially problematic as the abseils are often in the full flow of water. The canyon becomes more vertical at the end, with three pitches approaching 30m. The full descent is a long day out, with around 45 pitches in all. The dam marks the end of the descent.

RETURN

Follow the path right from the dam.

LAKE COMO

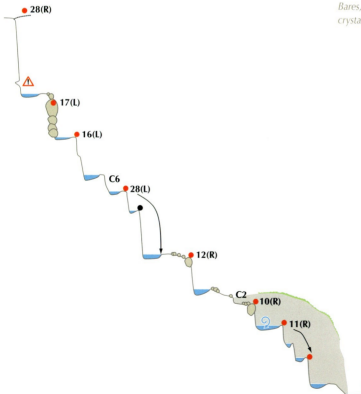

Bares, with its abundant, crystal-clear waters

ROUTE 44: BORGO

BORGO ★★★ ■ V3.A5.III

Alternative name	Valle di Darengo
Rock	Gneiss
Dimensions	Depth 309m (968m–659m); length 2000m
Ideal season	Late or well-established summer
Time	Approach 1hr 15mins; descent 3–4hrs; return 5mins
Shuttle info	N/A
Gear	2x20m
Technical notes	Very aquatic. Flow augmented in several places during descent. Assess flow at exit dam. Scarce, often hard-to-reach anchors (2009); jumps and delicate downclimbs obligatory. Beware of current among boulders and in plunge-pools.
Escapes	Improvised escapes up the steep left bank
Note	For map see Route 43

Torrente Borgo is a wild and aquatic alpine river. Open and without real interest to begin with, it becomes more steep sided and technical with descent. Cold, abundant water and sparse rigging mean that this is not a canyon for beginners, nor for anyone lacking jumping confidence.

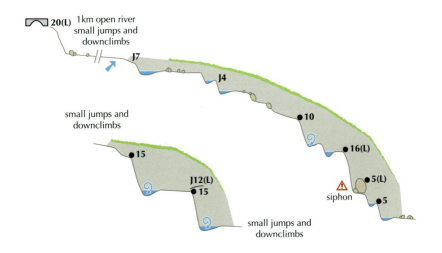

PARKING
As for Bares (Route 43).

APPROACH
(To check water levels at the exit dam, take a faint path above the restaurant and its out-buildings.) From Crotto Dangri, cross the bridge and follow the

LAKE COMO

Fun in the white water before the serious stuff begins (photo: Simon Flower)

main path to Baggio (a little cluster of buildings and a drinking fountain). Go left at the fountain, following signs for Rif Pianezza. Follow the path along the flanks of Valle di Darengo all the way to the bridge over the canyon.

DESCENT

The canyon begins open and horizontal; the first kilometre or so lacks real interest, aside from some optional jumps from boulders. As it begins dipping towards the valley, things become a bit more continuous. Six short but technical pitches stand between here and the end.

RETURN

At the dam, exit right to Crotto Dangri.

ROUTE 45: PERLANA INFERIORE

PERLANA INFERIORE  V3.3.III

Rock	Limestone
Dimensions	Depth 171m (450m–279m); length 1400m
Ideal season	Early to late season
Time	Approach 40mins; descent 2–3hrs; return 10mins
Shuttle info	N/A
Gear	2x15m ropes (2x20m ropes for the part after the bridge); head-torch useful but not essential; shorty wetsuits sufficient
Technical notes	Excellent rigging – double P-hangars (2010). Pleasant and sporty water levels, decreasing through summer.
Escapes	Numerous (see descent description)

For the most part this short descent is pleasant, but unremarkable. After toiling through the tourist traffic on Lake Como's western side, you may wonder if the effort outweighs the reward. Yet given the right mood, Perlana is worth the detour. Its central section is very pretty, with clean-washed limestone and beautiful deep pools, capped off with a unique cave passage complete with stalactites and tuffi. Sensible quantities of warm(ish) water and excellent rigging make this an ideal novice canyon.

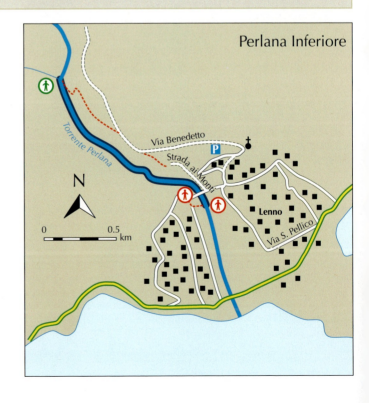

LAKE COMO

The sporting 12m toboggan prior to the cave section

ROUTE 45: PERLANA INFERIORE

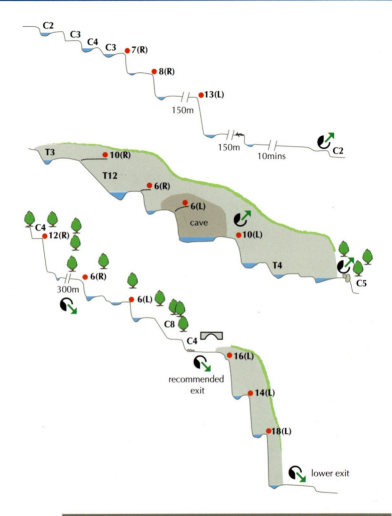

PARKING

Approaching from the north, take the first right in Lenno. If you reach the Sau Paulo Imi Bank you have gone too far. The road immediately splits at a confusing array of sign-posts. Take a left up Via S.Pellico, signposted to Santuario del Soccorso. Follow the road up hill to another split. Take the right for Sergio Ascentis and keep climbing. Park just before the monastery.

APPROACH

From the monastery take Via Benedetto, a tarmac lane that climbs steeply before becoming unsurfaced. After about 20mins take a reasonably obvious trail branching left into the woods (marked with ageing blue and yellow paint). There are a few turnings before this one, also marked, but these are

LAKE COMO

Perlana's cave-like section is worth a detour

less obvious and descend steeply. The correct trail skirts the wooded hillside, exposed in places but protected where needed with a chain.

DESCENT

The canyon begins with a few pleasant down-climbs and pitches in a steep-sided canyon passage. There is then a 10–15min march in the streamway, after which an escape can be made left. A 3m toboggan signifies the start of the interesting section. A further stunning 12m toboggan leads to the cave. This is two pitches long, but only the second (6m) is truly dark. Light can be seen filtering in 20m away, so although useful a light is not essential. A pipe catches water at this level, after which there is a further short enclosed section. Following this, an escape can be made left up a dry gully, just before a climb down between two boulders (path difficult to follow). From here there's another 30mins of more open stream to the road bridge, which signifies the end of the canyon (exit right).

Lower exit Just past the bridge the river becomes encased again and drops steeply in three pitches (maximum 18m). However, although pleasant they are not recommended. The water is of suspect quality, having picked up pollutants from the village, and the exit is tricky without scrambling through private land (although there may be a route over a wall up to the right).

RETURN

Cross back over the bridge. A few yards further on, take a pedestrian street (Strada ai Monti) on the left. After about 150m, branch right across the rear edge of an orchard. This brings you out at the road to the monastery. Take a left and climb back to the car.

ROUTE 46: BONDASCA

BONDASCA  V4.A4.III

Rock	Gneiss
Dimensions	Depth 234m (1070m–836m); length 1100m
Ideal season	Mid to late summer
Location	Switzerland
Time	Approach 30mins; descent 3hrs; return 0mins
Shuttle info	Shuttle not recommended
Gear	2x30m ropes
Technical notes	Rigging sufficient (2010); longer pitches rigged on double 10mm thru-bolts. Some slippery and awkward traverses needed. Most pitches rigged for high water, but second pitch in full flow. Glacial melt-water, so quite cloudy and very, very cold!
Escapes	None evident – improvised only

A sporting and reasonably technical outing in the freezing waters draining the northern slopes of Piz Badile. Although never dull, the canyon is initially discontinuous, with long sections of quite bouldery streamway. The obstacles slowly become more frequent and imposing, culminating in several encased and aquatic pitches towards the end. It is best to start around midday to maximise what little warmth this canyon receives.

⚠ **Dangerous dam upstream – tel +41 (0) 58 3196211 (or +41 (0) 81 822 6315/6311/6414/6211); failing that, try 058 3196971. The operators (if you get through) speak Swiss-German. Even if descent is permitted, commit to the descent only if the flow upstream of the dam is acceptable (around 300l/sec) – it seems the dam has unpredictable opening patterns.**

PARKING

Take the SS37 into Switzerland (passport required), then the turning into Bondo. Follow signs for the campsite. Park just after the bridge over the river, about 100m before the campsite.

OPTIONAL SHUTTLE

Possible parking near the dam, but not recommended. The toll road, which starts just beyond the church in Bondo, is disproportionately expensive (€9 or 12 CHF in 2010).

APPROACH

Take the path that climbs into the trees by the parking place (signposted to Cugian and Laret, marked with red and white stripes). After 15–20mins the path crosses over the toll road, then meets it again 10mins further on. Follow this up and take a right just before the dam, down to a little bridge over the canyon. Abseil 21m into the canyon from the bridge.

The second pitch is the most critical in high water (photo: Simon Flower)

ROUTE 46: BONDASCA

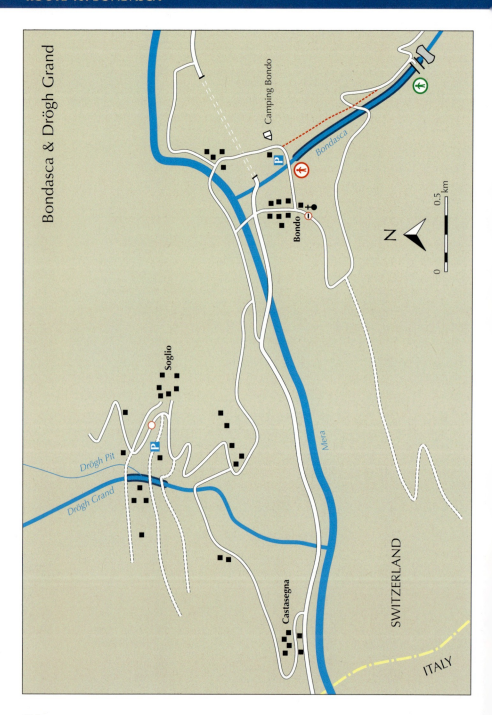

LAKE COMO

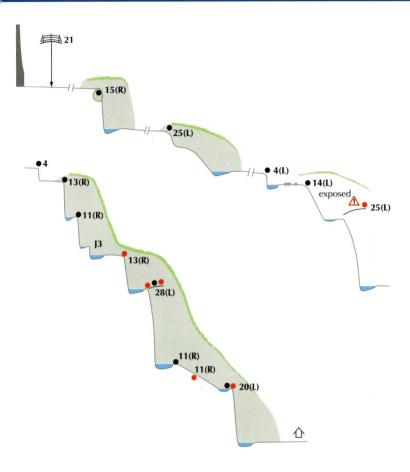

DESCENT

Ten minutes or so of quite bouldery going leads to the first pitch – a 15m drop into a deep pool. More walking and down-climbing leads to the second pitch – a narrow chute taking all the water (care required pulling through). More open going follows, then the canyon starts to become more continuous. A pitch of 14m is followed immediately by one of 25m (an exposed and often slippery traverse is required to gain the anchors). A short distance on, the canyon suddenly becomes more enclosed. Six atmospheric pitches follow. The greatest difficulty is the 28m pitch, requiring a slippery but protected traverse out left. Immediately after, an inclined rift (split into two pitches) leads to the final 20m abseil (anchors awkward to access). Exit just before the bridge over the river.

ROUTE 46A: DRÖGH GRAND

DRÖGH GRAND   V3.A1.II

Drögh Grand, just inside the Swiss border, provides a pleasant enough way to kill time, but the overriding impression is one of rubbly, log-strewn streamway.

Park in Soglio (2 CHF for 6hrs in 2010) and continue up the main road on foot (access for farm vehicles only). At the next junction take a left. At the second bridge, scramble in on the true left, on the upstream side. The canyon consists of 8 splashy pitches (max 20m), rigged on single anchors. Exit the canyon where it passes under the second bridge. Following the river further downstream leads (after two shorter pitches) to a spectacular, unrigged waterfall, about 50–60m high.

Drögh Grand – pleasantly encased in places (photo: Simon Flower)

ROUTE 47: LESINA

LESINA ★★★ (★★★★ when dam open) 🟦 to 🏴 V3.A4.III–V6.A5.III

Rock	Gneiss
Dimensions	Depth 220m (480m–260m); length 2000m
Ideal season	Early to late summer
Time	Approach 1hr 30mns–2hrs; descent 2hrs; return 0mins
Shuttle info	N/A
Gear	2x20m ropes
Technical notes	AIC rigging, but useful only for normal flow (usually minimal in summer). Other rigging exists for high water (single 8mm anchors, slings, etc), but be prepared to use naturals, do sketchy climbs and jump into very turbulent pools. One non-critical pitch in full flow of water.
Escapes	None evident after the first abseil

A short, playful canyon offering a string of jumping and tobogganing opportunities (including a very sporting toboggan of 14m). Some groups may hardly get the rope out at all. Although bouldery and discontinuous to begin with, the lower half of the canyon is more enclosed and imposing, and there is no escape is possible. As it has a large catchment area the canyon responds quickly to rain, and the character of the descent changes dramatically in high water. Inviting pools and playful toboggans are replaced with turbulent plunge-pools and fearsome pitches, and all the little down-climbs and jumps that you barely notice on a 'dry' descent suddenly require great care to negotiate. Evaluate the current carefully before committing!

⚠ **Dam upstream (opens after wet weather) – try phoning the guardian on +39 0342 685109**

PARKING

From the SS38, turn into Delébio. Find your way to the back of the village and park by the bridge over the canyon, next to the hydroelectric station. Assess the flow from the final flood defence – the river should be flowing over only the central portion, otherwise it is in high water.

APPROACH

Follow the road up by the hydroelectric station on the west side of the river. At the end of the road, follow the steep cobbled track that climbs on hairpins to the hydroelectric holding pond (30mins, authorised vehicles only). From here, follow the line of a pipe which contours the hillside. On the far side of a second tunnel, the pipe ends. A steep wooded scramble leads to the river in 10mins (follow the line of the gully, stepping right to negotiate an exposed down-climb at the bottom).

DESCENT

The canyon begins with a march in open stream, then four well-spaced pitches (including one 5m pitch in the full flow of water). Beyond this the canyon

ROUTE 47: LESINA

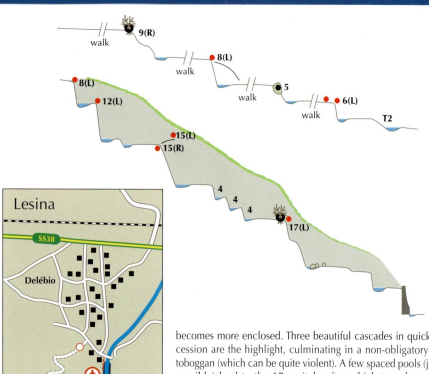

becomes more enclosed. Three beautiful cascades in quick succession are the highlight, culminating in a non-obligatory 14m toboggan (which can be quite violent). A few spaced pools (jumps possible) lead to the 17m pitch, after which two short drops (jumps possible) lead to the dam. Either jump or scramble down to the right. Clamber over the barriers back to the car.

Dam open – danger! (photo: Simon Flower)

ROUTE 48: FERRO

FERRO	★★★★ ■ V5.A3–4.III
Rock	Granite
Dimensions	Depth 200m (1300m–1100m); length 350m
Ideal season	Mid to late summer
Time	Approach 30mins; descent 2–3hrs; return 5mins
Shuttle info	Bus service obligatory, depending on season (see 'Shuttle service', below), or 2km walk
Gear	2x60m ropes (2x50m rope sufficient)
Technical notes	Rigging very good; double P-hangars, sensibly placed (2010). Current always strong and some abseils in full flow. Descent not always possible, even in summer.
Escapes	Improvised escapes only

There can be no doubt that Ferro is a beautiful and sporting canyon. The exhilarating pitches and gently sculpted, sun-soaked granite would be well worth the trip alone. However, it is the view over Val di Mello that makes this canyon special. For Europe, the scenery is unique – a climber's dream of granite boulders and smooth, towering faces; like Yosemite, only smaller. The canyon is vertically developed, and a number of abseils are potentially dangerous in all but low water conditions. Be prepared to abandon canyoning plans and do something else instead (bring rock-boots).

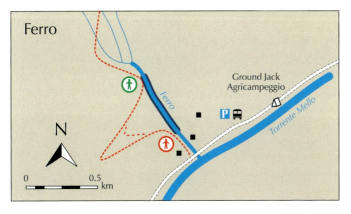

SHUTTLE SERVICE

From the end of June to the first Sunday in September an obligatory 2km shuttle service (no driving allowed) runs from the large car park at the entrance to San Martino into Val di Mello. Tickets are available from the tourist information kiosk (€1.50 per person and €5 for parking in 2011; service runs 8am–6pm). Outside peak season it is possible to drive, but a permit is needed, available from a machine near the information kiosk (€5 in 2010; only 80 available each day). It seems that all fees can be avoided by staying at the Ground Jack Agricampeggio campsite, just opposite the canyon.

ROUTE 48: FERRO

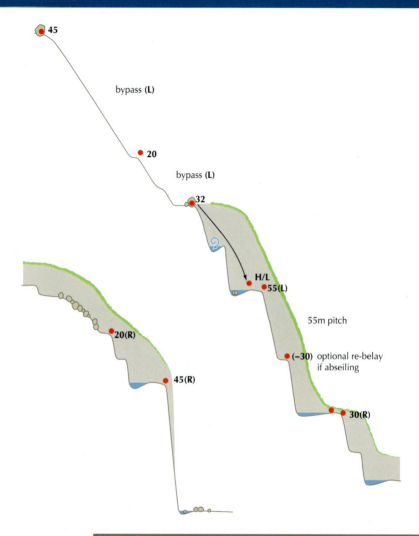

PARKING

From the SS38, take a left onto the SS404, signposted to Valmasino. Follow this road to the pretty holiday village of San Martino. If driving, continue through the village on the main road and take a right into Val di Mello. The track crosses over the canyon after 1.75km. Park 250m further on in the obvious parking place.

APPROACH

Climb on the marked path that flanks the true right of the canyon. Once in the trees, the path climbs away from the canyon, then turns back towards it (there is a short-cut, which is much steeper but not much quicker). As the canyon approaches, take a faint path that traverses over to it.

LAKE COMO

Sun-soaked granite scenery in Ferro

ROUTE 48: FERRO

Views over Val di Mello

DESCENT

A 45m inclined pitch can be bypassed easily, as can the following 20m pitch. The canyon begins in earnest just below the cable-way support (you could cut the approach walk short by entering here). The first anchors are hidden behind a boulder, providing a 32m pitch via a turbulent intermediate pool. The longest pitch follows, 55m, but a 50m rope will take you to a shelf from which it is possible to down-climb with care. The pitch can also be abseiled in the flow of water (re-belay on the right after 30m). Two short but very aquatic pitches follow, separated by a bouldery down-climb. A much more relaxing 45m pitch is the final obstacle.

RETURN

About 50m along the river from the last pitch, take a path on the right which leads back to the approach path.

It would be criminal to come all this way, to such a beautiful place, for such a short canyon and do nothing else besides. Val di Mello is a world-famous bouldering and climbing venue. Guidebooks are available from the gear shop in San Martino (Fiorelli Sport, tel +39 0342 641070, www.fiorellisport.com).

ROUTE 49: CORMOR

CORMOR ★★★★★ ■ V4.A3.V

Rock	Serpentinite
Dimensions	Depth 360m (1900m–1540m); length 1050m
Ideal season	Early to late summer
Time	Approach 2mins (Parking B); descent 4–5hrs; return 15mins (Parking A)
Shuttle info	Parking A to Parking B – 6.9km (1hr 30mins walk)
Gear	2x30m ropes; head-torches essential
Technical notes	Excellent, well-positioned rigging; double P-hangars and chains (2010). Dam regulates flow – no problems in upper part. A tributary mid-descent can create problems on 18m pitch of lower part. Flow cannot be assessed from Parking A – a large tributary joins after canyon finishes.
Escapes	One – mid-descent

Cormor is a unique, pitch-black experience – a cross between canyoning and caving. The canyon is formed in serpentinite, a shimmering green rock that is not too dissimilar to soapstone in appearance. Although serpentinite itself is not that uncommon in the Alps, serpentinite canyons are very rare indeed, with the only others clustered close by. But only Cormor is so enclosed as to be dark. Much of this darkness arises through bouldery infill, but rock arches and sections of cave passage do exist – a true geological anomaly and a testament to once powerful erosive forces. The river is now tamed behind two enormous dams, allowing the pitches and often complex passages to be explored in relative peace, but a few aquatic abseils and chest-deep wades serve as an icy reminder of the river's glacial origin.

⚠ **Dam upstream. Manoeuvres rare but phone the guardian – tel +39 0342 451260. Local inns normally informed of any manoeuvres planned.**

PARKING A

Driving east on the SS38, take a right just before Sondrio, signposted Valmalenco. Go left beneath the SS38 and follow this road up the hill, initially following signs to Chiesa, then Lanzada, then finally Franscia. The road passes through a series of tunnels, finally emerging in Franscia by a couple of restaurants. Park in the main square.

GETTING FROM PARKING A TO B

By car
Follow the road up to Campo Moro. Immediately after the last (eighth) tunnel take a left down a vehicle track (to the right of a chapel). Follow this for 800m down to a clearing directly beneath the dam. Park here.

On foot
Take the road north from the car park, which crosses first over the Cormor stream, then the Lanterna stream. By the second (Lanterna) bridge, take a path

ROUTE 49: CORMOR

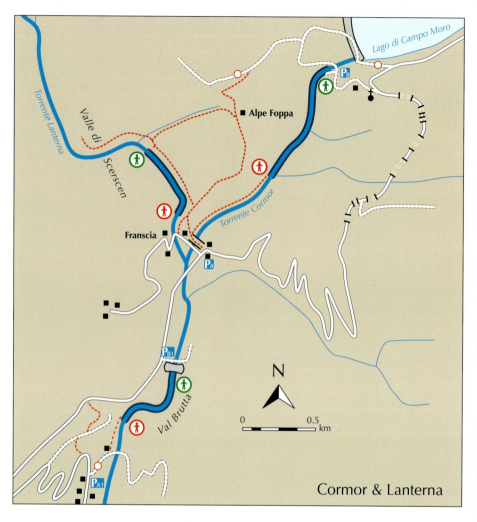

Cormor & Lanterna

right, signposted to Foppa. After 5–10mins, ignore the turning to Gole del Scerscen and continue on the main path. This climbs steeply on a stepped path to a beautiful grassy clearing with a couple of buildings (Alpe Foppa). Continue past this and take a right to Campo Moro. A short climb brings you to a vehicle track. Follow this right to a split, where both ways are signposted to Campo Moro. Take the right branch (the left is forbidden to vehicles), which brings you quickly to Parking B under the dam.

APPROACH FROM PARKING B

Take an abandoned vehicle track by the flood-warning sign. This eventually descends into the canyon.

LAKE COMO

Cormor's bouldery first pitch

ROUTE 49: CORMOR

DESCENT

Good route-finding and down-climbing skills are needed to negotiate the extensive boulder field at the head of the canyon. There are two sets of anchors on the first pitch (25m) – the best are on the far side, around to the left. The canyon then becomes steadily more enclosed, plunging into darkness for three pitches. There is a brief respite among sunny boulders, then more of the same. The first section ends with the 27m pitch, after which a well-marked escape is possible left. It is possible to follow this path for a short distance before dropping back into the canyon for the second section. The river has now at least twice the flow, having been augmented by a tributary entering left. The most difficult passage is the 18m pitch, whose awkward plunge-pool cannot easily be seen from above. This plunge-pool is desperate in high water – try to pendulum over to the exit slot on the true left and consider a Tyrolean for team-mates. Finally the canyon opens out. Scrambling and squeezing among boulders brings you to a significant tributary coming in left, which marks the end of the canyon.

RETURN

Look out for a marked path crossing over the river, at the level of the tributary. Take the path on the right bank, which takes you easily back to Parking A in Franscia.

25(L)
20(L)
−12(L)
7(L)
13(L)
18(R)
22(R)
C4
6
7
5
18(R)
5
problematic in high water
9
9
10(R)
5(R)
13(R)
27(R)
8(R)
12(R)

LAKE COMO

Strange sculpted rock in Cormor

TORRENTE LANTERNA (VALLE DI SCERSCEN AND VAL BRUTTA)

Despite being formed from the same strange rock as Cormor, these two canyons couldn't be more different in character. They are generally wide, bouldery and (in Valle di Scerscen at least) well exposed to the sun. They are much less vertically developed than Cormor, and what few pitches there are tend to be intimidating on account of the abundant icy waters thundering down them. While by no means classics, the Lanterna canyons are well worth the trip when in the Sondrio area – and, being less than 1km apart, are ideal in combination.

ROUTE 50: VALLE DI SCERSCEN

VALLE DI SCERSCEN ★★★⭒ V5.A4.III

Rock	Serpentinite
Dimensions	Depth 100m (1600m–1500m); length 550m
Ideal season	Late (or well-established) summer to autumn
Time	Approach 30mins; descent 2–3hrs; return 10mins
Shuttle info	N/A
Gear	2x20m ropes
Technical notes	Sufficient rigging, on single 8mm and 10mm thru-bolts. Double anchors on the 15m pitch (2011). High-flow glacial stream (very cold water).
Escapes	Scramble up left after the 15m pitch
Note	For map see Route 49

Sunny, open and sporting, with a troublesome crux mid-descent.

⚠ **Dam upstream – no information available. Flow in canyon appears to be unpredictable. Recommended on cooler days after a long period of stable weather or in autumn, when glacial melt is less.**

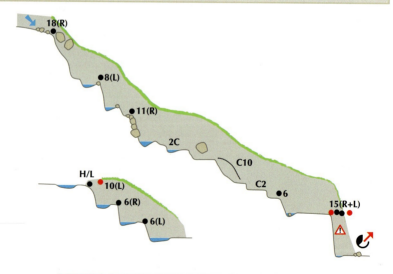

PARKING

As for Cormor Parking A (see Route 49).

APPROACH

Take the road north towards the houses. It crosses over the Cormor stream then the Lanterna stream. By the second (Lanterna) bridge, take a path right,

LAKE COMO

At the head of Valle di Scerscen

signposted to Foppa. About 5–10mins further on, take a path left, signposted to Gole del Scerscen/Foppa. The path climbs on some rocky slabs (follow the yellow markers) before entering the trees again. Continue on the path as far as a large boulder on a shoulder, just after crossing a significant tributary. Leave the path here and continue onto the shoulder, trending rightwards into a little gully. There is no path from here – just scramble down the boulders into the canyon (care required). Alternatively it is possible abseil the final 10m from a tree.

DESCENT

Three short pitches out of the main flow of water lead to a more horizontal section, with awkward down-climbs in a narrow passage – take care as the pools are full of boulders (not visible owing to turbid water). The 15m pitch that follows is the crux of the descent. There are anchors for installing hand-lines on the right and left, but neither is easy. In 2011 a Tyrolean traverse was in place; but, if absent, the direct descent goes behind the waterfall. Three less troublesome drops lead to the end. Again, a Tyrolean was in place for most of this last section, but only for the purpose of pleasing paying tourists.

RETURN

Where the canyon opens out, aim up and left to a rounded rocky outcrop. Drop over the back of this and follow a faint path back to Franscia.

It is 700m along the road from Franscia to the start of Val Brutta.

ROUTE 50: VALLE DI SCERSCEN

One of Val di Scerscen's many icy pools

ROUTE 51: VAL BRUTTA

VAL BRUTTA		★★★↙	V4.A3.III
Rock	Serpentinite		
Dimensions	Depth 310m (1450m–1140m); length 850m		
Ideal season	Late (or well-established) summer to autumn		
Time	Approach 0mins (Parking B1); descent 2–3hrs; return 5mins (Parking A1)		
Shuttle info	Parking A to Parking B – 4.7km (50–60mins walk)		
Gear	2x30m ropes		
Technical notes	First six pitches rigged largely out of water on single anchors (including a piton). The 25m pitch is in full flow (can be assessed from the road just prior to the last tunnel).		
Escapes	One – after the first six pitches, before the crux 25m pitch		
Note	For map see Route 49		

The more geologically interesting of the two Lanterna descents, this is reminiscent of Cormor in its lower reaches.

 Dam upstream – no information available (see Route 50)

PARKING A1

Driving east on the SS38, take a right just before Sondrio, signposted Valmalenco. Follow this road up the hill, initially following signs to Chiesa, then Lanzada. Some 500m beyond Lanzada, just before the first hairpin bend up the hill, look out for a tower-like electricity substation on the right (marked with a sign to Alpe Brusada). Park here, just before the private track down to the river (there is a spring with drinking water at the junction).

GETTING FROM PARKING A1 TO B1

By car
Continue up the hill. Pass through a series of tunnels and park by the first dam.

On foot
Follow the road up initially, then take a path signposted 'Franscia' (marked with red and white stripes). It meets an unsurfaced track further up. Follow this for a few hundred metres, but do not miss the path off this on the left, which climbs past an old mine back to the main road. Follow the road through the tunnels to the dam.

DESCENT

Four to six pitches (two are climbable) out of the main flow of water bring you to an open area – escape possible left. An 8m abseil gains the head of the 25m pitch (slippery – care required). This is the crux pitch, in the full flow of

ROUTE 51: VAL BRUTTA

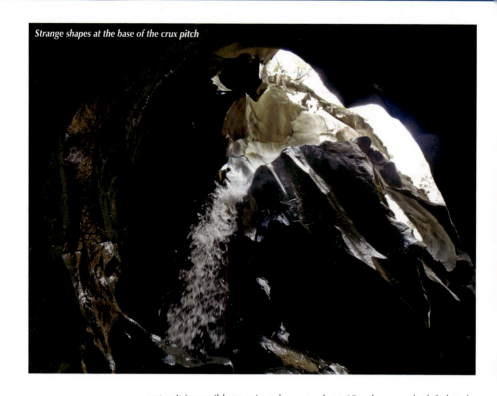

Strange shapes at the base of the crux pitch

water. It is possible to gain a dry route about 15m down on the left, but the traverse required is very greasy. It is better to continue down – much of the jet can be avoided, and the landing presents no great problems. A geologically curious cave inlet enters here, delivering the remainder of the water back to the canyon. After two short down-climbs (care required) things open out. Down-climb among boulders, aiming for a scree slope on the right at the head of the final pitch (unrigged). Traverse this to a track, which leads quickly to the hydro-electric substation at the base of the canyon.

RETURN

Walk up the track to the main road and continue back to Parking A1.

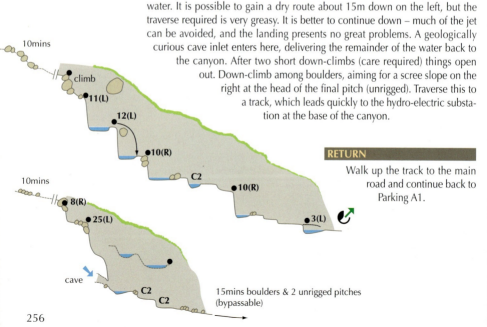

The first stretch of canyon in Val Brutta

ROUTE 52: ESINO INFERIORE

ESINO INFERIORE ★★★ ▪ V2.A2.III

Alternative name	Orrido di Vezio
Rock	Limestone
Dimensions	Depth 100m (310m–210m); length 600m
Ideal season	Late spring to late summer
Time	Approach 20mins; descent 1hr; return 5mins
Shuttle info	Optional (3km)
Gear	2x10m ropes
Technical notes	Rigging sufficient; mix of single and double thru-bolts (2010). A minimal flow in summer belies a large catchment area (presumably much sinks underground) – avoid in bad weather.
Escapes	After first enclosed section (not verified)

Although not worth going out of your way for, this canyon provides a worthwhile addition to a day spent in Boazzo (Route 53). There is more canyon here than would perhaps be expected for such a short walk-in, and what is there is very well formed.

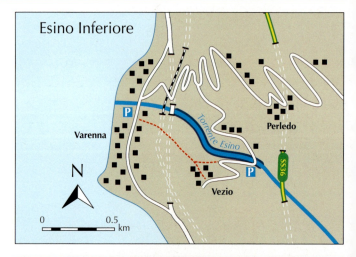

PARKING

From the SS36, take the turning to Bellano, then follow the signs for Varenna. Drive into Varenna and park as near as possible to the river. This is awkward in summer – Varenna is a very busy tourist town.

SHUTTLE (OPTIONAL)

If you really must (or you can't find parking in Varenna), take the road immediately to the north of the river, which climbs the hill on hairpins. Take a right turn,

LAKE COMO

signposted to Vezio. Park where the bridge crosses the canyon, about 750m further on.

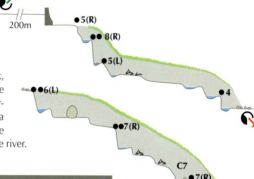

APPROACH

Take a path signposted to Vezio/Perledo, located about 75m south of the river on the main road through Varenna. Climb on a cobbled path, which goes over a private vehicle track, to Vezio (15mins). In Vezio the path splits. Take the left turning, signposted to Orrido di Vezio. This intercepts the private track, which is now followed up to a tarmac road. Follow the tarmac road downhill to the canyon. Access is just upstream on the true left of the river.

DESCENT

Three pitches by the bridge precede a long march in open, vegetated streamway. The canyon then closes down for a series of well-sculpted pitches and narrow passages. It finishes at the road bridge.

RETURN

Follow the river down to Varenna.

Tranquil canyoning in Esino

ROUTE 53: BOAZZO

BOAZZO ★★★✦ V3.A4.III

Alternative name	Torrente Caldone
Rock	Limestone
Dimensions	Depth 420m (820m–400m); length 1100m
Ideal season	Early to late summer
Time	Approach 10mins (Parking B); descent 3hrs; return 10mins (Parking A)
Shuttle info	15km (1hr 20mins walk)
Gear	2x25m ropes
Technical notes	Excellent rigging, on dual P-hangars and chains (a bit mixed below the dam). Flow always considerable – problematic in spring or after rain. Very dangerous siphon, but rigging helps avoid it. Very little flow below dam.
Escapes	One, mid-descent – watch for a rope on the right after first encasement (not verified). At the dam, go right to rejoin approach path.

Valle Boazzo is one of the few really worthwhile limestone canyons in the Lake Como area, and has been an established classic since the 1980s. It is divisible into two distinct parts – an aquatic upper part characterised by a number of well-formed but discrete enclosed sections, and a beautifully sculpted lower part, which as a result of a dam is sadly almost devoid of running water. The upper part has a few technical passages and should not be underestimated, particularly in times of high water.

 Dam mid-descent (no info)

PARKING A

Finding the parking spot is not straightforward, a task made no easier by the 2004 edition 1:50,000 Kompass map, which is inaccurate. From the SS36 on the northern fringes of Lecco, take the exit to Valsassina (the exit is inside the San Martino tunnel). Note that there is an alternative well-signposted route up to Valsassina from Lecco itself that does not go via the canyon – avoid this. Keep following the signs for Valsassina/SP62, which takes you through Lecco. When the road starts climbing, look out for a right turn down Via Don L. Monza, which is on a sharp left-hand bend (signposted to Casa del Clero Ville Alde). Follow this for 1km or so until a T-junction by a church. Take a left up Via Piloni and park just before the road turns into a gravel track (forbidden to unauthorised vehicles).

GETTING FROM PARKING A TO B

By car
Go back to the Valsassina road. Follow the road up the hill on hairpins. At the top, take a right on the SP63, signposted to Morterone. This road climbs a further hill on hairpins. Where it levels off, just after a left-hand bend, look out for a sign for via ferrata on the left. Park in one of the lay-bys nearby. If you

Boazzo's more aquatic upper reaches (photo: Simon Flower)

pass a vehicle track on the right (forbidden to unauthorised vehicles), you have gone too far.

On foot

Follow the gravel track upstream, along the true right of the river. Take a left where the track splits. This climbs a little and crosses a side-stream (Torrente Grigna) before terminating. From here, climb on the path (signposted to Passo del Lupo/Bellabio/Versacio) and take a left where it splits (right goes to the dam two-thirds of the way down the canyon – allow 20mins for access from Parking A). The path emerges on a broad gravel track. Take a right in the direction of the tunnel. After about 50m, take a much fainter path on the left which continues up the hillside. It passes among some ruined buildings before emerging on the SP63. Follow the road up to the upstream parking spot (a short section of road can be avoided by taking a path on the first left-hand hairpin bend, although it is debatable whether this helps much).

APPROACH FROM PARKING B

Take the vehicle track forbidden to unauthorised vehicles, then an immediate right onto a path in the woods. This descends very steeply to the river and is exposed in places. Alternatively, follow the vehicle track to Boazzo, where it is possible to enter the river directly (allow 30mins for the walk-in, then a long, boring section of open streamway).

ROUTE 53: BOAZZO

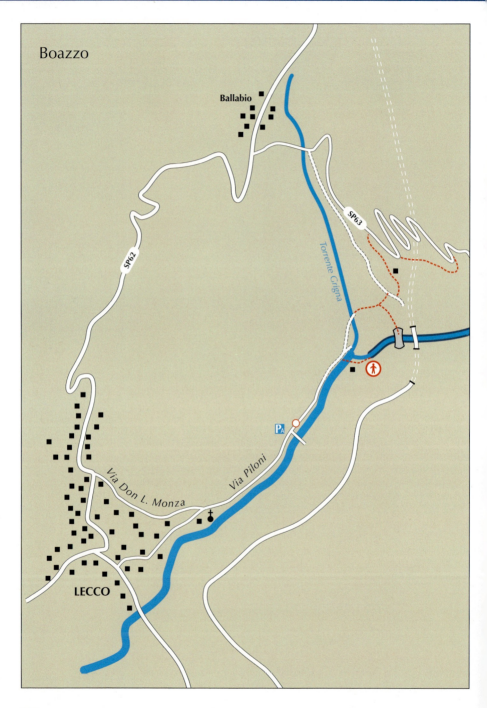

LAKE COMO

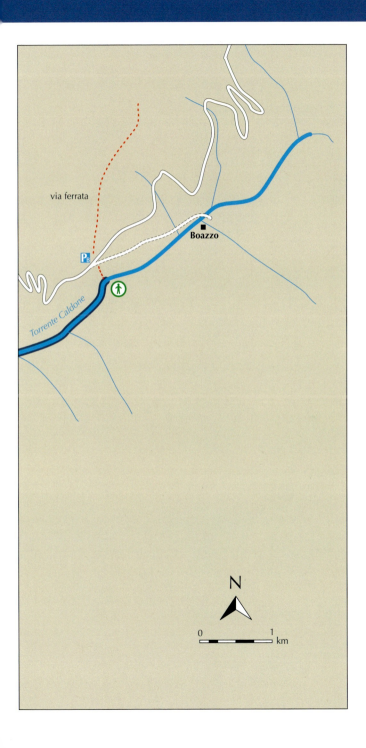

ROUTE 53: BOAZZO

DESCENT

The canyon begins with open streamway, then a few open pitches. A descent through boulders marks the start of an enclosed string of four pitches, the most critical of which is a pitch whose exit is barred by a siphon – care required, especially in high water. If in doubt, take the aerial traverse out right which provides a trouble-free hang. A second enclosed section follows more open streamway. Beyond the dam, the character changes entirely. The canyon narrows down, but is much drier. The final, very pretty cave-like pitch marks the end of the canyon.

RETURN

Where the canyon opens out, take a path on the left of the river. Follow the path down to the vehicle track and Parking A.

If you have some time on your hands, why not do via ferrata Simone Contessi, which starts by Parking B. This gains the long alpine ridge of Monte Due Mani (grade KS4-B).

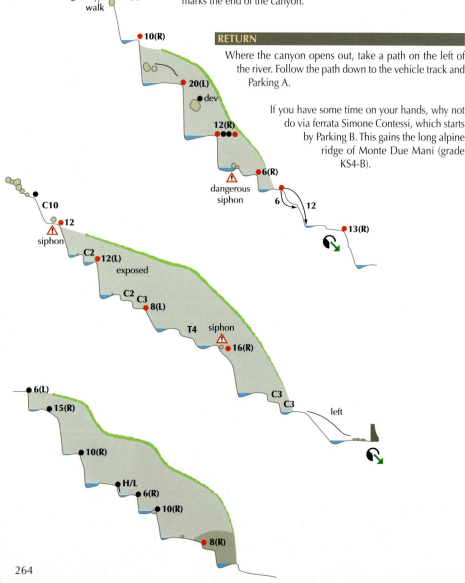

Standing atop the rock arch in Val dei Forti's third encasement (Route 56)

The Belluno and Friuli Dolomites

CANYONING IN THE ALPS

THE BELLUNO AND FRIULI DOLOMITES

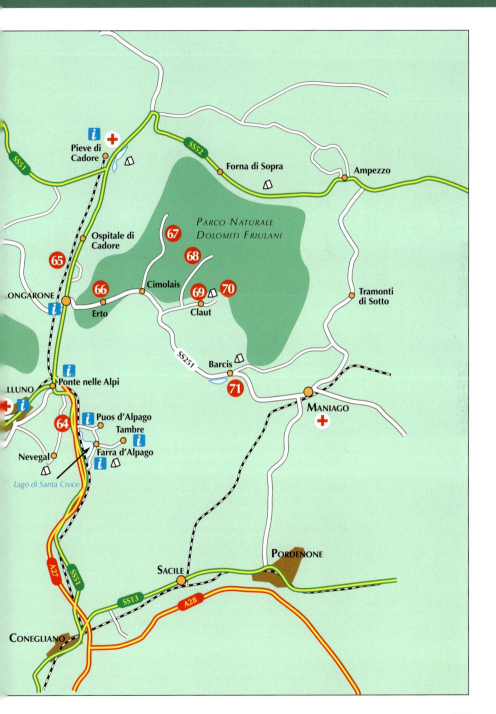

CANYONING IN THE ALPS

Fording the Cordevole river – the access route to Fogarè (Routes 61 and 62) (photo: Simon Flower)

The mountains of Belluno and Friuli form the least known corner of the Dolomites. They sit on the periphery of the range, bypassed by all for more prestigious playgrounds to the north and west. Few British tourists make it this far at all. Granted, the area around Belluno itself does little to inspire, with industry and commercial parks lining the valley floors. Yet the higher ground is a landscape of rolling pasture and precipitous rocky peaks. Furthermore, it is an area of national parks and natural reserves, untouched by the mass tourism or ski industry that taint the Dolomites elsewhere.

Dolomite is a type of limestone rich in magnesium, which forms a distinct canyon environment. Towering canyon passages and karstic features are common, just as in any limestone canyon, but the rock is frequently beige coloured – smooth, with a green shimmer like sculpted soapstone. Most canyons in the area offer fairly serious outings, being long and reasonably technical. Despite the abundance of classic canyons, the area remains surprisingly little visited. It is unusual to see too many fellow canyoners, and very rare indeed to see guided groups. A small number of canyons are suited to less experienced parties and provide light-hearted relief for quieter days.

Few roads climb into the mountains, which means that most of the canyons have stiff approach walks. To make matters worse the abundant deer population ensures a thriving tick community, hungry for human blood (see 'Warning', below). But don't be too put off – ticks are easily deterred by insect repellent, and the canyoning more than compensates for the walk-ins, which at least deter the crowds.

THE BELLUNO AND FRIULI DOLOMITES

CANYONING IN THE NATIONAL PARK

A number of canyons in the area are situated within the Belluno Dolomites National Park (including Mus, Fogarè, Clusa, Soffia, Pisson, Forti). A few years ago, the national park authorities declared the park off limits to canyoners, although the picture was never clear – there was no explicit signposting and the authorities seemed to turn a blind eye. In fact, certain canyons in the national park appeared to be well frequented. Sadly, all this has now changed.

The good news is that the Associazione Italiano Canyoning is trying to negotiate access rights for canyoners. They have requested that no canyoning takes place within the park, lest it jeopardise all the work done so far. The canyons in the national park have been included in the guide in the hope that one day they will again be open to all. Seek local advice before you go, or see the forum pages of the AIC website.

WHERE TO STAY

Belluno itself provides a convenient centre from which to explore the majority of canyons in the area. There are two campsites nearby at Farra d'Alpago (Camping Sarathei) and Nevegal. The lakeside campsite in Farra d'Alpago is popular with families and kite-surfers. It gets quite noisy at weekends and throughout August. There is a restaurant on site, a tourist information office just outside and shops close by. At an altitude of 400m, mild evening temperatures make excellent barbecuing conditions. Nevegal is 600m higher and attracts an older crowd on longer-stay vacations. It is cooler in the evenings, but considerably more peaceful. For details of all campsites in the area see Appendix C. Unfortunately the campsite by Lago di Mis, marked on walking maps, is closed at the time of writing.

Hiring an apartment can be an economical alternative to expensive Italian campsites, particularly for larger groups, but information is difficult to find online. Local tourist offices (see Appendix D) are able to provide lists. Inns, or *albergi*, are much more commonplace, but more expensive.

PRACTICALITIES

Shops and services

The biggest tourist centres are Feltre, Agordo, Belluno, Nevegal, Longarone and around Lago Santa Croce, but basic facilities can be found in most settlements of any size. There are grocery shops, a bank and a pharmacy in Farra d'Alpago, along with a handful of bars and restaurants. There is a supermarket in Bastia, just up the road. There are larger supermarkets along the SS50 into Belluno. Facilities are fewer east of the SS51, but Erto, Cimolais and Claut have restaurants, hotels, banks and grocery shops.

Gear shops

There are a few shops that sell climbing equipment, such as Intersport, on the SS50 between Belluno and Ponte nelle Alpi. A more dedicated outdoor shop can be found in the centre of Longarone (Tutto Sport – Via Roma 16, tel +39 0437 770429, www.tuttosportlongarone.it). They do not sell canyoning equipment, but may be able to order it on request.

Hospitals
The main hospitals in the area are in Feltre and Belluno, near the railway station, although there are smaller hospitals in Agordo, Auronzo di Cadore and Pieve di Cadore. There is also a hospital in Maniago, 15km east of Barcis.

Weather forecast
The most reliable weather forecasts can be found on the ARPA Veneto and Friuli websites – www.arpa.veneto.it (available in English) and www.meteo.fvg.it respectively. Longer range forecasts can be obtained from 3B Meteo (www.3bmeteo.com) and Il Meteo (www.ilmeteo.it).

The south-eastern Dolomites are among the wettest regions in Italy, sitting at a point where the warm, moist Mediterranean air meets the cool air of the mountains. Afternoon storms are relatively common, so it is important to keep an eye on the weather forecast and to choose canyons accordingly.

Maps
The whole area is covered at 1:25,000 by Tobacco mapping. Tobacco, Kompass and Freytag & Berndt cover the area west of the SS51 at 1:50,000, although Tobacco mapping is clearest.

TRAVEL AND TRANSPORT

Rail
Trains go to Belluno (car hire possible), either via Feltre to the west or Ponte nella Alpi just to the east (the latter is the best stop for the lakeside campsite, but still a long way on foot). The line continues north to Pieve di Cadore.

Driving
Roads in and around Belluno can seem complicated, and signposting is not always straightforward. If passing through Belluno, follow signs for Feltre if going west (eg to Maor and Grigno) or for Agordo if travelling to the canyons in the north-west (eg Soffia, Clusa). At rush hour the SP1 on the south side of the river is generally quieter than the SS50, which runs through town. At weekends, avoid the northbound A27 motorway where there can be a long (1hr) tailback as traffic attempts to merge with the SS51 heading north to Cortina.

OTHER ACTIVITIES

This being the Dolomites, there are plenty of things to do on a day off. The Schiara and di Zoldo ranges are the closest mountains for via ferrata (detailed in *Via Ferratas of the Italian Dolomites Vol 2*, Cicerone Press). Protected paths also exist around Puos d'Alpago (sentiero Rino Costacurta) and Erto (sentiero Osvaldo Zandonella), but details are available only in foreign-language guidebooks – see Appendix B. Sport climbing is possible in a number of places.

THE BELLUNO AND FRIULI DOLOMITES

The imposing 27m pitch in Clusa's aquatic lower reaches (Route 59)

www.planetmountain.com has details of the crags at Casso and Erto (near Val Zemola), where the climbing is generally steep and powerful. Tutto Sport in Longarone has details on other crags in the area. Only two climbing guidebooks are easily available in the UK – *Classic Rock Climbs in the Dolomites* (Baton Wicks) and the Italian-language *50 Classic Routes in the Dolomites* (available through Cordee in the UK or direct from the publisher at www.versantesud.it). These books cover mostly longer routes on the big faces further north. For walking and summit-bagging in the national park, try *Sulle Tracce di Pionieri e Camosci. Vie Normali nel Parco Nazionale Dolomiti Bellunesi* by Vittorino Mason, available direct from the publishers (www.versantesud.it).

PROTECTED AREAS

Parco Nazionale Dolomiti Bellunesi (www.dolomitipark.it)
Parco Regionale delle Dolomiti Friulane (www.parcodolomitifriulane.it)

WARNING

TICKS, LYME DISEASE AND TICK-BORNE ENCEPHALITIS
Unfortunately ticks are rife on many of the approach walks in this area. Without suitable protection, tick bites are virtually guaranteed. Ticks can carry unpleasant diseases – Lyme disease, tick-borne encephalitis (TBE), babesiosis and human granulocytic anaplasmosis (or Ehrlichiosis) are all endemic to north-east Italy. Although rarely fatal in healthy individuals they can be serious, with severe, prolonged, or even permanent effects. What's more, they may masquerade as simple viral illnesses in their early stages, which means that diagnosis can be difficult.

Preventing bites
Apply a DEET-containing insect repellent to skin and treat clothing with permethrin. This measure alone is extremely effective. Just wearing long trousers only delays the tick bite, although they make it harder for the little blighters to crawl up into your groin (a favourite spot). Inspect yourself and your team mates frequently, remembering that juvenile ticks (or nymphs) are the size of a pinhead.

If bitten
Remove ticks as soon as possible to reduce the risk of infection (see below). The risk of Lyme disease, for example, is reduced to around zero if the tick is removed within 24hrs. In the US, a single dose of an antibiotic taken within 72hrs of a tick bite has proven effective in reducing the risk of Lyme disease. It is not clear whether this strategy would be effective against the European form of the disease and is not generally recommended. With regards to preventing TBE, post-exposure immunoglobins are no longer recommended in Europe. If you become unwell, or develop an odd rash within a month of returning from this corner of Italy, seek medical help.

Removing ticks
Barbed mouth parts and a special glue make ticks difficult to remove, particularly if small. Incomplete removal can lead to skin infections. Grasp the tick as close to the skin as possible with fine-tipped tweezers and pull in a slow, steady motion – no jerking or twisting – ensuring the mouth parts are removed completely. Try to get underneath the tick rather than squeeze the actual body. The tick should still be alive when removed. A number of specialised tick-removing tools are on the market which advocate a twisting action. These apply less pressure to any one area of the tick, reducing the risk of the tick breaking. If the tick breaks, remove the mouth parts with the tip of a clean knife, tweezers or, better still, a sterile needle. It is no longer recommended to smear Vaseline on ticks or burn them off. This may cause the tick to regurgitate its stomach contents, increasing the risk of infection.

Advice changes
Updates can be found on the National Travel Health Network and Centre (NaTHNaC) website www.nathnac.org.

Tick rating
In this and the following chapter each canyon is given a tick rating, dependent on the chance of encountering ticks during approach walks. Walks are graded 1 = small risk to legs only, 2 = bites to legs guaranteed without protection, or 3 = bites above waist a possibility.

It is worth mentioning that the author took a very laissez-faire approach to ticks in this area, removing 15 over the course of a week before deciding to use insect repellent. Consequently he developed Lyme disease on his return to the UK. Be warned!

ROUTE 54: GRIGNO

GRIGNO ★★★★↲ ■ V5.A6.IV

Alternative name	Apocalypse Now
Rock	Limestone
Dimensions	Depth 210m (510m–300m); length 3000m
Ideal season	Early to late summer
Time	Approach 15mins (Parking B); descent 4hrs; return 15mins (Parking A)
Shuttle info	21km (1hr 15mins walk)
Tick rating	1
Gear	2x35m ropes
Technical notes	AIC rigging (good condition 2009). Pitches are sensibly rigged for the volume of water, but prone to damage from rock fall. Beware of undercurrents and concealed boulders.
Escapes	None in the enclosed section

Few other places combine sport and beauty in such equal and abundant measure. Barely an arm-span across in places, Grigno's looming walls and pounding river create a unique and intimidating atmosphere. In short, it is an immense, sparsely lit corridor of beige–white limestone, with a fearsome volume of water in it. Extreme care must be taken in plunge-pools, which are teeming with waves and undercurrents. Thankfully, there are ledges in critical places and the rigging is excellent throughout. Grigno is a wet, loud, exhilarating descent, suitable for experienced parties only – a 'man against river' experience. It loses half a star for the dull and laborious final part.

 Dam upstream (no information available). Flow rate varies daily. It was doubled in 2009 to around 500l/s, although values as high as 600l/s, and even 1000l/s, have been reported. Check the AIC forum for updates. The current flow rate can be found at www.floods.it/public/PreDati.php.

PARKING A

This is the furthest canyon from Belluno (about 1hr 20mins). From Belluno take the SS50 west towards Feltre. At Arsiè the road enters a long tunnel. Just as the tunnel ends take the exit onto the northbound SS47 (signed for Trento). From the SS47 take the turning to Grigno. At Grigno, cross the bridge over Torrente Grigno and enter the village by the road which flanks the river's west bank (Via Venezia). Follow this to a square with a fountain (drinking water) and a large hotel (Albergo Conca d'Oro). There is more parking in the square by the church. Do not change in the village.

GETTING FROM PARKING A TO B

By car
From Grigno take the minor road east (the SP75bis or Viale Trento). Cross the Torrente Grigno and take a left to Castello Tesino. The road climbs steeply on

ROUTE 54: GRIGNO

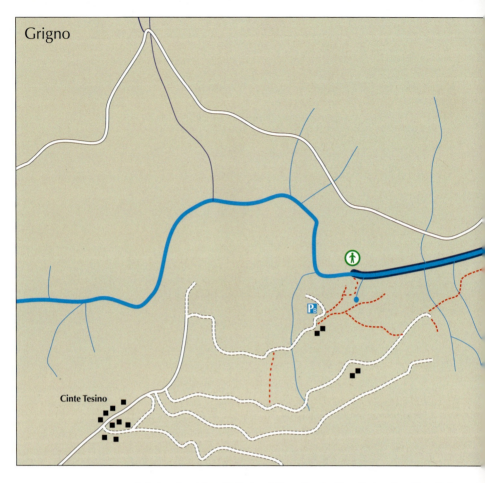

hairpins. From Castello Tesino, follow signs to Pieve Tesino then Cinte Tesino. Pick your way through Cinte Tesino. Once past the main village, pass three turnings on the right in quick succession. Take the fourth right, which is a little further on, where the road turns into a gravel track. The track contours the hillside before entering woodland and descending steeply. Pass a house and park in the wide grassy area on a sharp left-hand bend. There is sign for Forra, some blue and white markings on trees and a derelict car just out of sight from the road.

On foot

From the square, follow Via Cinte to its end, then take a broad track which ascends gradually in woodland. After 5–10mins the track hairpins back left. Here, a path continues (signposted 'no entry' in 2010, but don't be too put off; the path is not as damaged as the sign would make out). After a short distance (at the sign for 'Cinte T. 6km'), the path drops down to a wooden bridge,

THE BELLUNO AND FRIULI DOLOMITES

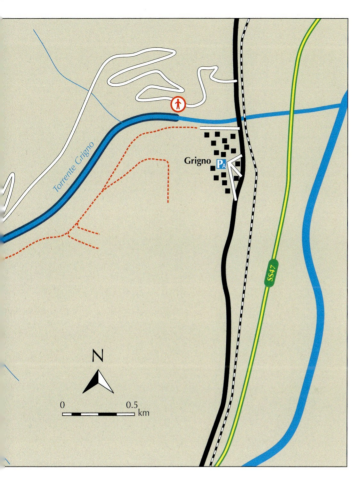

after which a steep climb on scree leads to an exposed shelf. From here the path gradually improves, becoming a vehicle track again where it levels out. Ignore the track off left. Contour around the hillside. Eventually reach a bridge that passes over an artificial water channel. It is 300m from here to where a difficult-to-see but well-trodden path slips off right into the woods (if you reach some pretty houses you've gone 3mins too far). Descend for 10mins on this to a wider path, then take a left. This path leads to a house, 'Micillini'. Just past this, a road is visible 3m down to the right – gain this via a sketchy down-climb just past the house. Don't be tempted to go further on this path – it is private property. The hairpin bend a few metres downhill is Parking B.

APPROACH FROM PARKING B

Follow the track into the woods, where it turns into a path. Descend gradually on a deteriorating path to a blunt ridge crest. Here, minor paths split off left

ROUTE 54: GRIGNO

Traversing high above the second pitch

THE BELLUNO AND FRIULI DOLOMITES

then right. Follow the right-hand path which descends steeply to a small stream (an inlet of Grigno). Trend downstream (there is no obvious path here – stick to a point about 10m above the water). The path then reappears and skirts left under a rocky bluff away from the inlet. Follow this to the main Grigno streamway.

DESCENT

The canyon begins with a 20m abseil well clear of the water. From here there is no return. You are committed and, in all likelihood, feeling a bit nervous. Next is the biggest pitch, the 25m Cascata delle Valchirie. It is rigged almost clear of the water from a ledge along left (2x35m rope needed). A short hand-line leads around an area of recent collapse into a passage that has a cathedral-like ambiance. From here the canyon becomes more enclosed, with only tiny filaments of light penetrating the depths. Typical dolomite canyon passage ensues, with smooth, green-tinged, totally vertical walls. The rock is of sound quality and reassuringly grippy. Two pitches follow, which get you closely acquainted with the torrent but avoid much of the danger. The next two pitches require care in the plunge-pools (strong undercurrents). The passage then widens out and the difficulties ease. By now the worst of things are over, although turbulent plunge-pools continue to threaten. Another beautiful enclosed section ends all too soon, and the bouldery walk-out begins (1hr from here). Two big but uninspiring pitches in open streamway punctuate the tedium, both rigged well clear of the water.

RETURN

Walk downstream to the concrete flood defences, picking your way along paths in the trees where possible. At the dam, climb down on the right and take the path to Grigno. Follow your nose back to Parking A in the village (but get changed beforehand).

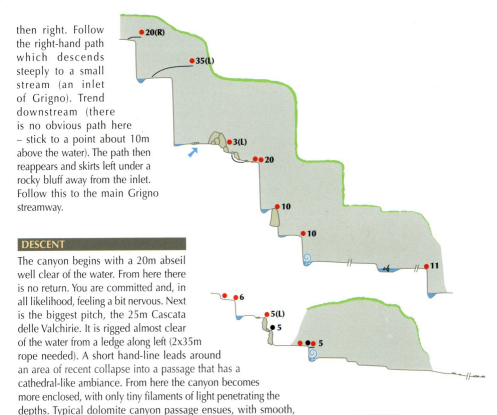

ROUTE 54: GRIGNO

A calm moment to take in Grigno's impressive canyon scenery

ROUTE 55: LA SOFFIA

LA SOFFIA   ★★★★↙ ▮ V4.A4.IV

Rock	Limestone
Dimensions	Depth 350m (780m–430m); length 1600m
Ideal season	Summer
Time	Approach 1hr; descent 4hrs 30mins; return 2mins
Shuttle info	N/A
Tick rating	1–2
Gear	2x40m ropes
Technical notes	Generally very good rigging, sensibly placed for trouble-free abseiling (2009). Some awkward down-climbs required. Water levels double after Pisson, but obstacles are far less threatening.
Escapes	Only one evident (see descent description)
Access restrictions	Canyoning currently forbidden in Belluno Dolomites National Park

Soffia is widely considered to be one of most beautiful canyons in Europe. The colossal scale of the place and the smooth, towering encasements are almost worthy of the five-star rating alone. That said, while it scores on aesthetics, it falls down a little on sporting interest. Although by no means a beginner's canyon, there are few jumps and toboggans, and the considerable current never really gets the adrenaline going. Nevertheless, go with your sight-seeing hat on and you won't be disappointed.

PARKING

From Belluno, follow signs to Agordo. Drive through Mas and take a left over the bridge towards Sosporilo. Follow signs for Lago di Mis. At the far end of Lago di Mis, cross the bridge and take a right to Bar alla Soffia. Park in the grassy lay-by just before the bar car park. **Warning** It can get very busy on summer weekends.

APPROACH

Follow the steep road, closed to traffic, which climbs from just before the bar. The tarmacked section finishes at a spring at Gena Alta (just a little cluster of houses). From the spring take a dirt track which contours the hillside towards the canyon (do not take the marked path which climbs above the spring). The track goes directly to the canyon. Beware of large spiders which sit in webs across the track.

DESCENT

The descent can be split into two distinct parts – before and after the confluence with Val Pisson. The first part is characterised by two beautiful encased sections, the second of which begins as an airy 24m pitch into a cave-like passage. The 31m pitch at the confluence with Val Pisson can be rigged away from the water, if needed, by traversing out to the right. After the rivers meet, the

ROUTE 55: LA SOFFIA

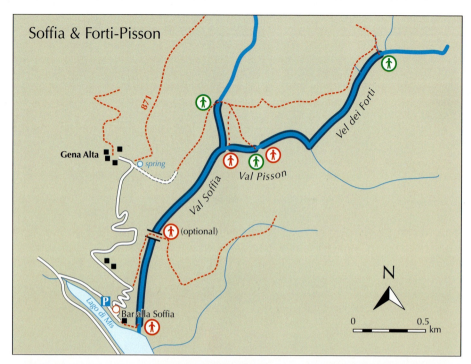

The first of two beautiful encased sections

THE BELLUNO AND FRIULI DOLOMITES

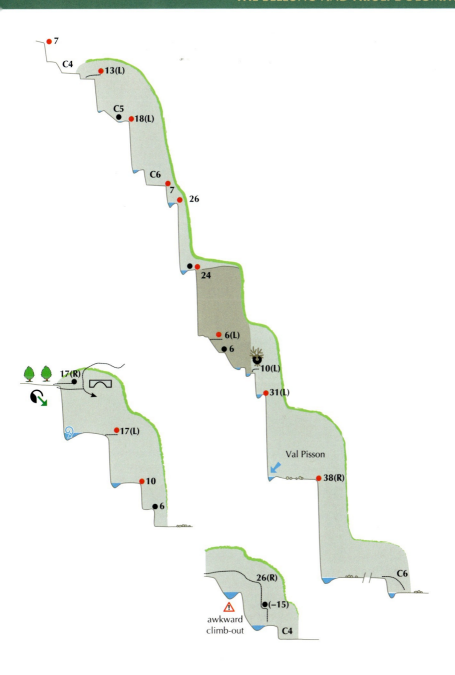

ROUTE 55: LA SOFFIA

The meeting of the waters – the junction of Soffia and Pisson (photo: Pete Talling)

canyon widens and becomes less continuous, although the scenery remains grandiose. The two 17m pitches following this have turbulent pools in high water. It is possible to escape at the top of the first (a faint path contours the canyon on its right bank – follow it down to the approach road). The going becomes a little tedious towards the end, when slippery rock and boulders slow progress. Avoid jumping into the first pool of the final enclosed section – it is very inviting but the climb-out is awkward.

RETURN

Exit at the tourist path. The tourist section beyond is not recommended, given the canyon's location in the national park.

FORTI AND PISSON

Pisson, a tributary of Soffia, is really a one-pitch wonder. It has perhaps the single most memorable pitch in the Dolomites, over 100m, split at two atmospheric spray-lashed ledges. This one pitch is well worth the walk-in alone. Val dei Forti, upstream of Val Pisson, is a relatively recent addition to the outing. It attracts far fewer people, a fact reflected in the overgrown walk-in and sparse rigging. It consists of a series of three vertically developed encasements, offering pleasant abseiling in striking rocky scenery. For experienced parties only.

PARKING
As for Soffia (see Route 57).

APPROACH
In the summer the sun hits the slopes shortly after 9am – arrive before then because the approach is steep and unrelenting. Follow the description for Soffia (see Route 57). Then cross the Soffia stream, taking a little-seen path about 15m back from the first pitch. Ascend in the woods for a minute to a barely visible split in the path. The right fork contours around to Pisson (10mins, exposed in places). The left fork continues to Forti (marked with a discreet wooden sign 'V. dei Forti'). The path ascends brutally for 1hr. It is faint and overgrown at times, although the occasional red spot provides some reassurance. At last, the path trends more or less horizontally. Follow this for 20mins (occasionally a little exposed) until it crosses a dry tributary. The red spots encourage you on, but a cairn and another discreet wooden sign (marked 'canyon') signify that it's time to descend. Descend to the stream (5mins).

ROUTE 56: FORTI

FORTI	★★★★ ■ V4.A2.IV
Rock	Limestone
Dimensions	Depth 350m (1150m–800m); length 1000m
Ideal season	Summer
Time	Approach 2hrs 30mins–3hrs; descent 3–4hrs; return 45mins
Shuttle info	N/A
Tick rating	3
Gear	2x50m ropes
Technical notes	Poor-quality rigging (2009). Usually single 8mm thru-bolts, sometimes well hidden or damaged (bolting kit advised). Double anchors on big pitches. **Beware** Two pitches often rigged together – check before pulling through. A number of pitches in full flow, but cause few problems in summer. Not rigged for high water.
Escapes	One probable (see descent description)
Access restrictions	Canyoning currently forbidden in Belluno Dolomites National Park
Note	For map see Route 55

The remote Val dei Forti provides an adventurous, and at times spectacular, outing.

The aquatic 48m pitch at the end of Forti's second encasement

THE BELLUNO AND FRIULI DOLOMITES

DESCENT

Forti consists of three enclosed sections that become shorter but more interesting with descent. After the first section, which is unremarkable and poorly rigged, you may well be wondering why you made the effort. When it opens out, yellow paint signifies a possible escape to the right (not verified). The following section is more imposing, with a tall, twisting canyon passage and an impressive 48m pitch. The canyon opens out briefly before the final enclosed section. This section is short, but impressive, with a fine rock arch at the end. A long section of boulder-hopping in open river precedes the final 20m pitch. It is possible to escape a few hundred metres further on via the Pisson approach path. This is on the right about 30m back from the 5m pitch/jump that signifies the start of Pisson. Beware – it is easy to miss.

ROUTE 57: PISSON

PISSON ★★★★✓ V5.A3.IV

Rock	Limestone
Dimensions	Depth (to Soffia escape) 230m (800m–570m); length 1000m (1500m with Soffia)
Ideal season	Summer
Time	Approach 1hr 30mins; descent 2hrs (to escape point in Soffia) or 4hrs (including Soffia); return 20mins (2mins if Soffia completed)
Shuttle info	N/A
Tick rating	2
Gear	2x50m ropes
Technical notes	Double 10mm thru-bolts and chains on 105m pitch (well placed, but ageing). Tricky 5m jump obligatory. The 105m pitch is largely out of the flow of water.
Escapes	One (see descent description)
Access restrictions	Canyoning currently forbidden in Belluno Dolomites National Park
Note	For map see Route 55; for topo see Route 56

Pisson's 100m pitch provides a breathtaking route into Soffia's lower reaches.

The calm before the storm

ROUTE 57: PISSON

DESCENT

The canyon begins with a tricky 5m jump, after which the rigging greatly improves. Pitches of 35m and 11m precede the 105m pitch. This is split at 20m down (room for two people only) and after a further 45m (three or four people at a push). It is possible to escape at the base of this pitch by climbing steeply in the woods up to the Pisson approach path. However, it is a route best avoided unless necessary. There is no path as such, and the Pisson approach path, faint at best, would be easy to miss. Continuing downstream, a 3–4m climb (not reversible) leads to the final pitch that meets with Soffia (37m). This can be split after 16m to ease rope retrieval. Continue by following Route 55 – remember that the trip can be cut short by escaping right at the head of the first 17m pitch, two pitches further on.

ROUTE 57: PISSON

Looking down the 100m cascade in Pisson

CLUSA

Clusa offers one of the finest sporting trips in Italy, demanding efficiency and a good level of physical fitness. The descent is always aquatic, but becomes exhilarating and very technical in high water, when the inexperienced are better off staying well away. The canyon is beautifully encased from start to finish and, bar one short horizontal section, vertically developed – a tremendous roller-coaster ride of abseils and jumping possibilities. It combines all the ingredients of a great alpine descent. The canyon can be divisible into a long upper part (Clusa Superiore) and a short but intense lower part (Clusa Inferiore).

CLUSA SUPERIORE	★★★★↗ V4.A4.V
Rock	Limestone
Dimensions	Depth 280m (900m–620m); length 1500m
Ideal season	Summer
Time	Approach 1hr 30mins; descent 3hrs 30mins–5hrs; return 30mins
Shuttle info	N/A
Tick rating	1
Gear	2x40m ropes
Technical notes	Very good rigging; mostly double P-hangars and chains, intelligently placed for wet conditions (2009). Be prepared for some 7–8m jumps. A few abseils in flow of water. Water levels double or triple after the confluence with Val del Canton de i Pez. Very enclosed – wait for settled weather.
Escapes	Dry gully on right halfway down (cairn), then path on right six pitches further on (not verified)
Access restrictions	Canyoning currently forbidden in Belluno Dolomites National Park (only the left bank)

A long, continuous descent, full of sporting variety.

PARKING

From Belluno, follow signs for Agordo. The route passes through Mas, where the SR203 starts. This road has posts every 100m. Follow it north and park in the lay-by at the '18 II' marker post, just after entering La Muda.

APPROACH

Take Path 546, signed for Val Clusa, marked with red and white stripes. A bifurcation is met a few minutes in, but the two arms meet up later on. After 25–30mins, a path on the right leads to the dam – the start of Clusa Inferiore. After another 25–30mins more climbing, leave the 546 and follow signs for Val

ROUTE 58: CLUSA SUPERIORE

Clusa. The path now contours the hillside, with a brief exposed section protected by cables (excellent condition 2009). Eventually the canyon rises up to the level of the path. Get in where possible (there may be a pitch or two above if you get in too early, but you won't be missing anything). Beware of ticks.

DESCENT

Except for an open and uninspiring start, Clusa Superiore provides an almost constant stream of pitches, around 30 in all, with barely any walking between them. Of special note is the 32m pitch with an S-bend. This requires an abseil in the full flow of water, although much can be avoided by a re-belay around to the true left at the level of the first lip (if you can reach it). The longest pitch is the 35m pitch at the confluence with Val del Canton de i Pez. The canyon then becomes more horizontal and much more aquatic (two to three times the volume of water). The two short pitches may pose problems in high water. The second (12m) is of particular mention – it requires a delicate traverse to gain the pitch-head, and the plunge-pool can be problematic to cross in high water. Once past this, get out and follow the obvious path right. Don't be tempted to continue beyond this – if the water levels in the reservoir are low it may not be possible to climb out.

RETURN

Follow the dam path back to the approach path.

Clusa becomes steadily more enclosed with descent

THE BELLUNO AND FRIULI DOLOMITES

One of Clusa Superiore's innumerable abseils

ROUTE 58: CLUSA SUPERIORE

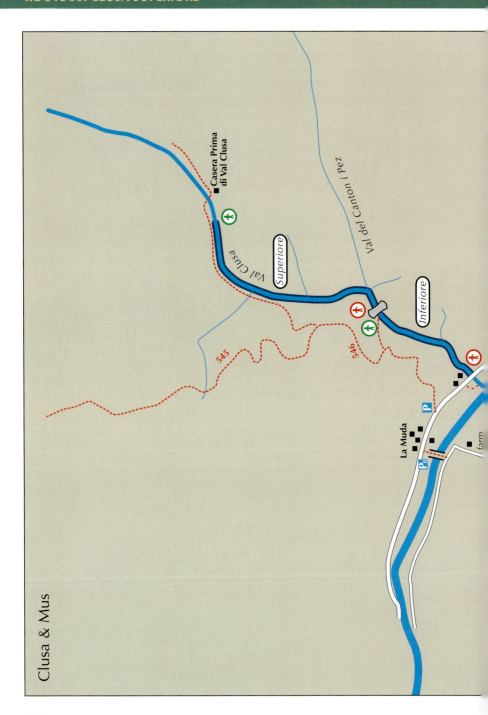

THE BELLUNO AND FRIULI DOLOMITES

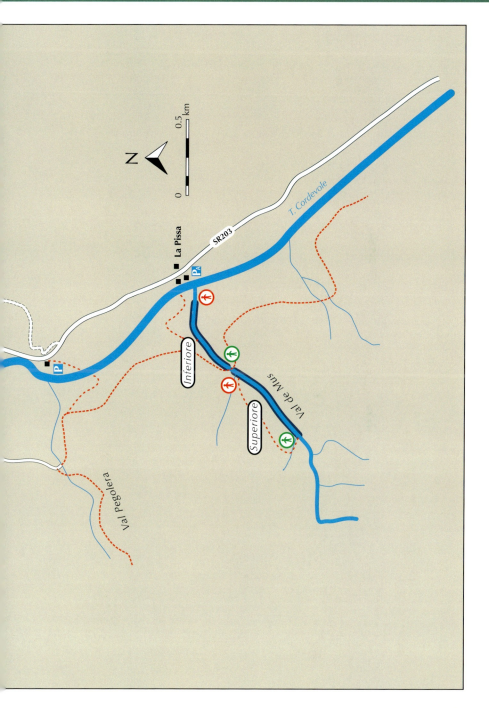

ROUTE 58: CLUSA SUPERIORE

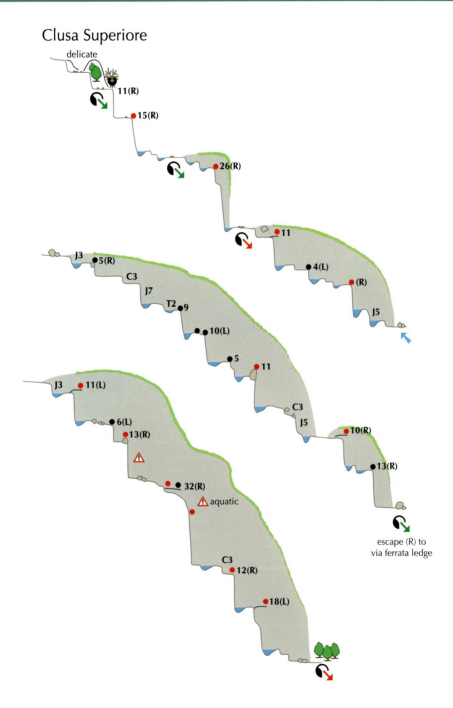

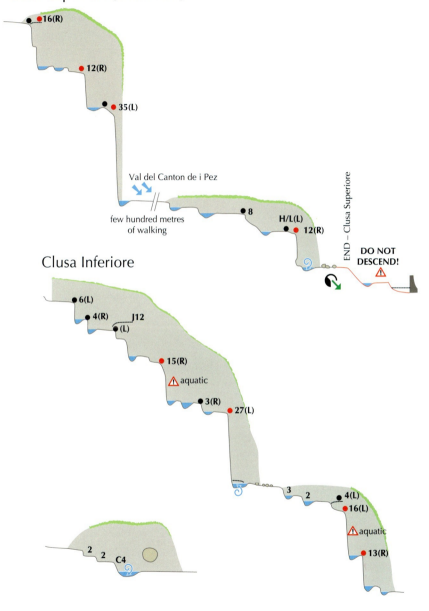

ROUTE 59: CLUSA INFERIORE

CLUSA INFERIORE	★★★★★ (in high water)	■ V5–6.A5–6.III
Rock	Limestone	
Dimensions	Depth 280m (900m–620m); length 1500m	
Ideal season	Mid to late summer	
Time	Approach 40mins; descent 2–3hrs; return 5mins	
Shuttle info	N/A	
Tick rating	1–2	
Gear	2x30m ropes	
Technical notes	Double anchors in critical places (2009). Water levels variable depending on amount removed at dam. In high water (ie when no water removed) the descent is intimidating and some plunge-pools are rather exciting.	
Escapes	None	
Access restrictions	Canyoning currently forbidden in Belluno Dolomites National Park (only the left bank)	
Note	For map and topo see Route 58. Lower grade applies when dam not emptying.	

Clusa's short but intense lower section is not for the faint-hearted.

⚠ **Automatic dam upstream – can open without warning. No information available. Safest when reservoir behind it is empty, but canyon very aquatic in these conditions.**

DESCENT

Climb back in at the dam. The canyon quickly becomes vertical again, in the same vein as before but with more water. An intense descent in high-water conditions, with only the tiniest of breathers halfway down.

RETURN

Pass under the road bridge and escape right. Walk 300m back along the road to the car.

THE BELLUNO AND FRIULI DOLOMITES

Clusa Inferiore's high water levels demand respect

ROUTE 60: MUS INFERIORE

MUS INFERIORE ★★★★ V4.A3.IV

Rock	Limestone
Dimensions	Depth 296m (706m–410m); length 600m
Ideal season	Early to late summer
Time	Approach 45mins (Parking B); descent 3hrs; return 5mins (Parking A)
Shuttle info	Parking A to Parking B – 2.3km (30mins road-walk)
Tick rating	1
Gear	2x65m ropes (2x45m ropes sufficient – see descent description)
Technical notes	Excellent rigging, although a few awkward down-climbs necessary. Splashy stream in summer should not cause problems. Flood debris evident in narrower parts.
Escapes	One, mid-descent (see descent description)
Access restrictions	Canyoning currently forbidden in Belluno Dolomites National Park
Note	For map see Route 58

Mus is an established classic, memorable for its sculpted pitches and beautiful deep pools. The current is splashy without being any great threat, and its small catchment area makes it a possibility after rain. There is also an upper canyon, Mus Superiore, described in brief below. It is pleasant enough, but unremarkable and barely worth the walk-in, which is unpleasant and exposed.

One of Mus Inferiore's glowing green pools

THE BELLUNO AND FRIULI DOLOMITES

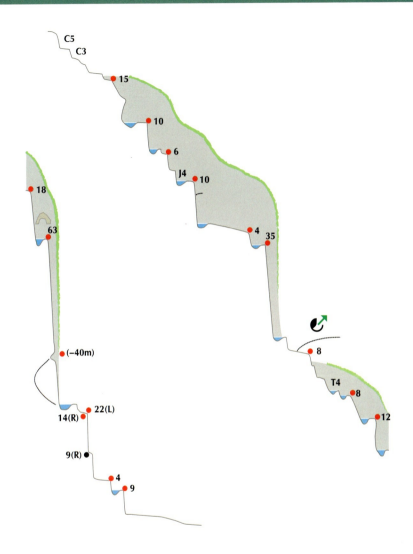

PARKING A

From Belluno, follow signs for Agordo. The route passes through Mas, where the SR203 starts. This road has posts every 100m. Park by the 16km road marker (bus stop), which is opposite the exit to the canyon.

GETTING FROM PARKING A TO B

Drive to La Muda and park in the car park just beyond the footbridge in La Muda (unmarked turning on the left at around the '18 III' marker).

ROUTE 60: MUS INFERIORE

The 63m pitch

THE BELLUNO AND FRIULI DOLOMITES

APPROACH FROM PARKING B
From La Muda, cross the footbridge and turn left. Just before the farm take the track on the right. Follow this, skirting the base of the hillside and ignoring tracks on the left which lead into fields. The track crosses another footbridge before climbing steeply in the trees to the head of the canyon.

There is a more direct approach from Parking A, which reduces the walk-in time to 30mins, but the route is difficult to find and tick infested. Ford the river, aiming for a place just north of the canyon mouth. Enter the trees and pick up a faint path that leads above the first rocky bluff. It first climbs to the north, then back south at the next bluff. At a shoulder, pick up a pylon-path heading straight up slope (marked with red paint). Follow this until it intercepts the main approach path. The woods are tick infested, and bites are all but guaranteed without insect repellent.

DESCENT
The canyon begins with a couple of sketchy down-climbs, after which the protection greatly improves. Many of the pitches can be jumped or tobogganed, having wonderful clear-green pools at their base. The 35m pitch marks the half-way point, after which there is a marked escape route on the left (red paint). The canyon then closes in again. After a series of pools and toboggans it becomes increasingly vertical, culminating in the 63m pitch (room for two or three people at the pitch-head – the remainder must tread water). The pitch can be split at –40m at a greasy ledge, but it is better to continue to the bottom. The canyon then widens and a few uninspiring pitches lead to the exit.

RETURN
Ford the Cordevole river back to Parking A. Beware of the current in high water.

ROUTE 60A: MUS SUPERIORE

| MUS SUPERIORE |  V3.A2.IV |

The drier upper reaches make for a wild, if rather dull, addition to Mus Inferiore.

From the Mus Inferiore entry point, go up the stream bed to a dry inlet on the right (the true left of the river). Follow a barely visible path which snakes its way up between the inlet and the main stream. From here on, the path is steep and exposed, with frequently poor footing and few handholds except clumps of grass. At the end of the first cable (very poor condition 2009), take a barely visible right turn, which doubles back above the path. This gains a second cable. After this the way gets even steeper and more exposed, climbing higher and higher above the canyon, with the odd bit of rusted cable for psychological support only. After a bad step (iron stake for assistance), the path becomes much easier. A final protected section (bizarrely in excellent condition in 2009) leads into a dry gully, from where it's an easy scramble down to the stream bed. Check yourself well for ticks afterwards (tick rating = 3). Allow a further 1–1hr 30mins for this part, plus 2hrs for the descent. The canyon is initially dry (it meets a resurgence lower down), the highest pitch is 26m, and the rigging is minimal – on 8mm spits and pitons.

FOGARÈ

Fogarè is a long and varied alpine canyon which is quite aquatic in its lower reaches. The approach walk is brutal but worth it (at least once anyway). The canyon is strongly encased for almost all its length, consisting of small pitches and horizontal passages that become more interesting with descent. It has a remote and serious feel, owing to the lengthy walk-in, sparse rigging and lack of escape routes. The lower canyon can be done alone, taking only a few hours to cover the prettier parts, at the cost of far fewer calories.

PARKING

From Belluno, follow signs for Agordo. The route passes through Mas, where the SR203 starts. This road has posts every 100m. Park in the car park on the left by the '12-I' marker post (signposted 'Area picnic & Ristoro').

ROUTE 61: FOGARÈ SUPERIORE

FOGARÈ SUPERIORE  V3.A3.V

Rock	Limestone
Dimensions	Depth 280m (880m–600m); length 1200m
Ideal season	Early to late summer
Time	Approach 2hrs 30mins–3hrs; descent 2hrs–2hrs 30mins; return 30mins
Shuttle info	N/A
Tick rating	1–2
Gear	2x35m ropes
Technical notes	Mostly single anchors (2009). Longer pitches usually rigged double, equalised with old rope or sling. Some awkward down-climbs obligatory. No problems with current in summer.
Escapes	None evident
Access restrictions	Canyoning currently forbidden in Belluno Dolomites National Park

The long and remote upper canyon just about makes up for the long and punishing walk-in, and makes the descent of Fogarè Inferiore that bit sweeter.

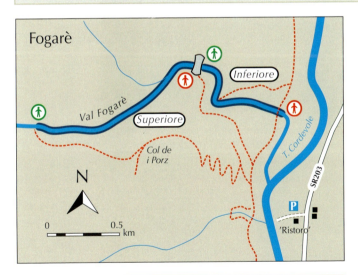

APPROACH

A complicated and punishing walk-in. The time quoted here allows for time spent getting lost, although waymarking may eventually improve. From the car, take the track down to the river. Ford directly over and enter the woods by a little stream inlet (this is not the canyon). Turn right and climb northwards on the clear path just inside the tree-line. Follow this for 5–10mins to where the path levels out, then take a path on the left heading upwards (signposted 'Col Porz').

ROUTE 61: FOGARÈ SUPERIORE

Fogare Superiore

After a few more minutes take another left turn ('Alta' written in red on a tree). If you miss this turning the path leads to a pylon after about 5–10mins (you may see the odd orange marker). Beware also of a second turning on the left.

Follow the 'Alta' path steeply upwards for about 90mins to reach Col de i Porz, following red and occasionally blue markers. Col de i Porz is a grassy, tree-strewn shoulder on the ridge, about 100m across. The path is easily lost here. Make your way to the far side of the col, where the path reappears and begins to rise again. After 100m or so the path splits; take the right branch (the left branch is signposted to 'Mont Alta'). Initially the path is a clear mule track, which descends slightly as it traverses the hillside.

Just before the track deteriorates, a little wooden sign with 'canyon' written on it directs steeply downwards. There is no path on this section. Descend the hillside with care, looking out for faint white markers on trees which direct further west. The path crosses two dry gullies (cairns) before breaking out of the tree-line below a cliff. Pick your way down to the river, trending left.

DESCENT

The canyon begins with four open pitches (maximum 30m) and a bouldery section. After this the canyon becomes steadily more enclosed. A dozen pitches up to 24m, with a few small obligatory jumps and down-climbs, lead to the dam.

RETURN

Escape right at the dam. Follow the path back to valley level or continue to Fogarè Inferiore.

END – Fogare Superiore
START – Fogare Inferiore

The inescapable and long Fogarè Superiore (photo: Simon Flower)

ROUTE 61: FOGARÈ SUPERIORE

Fogare Inferiore

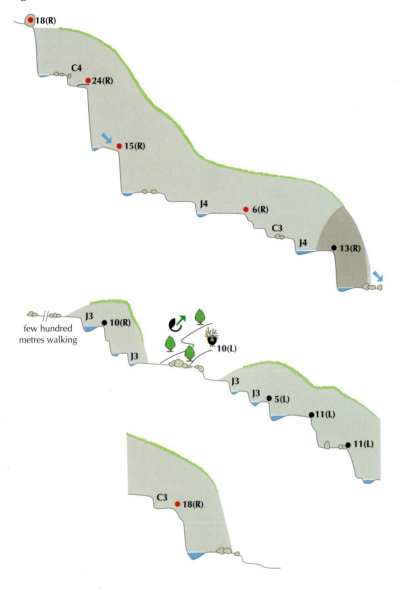

ROUTE 62: FOGARÈ INFERIORE

FOGARÈ INFERIORE

★★★★  V4.A4.IV

Rock	Limestone
Dimensions	Depth 184m (600m–416m); length 800m
Ideal season	Early to late summer
Time	Approach 40mins; descent 2hrs–2hrs 30mins; return 10mins
Shuttle info	N/A
Tick rating	2
Gear	2x25m ropes; no headlamp needed for the 'cave' section
Technical notes	Mixture of single and double anchors (2009). A few inlets augment flow of river by the dam. A few abseils in full flow of water – final (18m) pitch most critical.
Escapes	One (see descent description)
Access restrictions	Canyoning currently forbidden in Belluno Dolomites National Park
Note	For map and topo see Route 61

The shorter, more imposing lower canyon.

Impressive limestone scenery in Fogarè Inferiore

ROUTE 62: FOGARÈ INFERIORE

A typical splashy pitch in Fogarè Inferiore

THE BELLUNO AND FRIULI DOLOMITES

APPROACH
Start as for Fogarè Superiore (Route 61). On the main path, continue past the 'Col Porz' turning for a couple of minutes. Turn off onto a discreet rising path on the left (if the path starts to descend again you have gone too far). Climb for 15mins, passing a pylon, to where the path emerges from the trees to give a fine view over the canyon. From here it is 10–15mins walking along the line of an old water pipe to the start of the canyon (exposed and unstable in places).

DESCENT
From the dam the pitches continue, becoming more and more enclosed before plunging into semi-darkness for a pitch. After this the canyon opens out again, and a long walking section follows. After another brief enclosed section, it is possible to escape up left into the trees on a reasonable path (marked on the map). A tree belay marks the beginning of the final enclosed section. Two obligatory 3m jumps follow (care required), then a few pitches interspersed with walks and down-climbs. The final 18m pitch is the most critical in times of high flow. The pitch-head is slippery, and the anchors are tricky to reach. Rope retrieval can also be difficult.

RETURN
Ford the Cordevole river, aiming rightwards back to the car.

ROUTE 63: MAOR

MAOR		★★★★ ■ V2.A2.III
Rock	Limestone	
Dimensions	Depth 90m (470m–380m); length 1750m	
Ideal season	Late spring to mid-summer or after rain	
Time	Approach 0mins (Parking B); descent 2hrs–2hrs 30mins; return 30–60mins (Parking A)	
Shuttle info	Parking A to Parking B – 3km (50mins road-walk)	
Tick rating	0	
Gear	2x15m ropes	
Technical notes	Only one pitch, rigged from a tree. Small stream in summer. Although water is clear and odour free, avoid canyon in dry summers. Avoid if storms are brewing.	
Escapes	Improvised escapes possible up multiple dry gullies in first part. No escape is possible in second part.	

Situated in rolling countryside south of the Dolomites, Maor is a semi-urban canyon whose scale and beauty is quite unexpected. It consists of two short encased sections, the second of which is most striking. Here, deep pools of blue-green water alternate with constricted canyon passages, clean washed and virtually devoid of light. A meagre current and horizontal nature means the descent demands very little technical ability, making it an excellent canyon for beginners. It is marred by poor water quality in the first part and a monotonous walk-out.

⚠ **Makeshift WC at head of the canyon – incredible in 21st-century Europe that local authorities could allow such blatant pollution.**

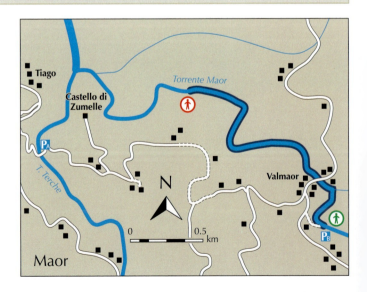

THE BELLUNO AND FRIULI DOLOMITES

Maor's clean-washed lower section

ROUTE 63: MAOR

One of Maor's deep green pools

PARKING A

Take the SP1 west from Belluno. At a roundabout just beyond Mel, take a turning left to Tiago. Drive through Tiago, down a steep hill and park on the left just after the bridge.

GETTING FROM PARKING A TO B

Whether driving or on foot, continue up the hill on the other side of bridge. The road, gravel in places, swings 90° left at the top. Turn left at a T-junction (signposted Belluno/Feltre). Take a right at the next T-junction in Valmaor. Take a left when the road splits, followed by another left to the sports field (*venostadio*). Park by the football field.

DESCENT

Try to ignore the slick emitting from behind the WC. The 10m climb from the flood defences provides the trickiest obstacle of the descent. Approach from the left (slippery – rope useful for the less experienced). A pleasant section of mainly horizontal passage follows, marred by fly-tipping from the village above. After about 30mins the canyon opens out. The stream disappears into the gravel during a 5min march in open streamway. It reappears at the dam, hopefully strained of its pollutants. Here, a 12m pitch leads via a short slippery section to the lower canyon. This part is beautiful and enclosed, becoming deeper and darker with descent. After 45–60mins the canyon unfortunately widens to give way once again to slippery and bouldery streamway.

RETURN

Follow the river downstream to where a similar sized river enters on the left (Torrente Terche). Follow the latter upstream as far as a 4m-high dam. This can be bypassed to the right (true left) by scrambling through the ruins of an old water mill. A path takes you quickly back to Parking A.

ROUTE 64: MAGGIORE

MAGGIORE	★★★ – ★★★★ ◢ V3.A3.III
Rock	Limestone
Dimensions	Depth 380m (760m–380m); length 2200m
Ideal season	Early to late summer
Time	Approach 1min (Parking C); descent 4hrs 30mins (2hrs from Parking B); return 0mins (Parking A)
Shuttle info	Parking A to Parking B – 3.5km (45mins road-walk)
	Parking B to Parking C – 2.5km (35mins road-walk)
Tick rating	0
Gear	2x25m ropes (2x20m if bypassing the 25m pitch); 2x15m ropes sufficient for upper half; foot-loop useful
Technical notes	AIC rigging (good condition 2009). Stream splashy in summer and is an option after rain.
Escapes	Many in upper half; only one (at the end) in the lower half – avoid if bad weather threatens

A low altitude, semi-urban canyon, Maggiore provides some light relief from the more serious descents further north. Although it lacks their splendour, it has a certain beauty and sporting interest of its own, and a small, low-lying catchment area makes it an option when everything else is too wet. It is divisible into two halves with similar character. The lower canyon is particularly worthwhile – there are plentiful jumps and toboggans and the rock is beautifully banded.

⚠ Beware of protruding cables in the final two pools – serious risk of impalement!

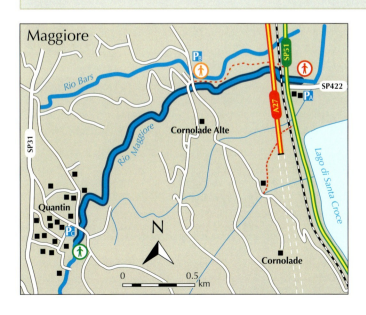

ROUTE 64: MAGGIORE

PARKING A
Park one car at the junction between SP51 and the SP422 (signposted to Lizzona, Bastia and Lago di Santa Croce).

PARKING B
Take the SP51 south. After about 1km take a right under the railway line (signposted to Cornolade). The road climbs steeply. When it levels out it crosses a bridge over the canyon. Park here.

PARKING C
Immediately after the bridge take a left (signposted Cornolade Alte), followed by an immediate right. The road again climbs steeply. At the top of the hill, just before the intersection with the main road (the SP31), take a left. This road takes you to the main square in Quantin. Park here.

WALK FROM PARKING A TO C (VIA PARKING B)
Although a path exists from Parking A to B, it is very overgrown and not easy to find. It is easier just to follow the road up. Maps suggest that the first corner can be cut by taking a path under the railway bridge about 200m south from Parking A. There are no signs forbidding use of the path, but it appears to pass through somebody's property.

APPROACH FROM PARKING C
From the square, follow the sign to 'Lavatoio', where it is possible to gain access to the river.

DESCENT
The beginning is unfortunately rather laborious. The first 500m or so is spent in open river, littered with shattered rock, cut branches and other detritus thrown in from above. Just when you're wondering why on earth you came, the canyon becomes enclosed and the fun starts, although metal barrels and motorcycle parts persist for a few pitches. The canyon consists of a number of discrete enclosed sections, which become more interesting with descent. The last section before the road is perhaps the most beautiful, with a number of jumps and toboggans and an entertaining sump passage (optional, but the clamber over the top is awkward – a foot-loop may be useful). The lower canyon also begins laboriously. An uninspiring 25m waterfall (easily bypassed around to the left) is followed by a dull march in the stream. The fun begins as it becomes more enclosed. Many short pitches follow, and the majority can be climbed or jumped. Two more sumps add optional entertainment, although you may not see them. Once the canyon opens out, a 20m abseil and a couple of jumps (beware of protruding cables – verify first) bar the way back to the car. This last part can be avoided by escaping right to the railway, then heading south to a path which passes beneath it.

THE BELLUNO AND FRIULI DOLOMITES

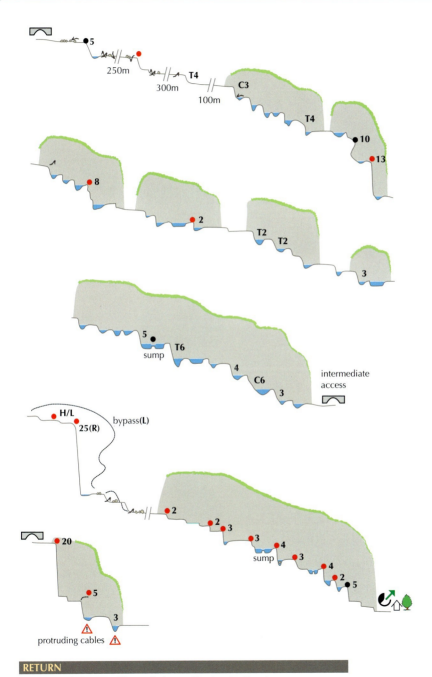

RETURN
Walk through the tunnel beneath the road back to Parking A.

ROUTE 64: MAGGIORE

In the lower reaches of Maggiore (photo: Simon Flower)

ROUTE 65: TOVANELLA

TOVANELLA ★★★★ V4.A3.V

Rock	Limestone
Dimensions	Depth 70m (570m–500m); length 500m
Ideal season	Summer
Time	Approach 15mins; descent 1hr 30mins; return 0mins
Shuttle info	N/A
Tick rating	0
Gear	2x25m ropes
Technical notes	Current quite powerful even in summer. The rigging leads away from the danger, but anchors are mostly old 8mm thru-bolts. Take a length of rope to replace the hand-line if needed.
Escapes	None

An excellent little outing, consisting of a continual stream of short pitches and deep pools. It is tight, aquatic and quite technical in places – not to be underestimated.

PARKING

Drive north from Longarone on the SS51. Pass through the Termine tunnel (2253m long) and take an immediate right on exit, signposted to Davestra and Ospetale. Take a right at the end of the slip road and park in the picnic area on the far (north) side of the bridge over the canyon.

ROUTE 65: TOVANELLA

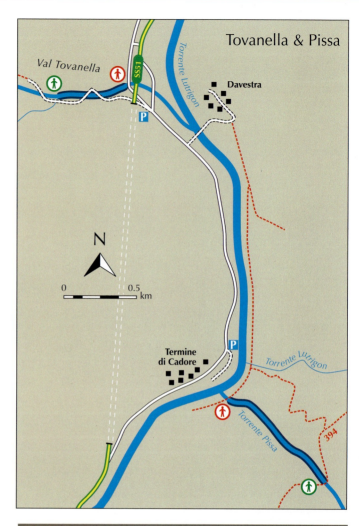

APPROACH

Go back over the bridge and take a steep track opposite the slip road. The track crosses the canyon twice. Where it begins to level out, about 100m before the third bridge, scramble down to the river where possible. The large metal flood defences signify the start of the canyon.

DESCENT

The canyon begins horizontally. Two short climbs and a 6m pitch (jump) punctuate the rocky going. Once under the bridge, the canyon begins in earnest, providing continual interest until the end. Four short drops precede two very atmospheric abseils, the first of which is accessed by an awkward traverse line.

THE BELLUNO AND FRIULI DOLOMITES

The final pitch (toboggan possible)

If you hear a worrying rumble here, don't worry – there's a rail bridge above the next pitch. The canyon ends with a 12m tobogganable pitch.

RETURN
Exit left to the car.

TORRENTE PISSA

An ultra-vertical canyon, culminating in the impressive 100m final pitch visible from the road below. Unfortunately the poor state of the *in-situ* equipment meant that our descent had to be abandoned. Those who wish to do it should go armed with 2x100m ropes, a drill and plenty of anchors just in case. Expect around 20 pitches over the course of 6hrs, including drops of 45m, 60m, 35m and 50m. Park in a large lay-by just north of Termine di Cadore. Take the track down to the river and ford the Piave river where sensible, aiming for a small inlet about 100m upstream (Torrente Lutrigon). Once inside the tree-line, start climbing on faint trails. These improve into a well-defined path with numbered turns. At turn 38 (500m higher up) the path deteriorates. Keep climbing, aiming for a broad grassy clearing just to the south. From here Path 394 (red-and-white markers) leads quickly to the canyon.

ROUTE 65: TOVANELLA

Tovanella, before the encased part

ROUTE 66: ZEMOLA

ZEMOLA ★★★★★ ■ V4.A4–5.IV

Rock	Limestone
Dimensions	Depth 180m (870m–690m); length 2000m
Ideal season	Mid to late summer
Time	Approach 20–30mins (Parking B); descent 4hrs; return 15mins (Parking A)
Shuttle info	Parking A to Parking B – 4km (45mins walk)
Tick rating	1
Gear	2x20m ropes; foot-loop useful
Technical notes	AIC rigging (good condition 2009). High water even in summer, and dangerous early in the season. Some abseils in full flow, but most rigged clear of danger. Beware of pools on fourth pitch and under rock arch.
Escapes	Two (see descent description)

Val Zemola provides one of the finest outings in Italy. It's a sort of 'Dolomites in miniature' – a tour de force of different canyoning styles, from technical white water and sporting sunlit cascades to sombre canyon passages and unique rock formations.

PARKING A
Take the SS251 east from Longarone. Park just before the bridge over Val Zemola (two to three spaces on either side of the road), just past turning for Erto.

GETTING FROM PARKING A TO B
Follow the SS251 back to Erto. Take the road signposted to local amenities at the 93-I marker, then an immediate right to Val Zemola/Rifugio Managio. Follow this road through the village, after which it turns into a single-file track. Park in the lay-by just past where the track swings 90° to the right (enough room for four cars).

APPROACH FROM PARKING A
Walk 50m back towards Erto and take a right by a water fountain. Take a dog-leg up to the houses and a left by a telegraph pole into a field. Skirt the right-hand edge of the field to a dry stream bed. Follow this for a short distance before crossing and climbing on the opposite bank (the path here is faint). When this is no longer possible, trend up and right to a water fountain by the nearest house. Take a left here, whereupon the path finally gets more obvious. Follow it through the woods to a house, where a right turn leads to a tarmacked road. It is 100m up here to the main road. Follow the main road up the valley to where it swings 90° right and descend the steep gully. This is best accessed via a

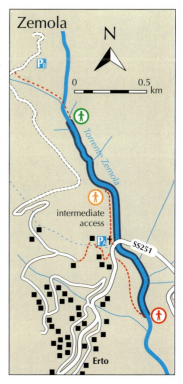

ROUTE 66: ZEMOLA

faint track 20–30m down from Parking B. The gully is rather loose and exposed in places. The first pitch is found a short march downstream.

APPROACH FROM PARKING B
Go back towards the 90° bend and follow the description above.

DESCENT
The descent can be separated into four distinct parts. The first is an enclosed section of four highly aquatic pitches. This is the most serious section and requires a head for white water. The last of these pitches has a particularly turbulent plunge-pool – care required. An escape can be made after this – go downstream a few hundred metres to where it is possible to scramble up to a water pipe on the right (10mins back to Parking A). A more open section of smaller jumps and pitches follows, which may seem like child's play after the previous section but still demands respect in high water. Then comes a more or less horizontal section of stunning cave-like passage, a hundred metres or so beneath the road. The canyon briefly opens out before two unique rock arches mark the beginning of the final section (escape possible left). Care is required in the plunge-pool of the first pitch – it is difficult to exit. The three pitches that follow are very aquatic, but present surprisingly little danger in 'normal' flow

THE BELLUNO AND FRIULI DOLOMITES

At the head of the fourth pitch

ROUTE 66: ZEMOLA

The exhilarating final pitch (some require acrobatic manoeuvres to rig traverse lines – a sling or foot-loop may be useful). In high flow some care is needed in plunge-pools to avoid getting swept over the next pitch.

RETURN
Some 50–100m after the canyon opens out, blue paint on a boulder signifies the exit (ascend the scree slope on the right) that leads back to Parking A.

INTERMEDIATE ACCESS
The canyon can be accessed at a point beyond the first enclosed section, reducing the descent time to 2hrs 30mins. From Parking A, follow a faint path which ascends behind the shrine. It meets with a path which follows a water pipe out of the canyon. The path is more or less level, but is rather exposed in places. It gains the canyon in 10–15mins.

ROUTE 67: PEZZEDA

PEZZEDA ★★★ V3.A4.IV

Rock	Limestone
Dimensions	Depth 390m (1440m–1050m); length 2500m
Ideal season	Summer
Time	Approach 3hrs; descent 3–5hrs; return 30mins
Shuttle info	N/A
Tick rating	2–3
Gear	2x20m ropes; bolting kit; length of cord/slings
Technical notes	Minimal rigging, notably absent in places (2010). Almost over-rigged in lower part. The beginning is splashy and pleasant (flow in both tributaries roughly equal). Current more forceful after confluence – not threatening in summer, but can cause problems on delicate down-climbs.
Escapes	Only where canyon intercepts approach walk

Pezzeda's isolation up a beautiful unpopulated side-valley gives it a distinct alpine flavour. However, its pleasant pools and impressive, towering enclosed sections are marred by logs and frequent bouldery sections. Some might argue that the canyon's modest length is not worth all the effort, and efficient parties will spend more time sweating up the steep slopes of the exhausting approach walk than they will in the canyon itself. There are two alternative starts via separate tributaries (east and west). The eastern tributary is described here.

Sparse rigging and slippery rock mean that this is not a canyon for beginners, nor indeed anyone not comfortable with obligatory and sometimes awkward jumps (up to 10m in the eastern tributary). Pezzeda is for experienced parties with extra calories to burn.

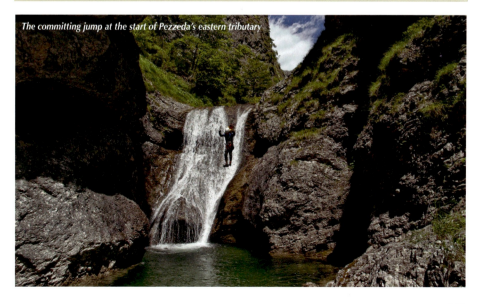
The committing jump at the start of Pezzeda's eastern tributary

ROUTE 67: PEZZEDA

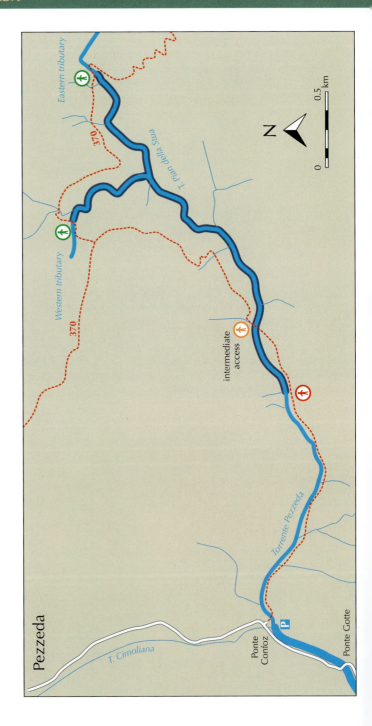

THE BELLUNO AND FRIULI DOLOMITES

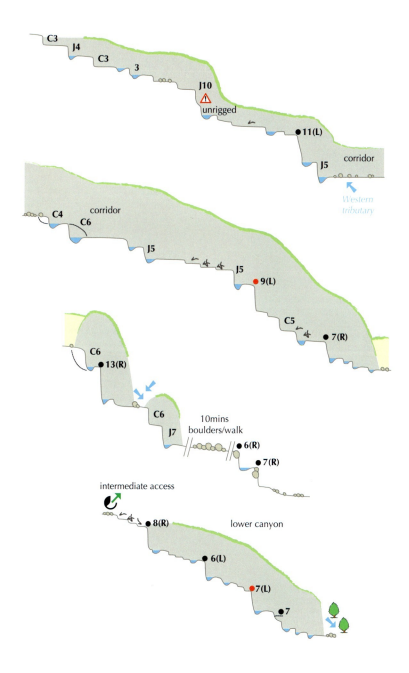

ROUTE 67: PEZZEDA

The pretty encased part in the lower canyon

THE BELLUNO AND FRIULI DOLOMITES

PARKING

On the SS251 east from Longarone, take a left at Cimolais (signposted Casa Anziani/Val Cimoliana). Park just before Ponte Confoz, 6.7km down this road. On weekends and public holidays, a modest fee is payable for the final 3.4km (€6 at the time of writing).

APPROACH

Cross Ponte Confoz and take a right on a strip of tarmac. From here a path leads to the river. Cross it and follow a faint track which heads up the valley (occasional red-and-white markings). After 20mins cross over a side-stream coming in from a valley on the right. After another 20mins the path crosses another tributary (canyon exit visible below) before entering the trees and descending to river level. This is the entry point for the **lower canyon** (1hr to here).

To continue, cross the river and head up the unlikely looking gully ahead. When it gets too steep, step back right (3m scramble on poor rock). From here it is 1hr 30mins of exhausting ascent, interspersed with exposed traversing on thin ledges. Eventually the path levels out and hits Path 370 (also marked with red and white, although the junction itself is unmarked). Follow this right, downhill to the river (5–10mins). This is the starting point for the **western tributary**. If your jumping skills are up to it, it is recommended that you continue for another 15mins to the start of the eastern tributary.

DESCENT

Eastern tributary A number of 2–3m climbs in loosely encased canyon passage precede the first pitch (10m). Being unrigged, this is essentially the key to the descent. The jump is certainly intimidating, with an awkward take off and a bulging lower wall. After this, a nice section of canyon passage leads to the confluence with the western tributary. The walls now loom progressively overhead. The remainder is a discontinuous series of down-climbs, small pitches and obligatory (although much less intimidating) jumps up to 7m. A long bouldery section leads to the approach path (escape/entry possible).

The lower canyon now begins. More boulders and debris lead to a nice but all too brief enclosed section, with two pretty pitches (maximum 8m) and some possible jumps. Allow 45–60mins for this part.

Western tributary (descent not verified). Nine mainly open pitches add an extra couple of hours to the descent time. Take 2x40m ropes (grade v4.a4.V).

RETURN

A stream-inlet on the left marks the end of the final encasement. About 100m further on, toil up left to the approach path, about 50m away.

ROUTE 68: CIOROSOLIN

CIOROSOLIN ★★★ ■ V4.A3.III

Alternative name	Val Cerosolin
Rock	Limestone
Dimensions	Depth 343m (1200m–857m); length 1600m
Ideal season	Summer
Time	Approach 1hr; descent 2hrs 30mins–4hrs; return 5mins
Shuttle info	N/A
Tick rating	1
Gear	2x50m ropes; bits of tape or slings
Technical notes	Longer pitches generally rigged double. Some anchors old. P-hangars and chains on 45m pitch (2009). Trickiest climbs often protectable, but some climbs compulsory. Many abseils/climbs in flow of water – 45m pitch would be tough in high water.
Escapes	Seemingly possible between encased sections

In an area of memorable descents there isn't a great deal to recommend this one. The beginning is mostly tedious going over slippery boulders, with abseils in open stream. The remainder is discontinuous, with open bouldery areas strewn with dead trees dividing sections of nondescript canyon passage. Only the final two enclosed sections are quite pleasant, providing some interesting climbs within clean-washed white canyon walls.

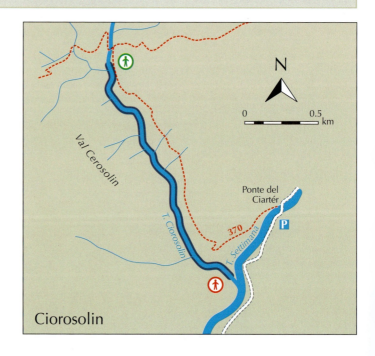

THE BELLUNO AND FRIULI DOLOMITES

Ciorosolin's aquatic 45m pitch

The hard-won pleasant section towards the end

ROUTE 68: CIOROSOLIN

PARKING
Take the SS251 east from Longarone, then the turning to Claut. Just before Claut take a left into the wide Val Settimana. Park by the third road bridge over the river (marked 'Ponte del Ciartér').

APPROACH
Take Path 370 signposted on the other side of the bridge. The path skirts the valley. Access the river when it is easy to do so.

DESCENT
The descent starts as a bouldery scramble with a few loosely enclosed pitches and down-climbs. Interest begins with a couple of short toboggans and jumps, which precede the 45m waterfall (anchors in place for a hand-line out right). Care is required, especially in high water, as all the water is channelled into a flume for the upper two-thirds of the cascade. An anchor at the base on the right can be used for a guide-line if needed. Two more bouldery sections and the unsightly black rock finally give way to classic white dolomite. The descent then becomes more interesting, with a few short climbs and abseils in a pretty canyon passage. This is followed by another similar, but shorter, section of enclosed passage. After this a cascade enters from the right, and it looks for all intents and purposes as though the canyon is over. A few hundred yards further on two 8m pitches with inviting pools mark the end. Cross the Settimana river directly to the road.

332

ROUTE 69: TORRENTE CHIADOLA

TORRENTE CHIADOLA   ★★★ V3.A2.III

Alternative name	Valle Ciadula, or 'Ciarfule' (to the locals)
Rock	Limestone
Dimensions	Depth 60m (660m–600m); length 160m
Ideal season	Late spring to autumn
Time	Approach 2mins; descent 45mins; return 5mins
Shuttle info	N/A
Tick rating	0
Gear	2x15m ropes
Technical notes	Excellent rigging with double anchors. One obligatory 3m toboggan. Current splashy in summer.
Escapes	Two

This is no-stress canyoning, with a handful of pleasant pitches in a nicely formed canyon passage. It is only really worth doing as a second canyon if you are canyoning nearby.

⚠ **Dam upstream (low risk)**

PARKING

Take the SS251 east from Longarone, then the turning to Claut. Enter Claut and take a right turn by the first bus stop (up Via GB Martini). Follow this for 600m to where the road crosses the canyon. Park just after, in the lay-by on the left (space for one car).

APPROACH

Take the rising path from the bridge. Follow it to a small dam, where the path ends.

DESCENT

A series of short splashy pitches, some of which can be climbed, jumped or tobogganed.

RETURN

Follow the left bank of the river until it is possible to take the tarmacked path back to the road.

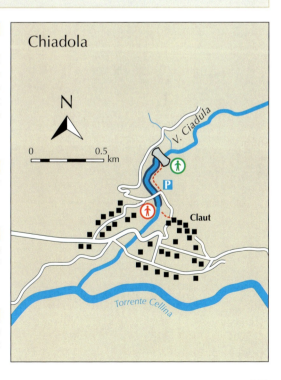

ROUTE 69: TORRENTE CHIADOLA

A splashy pitch in Chiadola's pleasant encased part

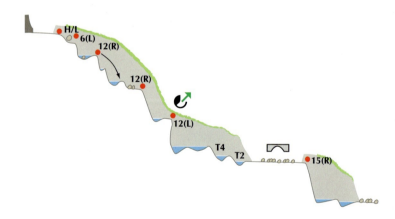

ROUTE 70: CIOLESAN

CIOLESAN ★★★↙ ■ V3–4.A3.III

Rock	Limestone
Dimensions	Depth 150m (825m–675m); length 850m
Ideal season	Summer
Time	Approach 45mins (60mins for upper canyon); descent 2h (+1h for upper canyon); return 10mins
Shuttle info	N/A
Tick rating	1–2
Gear	2x20m ropes (2x30m ropes needed for upper canyon)
Technical notes	Rigging generally very good (2009). Current poses few problems in summer. High water may cause problems in first narrow section.
Escapes	None evident

A short but sweet descent, suitable for the less experienced, water levels permitting. It consists of two pretty encased sections, with clean-washed walls and small splashy pitches. There is an upper canyon, but it is open and uninspiring, with little to recommend it.

The final few metres, calm and verdant

ROUTE 70: CIOLESAN

PARKING
Take the SS251 east from Longarone, then the turning to Claut. Drive through Claut to Lesis. Cross over the bridge and park by the grassy clearing (camping forbidden) at the end of the road.

APPROACH
Cross the footbridge and take the path on the right (true left) of the river. Where it swings right, take an immediate left, following a path which skirts the river for a few minutes. Ignore a small track on the left a little further on (this is the exit path) and start climbing. At a grassy clearing with two houses, take an immediate left. The path re-enters the woods and climbs steeply for 30mins. When the path levels out, a left turn at an obvious bifurcation descends directly to the canyon. The right fork leads to the upper canyon.

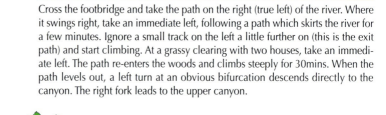

DESCENT
The **lower canyon** begins with a series of three pitches, which lead to the confluence with the main stream. An open section precedes an enclosed 10m pitch into a deep pool. This is followed by an exposed down-climb above two perched boulders (fixed hand-line in place) and a 10m pitch. A short walk in a more open passage leads to an 8m pitch which gives access the most beautiful section – a series of small jumps, climbs and abseils among sculpted rock scenery. A huge perched boulder across the canyon and the following 6m pitch lead to the exit.

The **upper canyon** (not shown) consists of five open pitches, longest 26m, separated by slippery walking passage. Only the first (a 4m jump) provides any great interest.

RETURN
Where the canyon opens out, a black water pipe hangs over the valley. The exit path follows this back to the beginning.

THE BELLUNO AND FRIULI DOLOMITES

The pleasant open section after the confluence with the main Ciolesan river

ROUTE 71: ALBA-MOLASSA

ALBA-MOLASSA ★★★ V1.A3.II

Rock	Limestone
Dimensions	Depth 39m (389m–350m); length 1200m
Ideal season	Early to late summer
Time	Approach 0mins; descent 1hr–1hr 30mins; return 30mins
Shuttle info	N/A
Tick rating	0
Gear	N/A
Technical notes	Current always considerable, but in summer poses few problems. Suspect water quality.
Escapes	At the tributary with Molassa, metal rungs provide a ladder out

Although a little out of the way (1hr 10mins from Belluno), the canyon's short length makes it good choice for a rest day or a second canyon. It is almost entirely horizontal, which is just as well given the considerable current in it. It is best appreciated floating on your back, gazing up the looming canyon walls. A lilo or rubber ring would be fun for the short rapid sections.

⚠ **Lago di Barcis dam upstream in Torrente Cellina (no information available)**

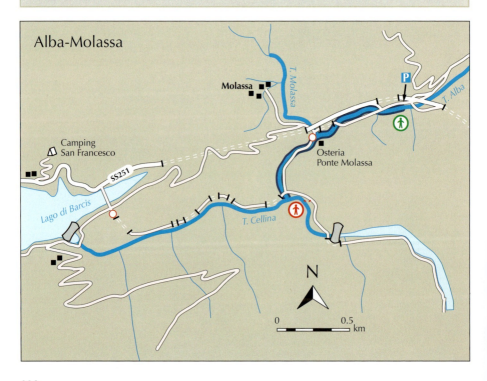

THE BELLUNO AND FRIULI DOLOMITES

Alba-Molassa: the perfect way to wind down

ROUTE 71: ALBA-MOLASSA

PARKING
Following the SS251 east, pass through the first kilometre of tunnel after Barcis. Take the exit marked Andreas. At the T-junction turn left towards Andreas. Follow this road as far as the bridge over the river and park in the lay-by just before it. Scramble down to the river.

DESCENT
The canyon begins a few hundred metres downstream. Progression in the river involves swimming, walking and the odd 1m down-climb. The tributary with Molassa is met about halfway down on the right (possible escape here). After this tributary the current increases, but causes few problems (only the odd turbulent section). The tall canyon passage continues, deep and imposing. The river finally emerges in Torrente Cellina, where the water is much cooler.

RETURN
Swim left (downstream). About 200m further on, just beyond the arches, it is possible to scramble up to the road on the left. Return along the road above the canyon (you may have to scramble over a gate at the far end).

Descending into the linear slot of Viellia 3 (Route 72)

Carnia and the Julian Alps

CANYONING IN THE ALPS

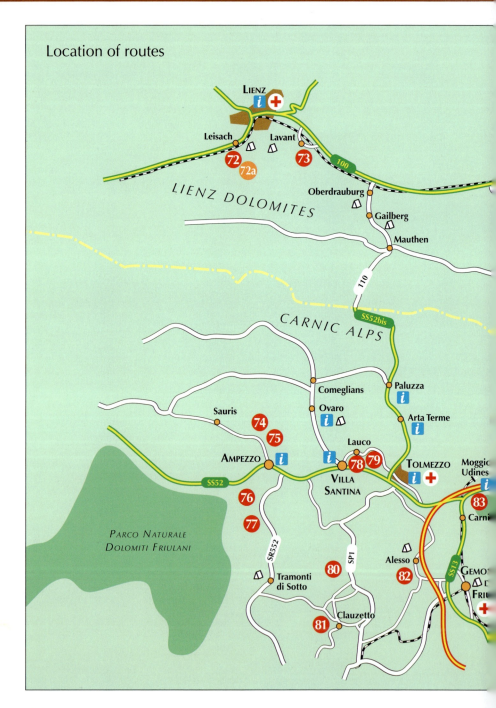

CARNIA AND THE JULIAN ALPS

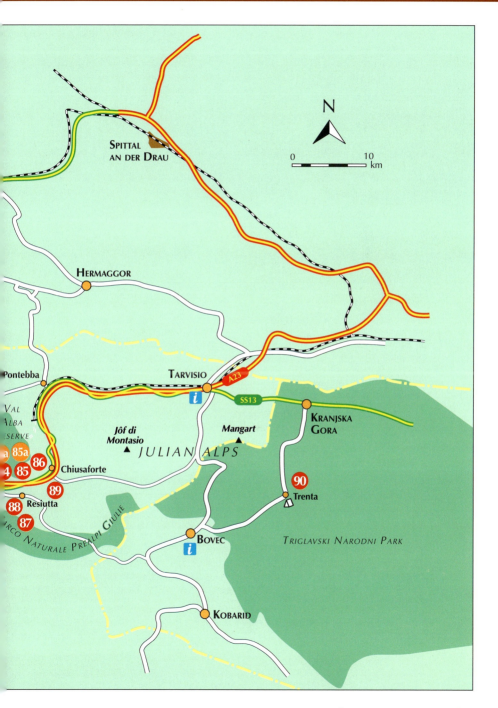

CANYONING IN THE ALPS

Overlooking the Fella river valley from the head of Cuestis's 70m pitch (Route 86)

Travelling north from the Venetian coast towards Tolmezzo, the flat monotony of the Po plain is broken first by the rolling pre-alpine foothills, then, quite suddenly, by the calcareous wall of the Carnic Alps. Further east, extending into Slovenia, are the Julian Alps, a flamboyant and much-celebrated full stop on the Alps' eastern extremity. Neither range is particularly high or glaciated. Their appeal lies in their isolation and tranquillity, being largely off the tourist map. They remain a hidden gem, almost entirely ignored by visiting walkers, climbers and mountaineers.

The region's canyons are conveniently clustered around the historic town of Tolmezzo, in and around the Tagliamento and Fella river valleys. For the most part, the region is an ideal destination for less confident canyoners and aspiring beginners. The majority of routes are relatively short or straightforward, with undemanding approach walks and plentiful shuttle-run possibilities. However, the tempestuous weather and a handful of recently discovered big-water descents lend the area a certain edge. A few technical descents can also be found just over the border, both in the Lienz Dolomites of Austria and the Triglav National Park of Slovenia. Regardless of country, the canyons are all limestone (or dolomite), so steep-walled passages and high waterfalls are characteristic.

WHERE TO STAY

In addition to campsites (see Appendix C), there are plenty of self-catering houses and apartments in the area, but details are quite difficult to come by. Good websites are www.viamalghe.com and www.carnia.it, and individual tourist

CARNIA AND THE JULIAN ALPS

offices can be very helpful (see Appendix D). A good balance of cost and comfort is found at the family-friendly Case per Vacanze Melaria in Preone (www.casevacanzemelaria.it), a little village of wooden huts that originally housed people displaced by the 1976 earthquakes. For a touch more luxury, try the Albergi Diffusi (www.clubalbergodiffuso.it), which are a network of self-catering houses and apartments clustered around a central office. The properties are interesting in that they are previously derelict buildings (many destroyed by the 1976 earthquakes), refurbished in authentic local style. There are offices in Ovaro, Lauco and Sutrio, each offering a number of lodgings in their area. There are also offices in Sauris, Comeglians and Clauzetto, but these locations are less convenient for canyoners.

The best places to find hotels are Gemona del Friuli, Tolmezzo, Villa Santina, Lauco, Ampezzo, Moggio-Udinese and Resiutta.

PRACTICALITIES

Shops and services

Tolmezzo is the political, economic and commercial centre of Carnia. It boasts a wide variety of shops and services while retaining a quiet, historical charm. There are also banks, hotels, restaurants and supermarkets in all reasonably sized settlements. The biggest supermarkets are on the outskirts of Tolmezzo and Villa Santina.

Rio Nero's aquatic final pitch (Route 88)

CANYONING IN THE ALPS

Gear shops
There are two gear shops within 200m of each other in Tolmezzo – No Limits (13 Viale Aldo Moro, tel +39 0433 40297, www.nolimitsextreme.it) and Angeli Sport (Via Linussio 24, tel +39 0433 2301, angelisport@gmail.com). No Limits sells a number of canyoning products.

Hospitals
There are emergency departments in Tolmezzo and Gemona del Friuli.

Weather forecast
This is one of the wettest regions in Italy, sitting at a point where the warm, moist Mediterranean air meets the cool air of the mountains. Afternoon storms are relatively common, so it is important to keep an eye on the weather forecast and to choose canyons accordingly. The best forecast can be obtained from www.meteo.fvg.it. Longer range forecasts can be obtained from 3B Meteo (www.3bmeteo.com) and Il Meteo (www.ilmeteo.it).

Maps
The only detailed maps covering this area are those produced by Tobacco. Owing to their 1:25,000 scale, a number of sheets are required to cover the whole area. For the canyons in Austria, use the 1:50,000 Kompass mapping. For Slovenia, there are a number of maps at varying scales available from Kompass, Freytag & Berndt and Slovenian organisations (both Slovenian Survey and the Slovenian Alpine Club).

Practicalities in Austria (Routes 72 and 73)
There is one campsite in Oberdrauburg and three around Lienz (one in Amlach, one by Tristacher See and one on the outskirts of Lienz itself). Lienz is a large town with all facilities, including a tourist information office and a hospital.

Practicalities in Slovenia (Route 90)
Camping Trenta is just down the road. A number of other campsites can be found further down the Soča valley. Bovec has a range of shops, hotels and other tourist facilities. There are magnificent one-day via ferrata opportunities nearby. The nearest hospital (*bolnišnica*) with an emergency department is in Jesenice, an hour's drive away.

TRAVEL AND TRANSPORT

Rail
The area is served by train, although the only convenient stops are in Gemona del Friuli, Venzone and Carnia. From Carnia, the train takes a subterranean route as far as Pontebba.

Driving
Apart from a couple of exceptions, the canyons are fairly well grouped together, so driving times are well under an hour in most cases. At the time of writing, the SS52 west of Tolmezzo was being widened and, in places,

CARNIA AND THE JULIAN ALPS

Beautiful cave-like scenery in Rio Cuestis (Route 86)

rerouted. The access routes to canyons along this road may therefore change.

The nearest car hire is in Udine, 50km south of Tolmezzo.

OTHER ACTIVITIES

Thanks to a general lack of industry, a limited population size and no fewer than four protected areas, nature in this corner of Italy remains largely unspoilt. However, as a visiting tourist, it is difficult to get the best out of the area. There are few roads that climb above the tree-line, and much time could be spent slogging up steep forested slopes seeing very little at all. A handful of pleasant ridge-top walks are evident on walking maps, but it's worth trying to get hold of a guidebook if you plan on doing any walking. Although there are numerous guidebooks to the Slovenian Julian Alps (including *The Julian Alps of Slovenia* and *Trekking in Slovenia*, Cicerone Press), none covers Carnia or the Italian Julian Alps in any depth. The bookshops in and around the central square in Tolmezzo (Piazza 20 Settembre) sell some interesting-looking Italian-language titles.

Carnia's most precipitous and impressive peaks are along the Austrian border, about an hour's drive north from Villa Santina. *Alpi Carniche: arrampicate classiche e moderne*, by Riccardo del Fabbro and Massimo Candolini, details 52 multi-pitch routes on the impressive-looking limestone faces around Sappada. The Julian Alps are another obvious choice for climbers, although information on the Italian side is far harder to come by. The staff in local gear shops may be able to point you in the right direction, as well provide details of more accessible valley crags in the area.

Via ferrata is another possibility. There is one difficult route on Zuc dal Bor in the Val Alba Reserve, but most are found in the Julian Alps (on both sides of the border) and along the Austrian border. For guidebook coverage, see Appendix B.

Finally, the land between Gemona del Friuli and Cividale to the south is wine-growing country, worth exploring if you're a wine-lover. The region is famed for its sweet Ramondolo wines and Tokai (a grape made more famous by the Hungarians).

PROTECTED AREAS

Parco Regionale delle Dolomiti Friulane www.parcodolomitifriulane.it
Parco Prealpi Giulie & Val Alba Reserve www.parcoprealpigiulie.org
Parco Intercomunale delle Colline Carniche www.parks.it/parco.colline.carniche
Julian Alps National Park (Slovenia) www.julijske-alpe.com

WARNING

Ticks, Lyme disease and tick-borne encephalitis
The warnings of the Belluno and Friuli Dolomites' chapter apply equally (if not more so) to Carnia and the Julian Alps.

ROUTE 72: LOWER RÖTENBACH

LOWER RÖTENBACH

★★★↙  V4.A2.V

Rock	Limestone
Dimensions	Depth 190m (920m–730m); length 350m
Ideal season	Summer
Location	Austria
Time	Approach 20mins (Parking C); descent 2–3hrs; return 10mins (Parking A)
Shuttle	Parking A to Parking B – 1.5km (25mins on foot)
	Parking B to Parking C – 1.1km (15mins on foot)
Tick rating	1–2
Gear	2x45m ropes
Technical notes	Well rigged on double P-hangars or 10mm thru-bolts. Current imposing, and a number of abseils are in the full flow of water. The canyon is badly flood prone – bolting equipment essential.
Escapes	None

A surprisingly little-known canyon given its location, Rötenbach offers a continual string of aquatic and sometimes intimidating pitches. It is a severe, imposing scene of bare white rock and waterfalls, without the rich colour of vegetation or plunge-pools. The faint, seldom trodden approach walk does little to temper the sense of isolation.

Only the lower canyon is described in detail here. The upper canyon lacks character and offers little reward for the black-rated approach walk. For those who have only one day in Austria, it might be better to combine lower Rötenbach with the lower part of Frauenbach (see Route 73), rather than do the full descent of Rötenbach.

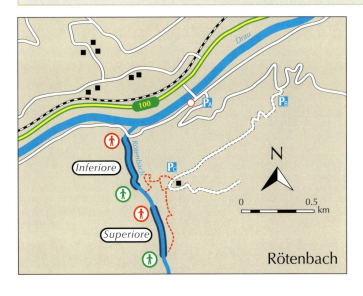

ROUTE 72: LOWER RÖTENBACH

PARKING A
This canyon is a 2hr drive from Tolmezzo. Follow the ss52bis into Austria. Continue through Mauthen to Oberdrauburg, then take a left towards Lienz on highway 100. In Lienz, follow signs for Bozen and Sillian (also on highway 100). Just after the 113km marker-post, turn left over a bridge (signposted to Kershbaumer Alm). Park at the T-junction or in the wide clearing to the left.

GETTING FROM PARKING A TO B
Follow the road up from the wide clearing. Park at the junction with a gravel track on a left-hand hairpin bend.

GETTING FROM PARKING B TO C
If your vehicle has good ground-clearance, continue up the gravel track (steep in places) and park just before the first hairpin bend left. There is a hidden hut just up on the left here (spring with drinking water).

CARNIA AND THE JULIAN ALPS

Start of lower Rötenbach

ROUTE 72: LOWER RÖTENBACH

Rötenbach – a harsh landscape of rock and water

APPROACH FROM PARKING C

Not easy to find. Take the grassy track on the right just before the hairpin bend. This turns into a path, which soon meets a wooden bird-spotters' shelter. Follow a faint trail down a broad grassy ridge to a point just above some makeshift fencing on the edge of the cliff. Aim right here. The path initially deteriorates to nothing, then reappears after about 100m when things steepen. About 10m further down, take a very faint trail left. This trail quickly improves – follow it down the ridge-line towards the broad gully on your left. Cross over the top of the gully (exposed; rope in situ in 2011) and descend on easier ground (initially a scree slope, then boulders) to gain the river about 200m before the canyon starts.

DESCENT

A continual string of enclosed pitches. Many of the abseils are in the full flow of water. A couple of pitches are difficult to assess from the top.

RETURN

Exit right where the canyon meets the main valley to return to Parking A.

ROUTE 72A: UPPER RÖTENBACH

UPPER RÖTENBACH   V3–4.A2.IV

This is the lacklustre upper canyon, whose sketchy walk-in is rather more memorable than the canyoning.

Allow 45mins to 1hr 15mins for the delicate approach walk. From Parking C, take a grassy track just above the hairpin bend. After a few metres a very faint trail snakes up into the trees. Follow this up to the watershed, where a faint hunters' path can be found. Follow this up-slope for 10–15mins. Where it gets too steep (just below a rocky outcrop), skirt down and right across a very exposed gully. The path descends a little then contours around to another very exposed gully, protected with a metal cable. There are remnants of a couple of tree-ladders here. Cross over the next gully and thrash through the dwarf pine to the river bed. Check for ticks (rating = 2). The descent (1hr 30mins–2hrs) consists of a series of enclosed pitches presenting no great difficulty or interest (in normal summer conditions). Maximum pitch 33m, rigged with single anchors, a few old and rusted. No escapes.

The opening pitch of upper Rötenbach

ROUTE 73: FRAUENBACH

FRAUENBACH ★★★↙ V4.A4.IV

Rock	Limestone
Dimensions	Depth 270m (950m–680m); length 300m
Ideal season	Summer
Location	Austria
Time	Approach 40mins; descent 3–4hrs; return 5mins
Shuttle	N/A
Tick rating	0–1
Gear	2x30m ropes
Technical notes	Double P-hangars and chains (2010). Flow in lower canyon sporting due to numerous resurgences, but silted pools mean current is rarely a problem. The flow can be checked at the final falls.
Escapes	After the first part and after the fourth pitch in the second part (not verified)

This is perhaps Austria's most celebrated canyon. Being just over an hour's drive from Tolmezzo, it is well worth the trip for anyone canyoning in Carnia. Frauenbach is a classic limestone canyon – steep, encased and continually interesting. While no single feature stands out above the rest, it offers a constant string of pleasant cascades from start to finish, with barely any time spent walking or boulder-hopping. The descent can be divided into two – a playful first part well suited to beginners (after which an escape is possible), and a more vertical and aquatic second. The twin falls at the end provide an opportunity to show off your rope skills to the tourists, who will be watching with a keen eye from viewing platforms.

 1 Dam upstream (no information available)

 2 Canyon in military exercise area. Open times posted in car park, but access guaranteed only at weekends.

PARKING

The canyon is a 1hr 30min drive from Tolmezzo. Head towards Lienz (see Route 72 for details). From highway 100, take a left turn by the 97.4 marker (signposted 'Frauenbach Wasserfall'). Once over the bridge and railway line, bear right where the road forks. Take a left just before entering Wacht (the turning is not signposted in this direction, but is signposted 'Lavanter Alm' from the other direction). Park in the large car park at the end of this road.

APPROACH

Continue up the unpaved track. It is a 25min walk to the second right-hand switch-back. A path heads off here to the halfway escape point (2mins to the stream). To get to the top of the canyon, continue up the track to a junction. Take the left to Lavanter Alm, which climbs to the water capture. Enter here.

A playful little toboggan in Frauenbach's first half (photo: Simon Flower)

ROUTE 73: FRAUENBACH

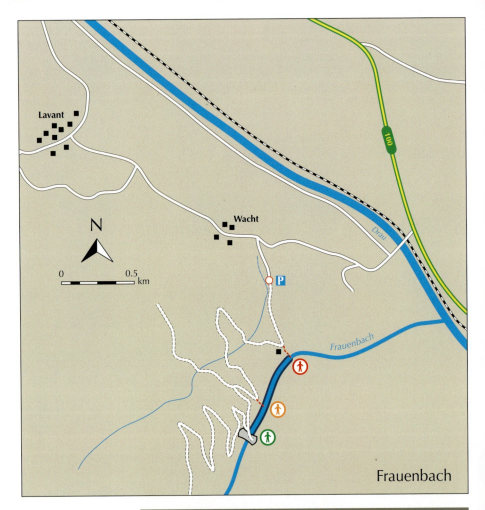

DESCENT

The upper canyon provides a string of short abseils and tobogganing opportunities (maximum pitch 15m). Be aware that some pools are quite silted. Exit left where the canyon opens out (a path leads in 2mins back to the approach walk) or continue down the lower canyon. A number of inlets and a more or less continual need for the rope means that this part is more technical. The twin falls at the end can either be done in a single abseil around to the right (2x50m ropes needed) or in two stages in the flow of the stream.

RETURN

After the look-out point, take a path on the left, just before the first concrete baffle.

CARNIA AND THE JULIAN ALPS

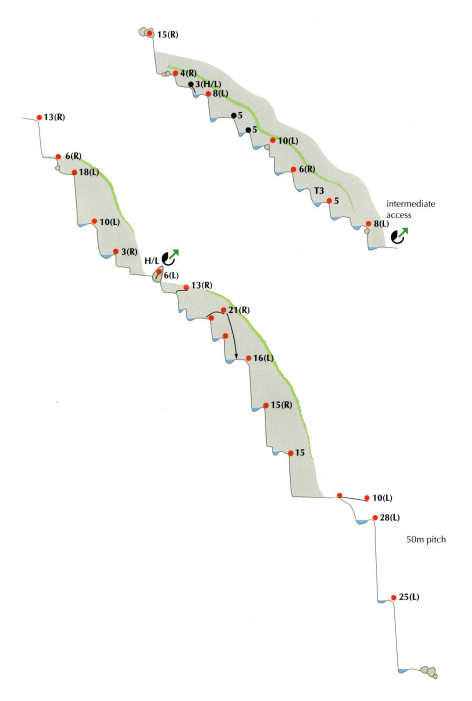

ROUTE 73: FRAUENBACH

More aquatic going below the escape point in Frauenbach (photo: Simon Flower)

CARNIA AND THE JULIAN ALPS

NOVARZA AND LUMIEI

Torrente Lumiei cuts a long and precipitous course through the limestone north of Ampezzo. Two separate descents are possible here, with the option of combining them. One is an impressive section of the Torrente Lumiei itself. This is mostly horizontal going in aquatic canyon passage. In places it is cathedral-like, its looming walls casting much of the first half into shadow. The other is Torrente Novarza, which is a major tributary of Torrente Lumiei but totally different in character, being much more vertically developed and virtually dry. Novarza instils mixed feelings. Its beginnings are certainly little to get excited about, but it gradually becomes more atmospheric and sombre. However the feeble stream, silted pools and detritus detract from the overall experience.

PARKING A
In Ampezzo, take the turning to Sauris on the SP73. Follow the road for 2.9km to the first hairpin bend left. The path from Lumiei exits here. Park in the lay-by on the left a little further on.

PARKING B
Follow the SP73 up through the 527m-long Clap della Polenta tunnel. A short distance before the Pala Pelosa tunnel, there is a large lay-by on the right, where the Lumiei access path starts.

PARKING C
Continue up the road, through the Pala Pelosa tunnel (314m long). At the far end the road passes over the impressive Lumiei canyon. Parking is available at either end of the bridge.

ROUTE 74: NOVARZA

NOVARZA ★★★ V4.A2.IV

Rock	Limestone
Dimensions	Length 309m (1000m–691m); length 1000m
Ideal season	Early to late summer
Time	Approach 20mins (Parking C); descent 2hrs 30mins–3hrs; return 15mins (Parking B) or walk to Lumiei 10mins
Shuttle info	Parking B to Parking C – 800km (10mins road-walk)
Tick rating	0
Gear	2x40m ropes
Technical notes	Double 8 or 10mm thru-bolts and spits, joined with rope (2010). Tiny stream in summer and all pools silted up.
Escapes	None

A vertically developed tributary of Torrente Lumiei – impressive in places but virtually dry.

⚠ **Dam upstream (no information)**

Novarza – imposing in its lower reaches but virtually dry

CARNIA AND THE JULIAN ALPS

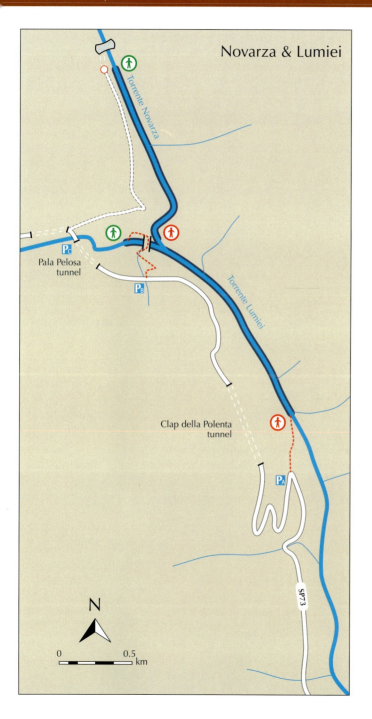

Novarza & Lumiei

ROUTE 74: NOVARZA

APPROACH FROM PARKING C
Follow the obvious broad track east on the far side of the bridge. The track ends by a tunnel (access forbidden). Skirt the hillside for 50m or so to an abseil station on a tree.

DESCENT
A 50m abseil from a tree gains a gully that descends to the stream bed. It is best split at −35m on a small ledge to the left (space for three; watch out for rockfall). Once in the canyon there is an almost continual string of abseils from start to finish (maximum 20m).

Where the canyon opens out, an obvious gully on the right signifies the return path. If you miss this a 16m pitch into the Lumiei canyon will be reached, 100m or so further on. Those intending to descend Lumiei should exit Novarza by the gully and start the descent of Lumiei from the beginning.

RETURN TO PARKING B/CONTINUE TO LUMIEI
At the top of the gully is the bridge over Lumiei. Either descend to the right just before the bridge and begin the descent of Lumiei (5mins) (see Route 75) or continue climbing to the road.

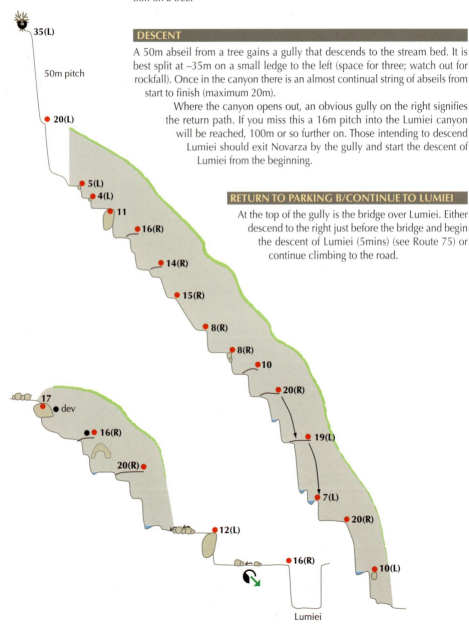

CARNIA AND THE JULIAN ALPS

A rare clean-washed section before the end

ROUTE 75: LUMIEI

LUMIEI	★★★⯨ 🟨🟦 V3.A4.IV
Rock	Limestone
Dimensions	Depth 170m (750m–580m); length 1900m
Ideal season	Early to late summer
Time	Approach 10mins (Parking B); descent 2hrs; return 15mins (Parking A)
Shuttle info	Parking A to Parking B – 3.2km (40mins road-walk)
Tick rating	0
Gear	2x20m ropes
Technical notes	AIC rigging (good condition 2010). Current quite powerful in places, but only the first pitch can really trouble.
Escapes	None until after encasement
Note	For map see Route 74

Straightforward and atmospheric, Lumiei is great for less experienced canyoners.

⚠ Dam and large reservoir (Lago di Sauris) upstream (no information)

APPROACH FROM PARKING B
Follow the path signposted 'sent. della Pedena del Buso' to a little bridge over the canyon. Cross this and take an immediate left down to river level (the path straight over is the Novarza exit path).

DESCENT
A short pitch/climb gains access to the main Lumiei pitch (16m). The main anchors are difficult to reach – the approach is best protected with a traverse line from anchors further back on the right. A section of impressive canyon passage then ensues. There are a couple of little jumps, climbs and toboggans, but the rope can now be stashed away. After what seems like a very short space of time, the canyon starts to open out and becomes more discontinuous. Look out for the exit path on the right. It is not obvious, but once found it is well marked with blue-on-white AIC markers.

RETURN
Follow the path up through the trees to the road and Parking A.

CARNIA AND THE JULIAN ALPS

Peering into the Lumiei canyon from the end of Novarza

ROUTE 76: RIO NEGRO

RIO NEGRO ★★★↙ V5.A6.II–III

Rock	Limestone
Dimensions	Depth 111m (642m–531m); length 1600m
Ideal season	Mid to late summer
Time	Approach 1hr 40mins; descent 2hrs 30mins–3hrs; return 40mins
Shuttle info	N/A
Tick rating	0–1
Gear	2x20m ropes
Technical notes	A handful of single anchors supplements mainly natural rigging. Always aquatic. Flow doubles just prior to the crux section. One pitch in the full flow of water into a very turbulent pool. This canyon is best done after a period of stable weather. Very slippery rock.
Escapes	Numerous before the final enclosed section

Discovered only in 2010, Rio Negro is Carnia's newest challenge. It might seem a long way to go for such a short canyon, but your efforts will be amply rewarded for the canyon's stunning final section. This sombre and aquatic passage provides a test of nerve for white-water enthusiasts, but a large, partially subterranean catchment area means that it requires a period of stable weather to come into condition. Come prepared to bypass this section all together.

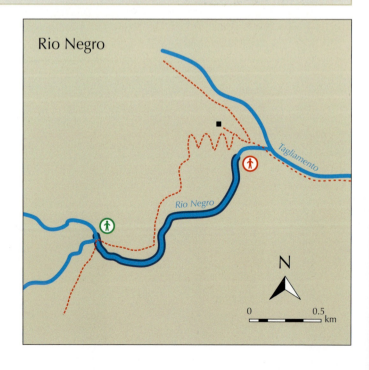

CARNIA AND THE JULIAN ALPS

No room for error – the final turbulent pitch

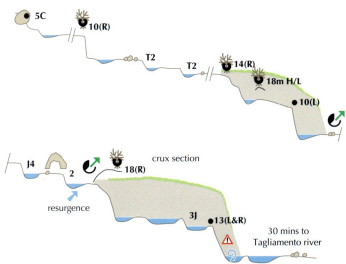

ROUTE 76: RIO NEGRO

Committing to Rio Negro's crux section

CARNIA AND THE JULIAN ALPS

PARKING
Follow the SS52 west from Tolmezzo. Cross Torrente Lumiei, then take an immediate left turning to Tramonti/Priuso (SR552). Go over a small pass to meet the Tagliamento river again. At the far end of the reservoir take a vehicle track just before the road crosses the river. Follow the vehicle track to the end. Alternatively, take a gravel track 400m beyond the bridge, where it is possible to park in the shade.

APPROACH
Follow the unshaded gravel bed of the Tagliamento, fording the stream a number of times where needed. The Rio Negro enters at an apparent forested island after about 40–45mins walking. Take the left side of the island, following the watercourse back to where it swings left at the base of the hill. Here, hunt around just inside the tree-line for a faint path marked with red and white stripes. Follow it steeply uphill for 15mins, after which it flanks the river (exposed at times). Enter where the path meets the river.

DESCENT
To start with the river is quite open. The first pitch is down-climbable to the left with care (bolt in situ). The second pitch is rigged off a tree to the right. The canyon then becomes more defined. It closes in for two pleasant pitches, the second of which has a precarious approach in high water conditions. If a strong current dictates that you need to use the tree belay high on the right (very awkward climb required), then the crux section is probably too wet. A 4m jump/toboggan follows, then another small jump into a pool. A resurgence enters underwater here, doubling the flow of the river and halving its temperature. The canyon narrows down for the crux section – escape is possible just prior to this. A tree belay around to the right (exposed) provides access to the slot. Exit is via an aquatic abseil into a very turbulent pool, with anchor on the left – great care required. From here it is much easier going. Two small climbs/jumps and a lengthy swim break up 30mins of slippery boulder-hopping.

RETURN
Follow the Tagliamento back downstream. Take lilos!

ROUTE 77: VIELLIA

VIELLIA

Rock	Limestone
Dimensions	Depth 770m (1220m–450m); length 5500m
Ideal season	Mid to late summer
Time	Approach 1hr/1hr 30mins/1hr 50mins/2hrs 30mins; descent 8–10hrs (2–3hrs + 1hr 30mins + 1hr 30mins + 3–4hrs; return 20mins
Shuttle info	(optional) 1.5km
Tick rating	1–2
Gear	2x40m ropes; 2x25m sufficient for Viellia 2, 3 and 4 – but may change as rigging improves. Prusiking kit useful for Viellia 1.
Technical notes	First-descent rigging (mono-points, pitons or absent). Current can cause problems in Viellia 1 and 2. Viellia 3 is much less aquatic. Viellia 4 is a sizeable stream with a strong current – dangerous in places. Climbs, jumps and toboggans, many intimidating from the top, are frequent and obligatory.
Escapes	Numerous (improvised or obvious) in Viellia 1; the enclosed section in Viellia 2 can be bypassed; no escapes evident in Viellia 3; only after the difficulties in Viellia 4

A comparatively recent 'discovery', Viellia is set to become a regional classic. Done in its entirety it is a long alpine adventure with all the key ingredients of a memorable descent. A strong current and bare-bones rigging mean that the canyon should not be underestimated; obligatory jumps and slippery down-climbs are frequent.

The descent is easily divisible into four parts, separated from each other by a few hundred metres of open river. Parts 2 and 3 are shortest and most straightforward. Part 4 is longest and most serious, having perhaps twice the volume of water of the parts preceding it. It is sporting and spectacular – a must for experienced parties (others should probably stay away unless the rigging improves). Part 1 is most vertically developed, but is the least aesthetically interesting overall. Anchors, where present, are often in unusual or hard-to-reach places, and a disproportionate amount of time will be spent picking the right line down the canyon. This part will appeal to purists, but there is little reward for a lot of extra effort, and it may well mean doing the more spectacular lower parts of the canyon in failing light.

PARKING

From the SS52 just east of Ampezzo, take the SS552 towards Tramonti. It climbs laboriously over the pass, then continues down the other side. Park about 100m beyond the 24km marker sign, where the path begins.

APPROACH

Take Path 377 signposted to Casera Chiampis. Climb to a broad col in about 30mins. Over the next 30mins, the path gently descends virtually to river level. **Viellia 4** is a 5min walk downstream from here. After 30mins of steady climbing, a bouldery river bed can be seen about 30m below – this is the start of **Viellia 3**. Climb again for 20mins. Where the path levels out, a walled

CARNIA AND THE JULIAN ALPS

The delicate, unrigged 14m pitch in Viellia 1

Committing to the aquatic and technical Viellia 4

ROUTE 77: VIELLIA

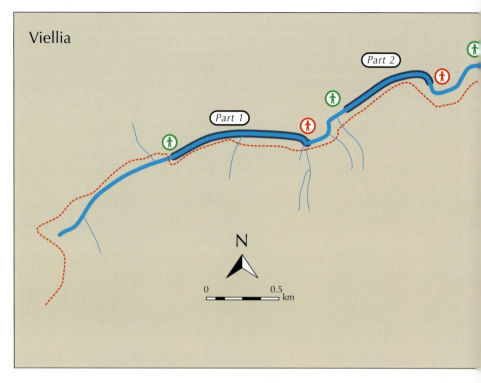

enclosure marks the start of **Viellia 2**. After a few minutes of gentle ascent, the path now steepens. Climb for 30mins to where the path reaches a broad valley, where **Viellia 1** begins.

DESCENT

VIELLIA 1 ★★★ V5.A4.III

A few loosely enclosed jumps and abseils precede an obvious fissure, accessed by a hand-line then a 10m abseil. Escape past the perched boulder at the far end is awkward and committing (take prusiking kit just in case you don't fancy it). It is another 30m to the floor from here. It might be better to bypass the fissure to the right, but the anchors for the following pitch are in very exposed positions part-way down (difficult to see from above). After this, things improve a little with a pretty but short enclosed section. The first pool here is difficult to escape – better to traverse around to the right. The going is then more open (escape possible right). Things get tricky again with a very thin climb, then jump, down a 14m pitch (very slippery at the top – no anchors evident). The

CARNIA AND THE JULIAN ALPS

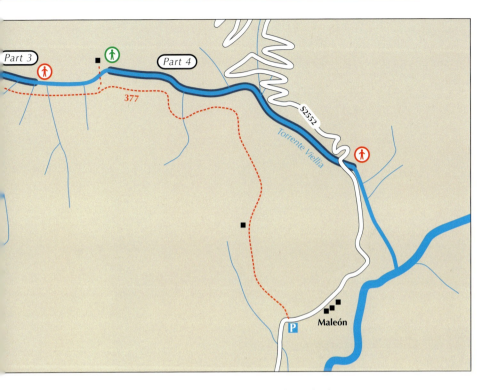

next and last major obstacle is the 60m pitch, divisible into three. The first is a 15m abseil off a single piton to a shelf, from where an exposed down-climb leads to double anchors. These can be used to gain the floor direct (2x50m rope useful for pull-through) or to gain a shelf 15m down, where a single anchor gives a 20m abseil to the floor. An escape right can be made at the second re-belay. At the end of the canyon, escape right to the approach path and follow it to Viellia 2 (5–10mins).

| VIELLIA 2 | ★★★★ | V4.A4.II |

Things begin playfully with a couple of small jumps into pretty pools. The fun then begins with an airy 12m jump into a deep pool, followed by a spectacular section under a rock arch (rigged with two pitons). This whole section can be bypassed around to the right. The final obstacle is an open 35m pitch. The single anchor is gained by clambering down to a shelf, which provides a 22m abseil to a ledge (pull-through awkward). From here it's an easy scramble down to the base of the waterfall. A few boulders and you're done. Escape right onto the approach path, where possible, and follow it down to Viellia 3 in 10–15mins (boulder-hopping downstream takes 30mins).

ROUTE 77: VIELLIA

Viellia 1

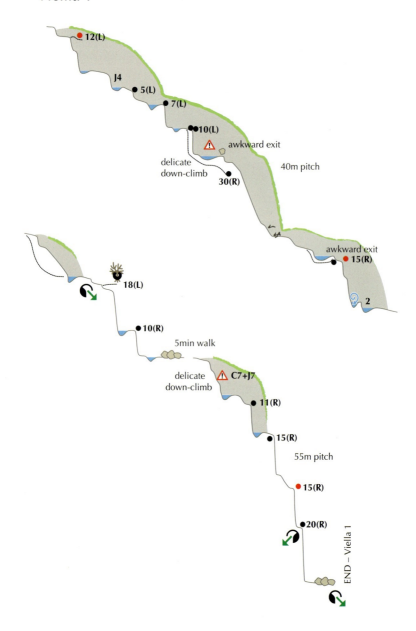

CARNIA AND THE JULIAN ALPS

VIELLIA 3 ★★★★ V4.A4.III

A couple of small pools signify the approach to the first encased section. The first pitch can either be down-climbed in the centre (very exposed) or abseiled on a tree to the right. Two obligatory jumps of 4m and 7m precede the main feature – a dramatic linear slot, where some water resurges along the left-hand wall to spray the depths below. Entry is by a 23m pitch (a longer tail is better for pulling through); exit by an obligatory jump of 8–10m into a huge pool. A large, very cold resurgence then enters from the right. Escape right or continue downstream to Viellia 4 (5–10mins).

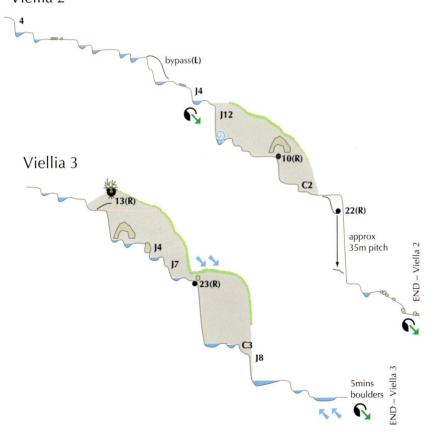

ROUTE 77: VIELLIA

VIELLIA 4 ★★★★

Do not take this section lightly. Of particular note is an aquatic and slippery chute midway down the second enclosed section. A very wet (and obligatory) 10m toboggan follows, but this is impossible to know from above, and the first person may wish to enter the chute by means of a body belay from the preceding pool. The third enclosed section also has a couple of problematic features, including a frothing siphon beneath a large boulder barring the way on (use a rope to access the right side) and a 3m frictionless climb in the stream a little further on. After a serene 100m swim, things ease greatly. The pitch that follows can be rigged safely from a tree around to the left. Where things open out, an escape can be made to the left, but all that really remains is the final enclosed passage, about 30mins long and child's play in comparison to the preceding few hours. Finally, pass under the bridge and take a path immediately on the right up to the road. From here, it is a 15min walk back to the car.

Viellia 4

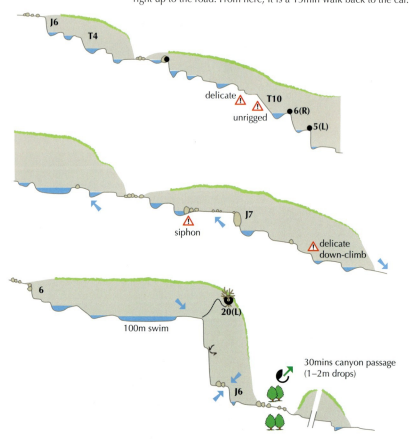

CARNIA AND THE JULIAN ALPS

Leaping into Viellia 2

VINADIA (VIA PICCHIONIS AND CHIANTIONE)

Torrente Vinadia is one of north-east Italy's most imposing canyons, cutting an immense cleft through the limestone north of Villa Santina. Two rivers join the Vinadia upstream, Picchionis and Chiantione, both canyoning trips in their own right. Chiantione is the most dramatic and continuous, with its vertical walls towering 100m overhead in places, barely an arm's width apart. The canyon is let down considerably by the sheer quantity of human detritus strewn along its length, from litter and household commodities to metal barrels and mechanical parts. The minimal flow in the canyon means that the water quality inevitably suffers. Picchionis, by contrast, is aquatic. It has a sporting pitch series and an impressive slot canyon, but is itself let down by long sections of open river and boulders. Below the dam (which thankfully filters the Chiantione detritus), the Vinadia canyon itself has some nice clean-washed passages, with some pleasant pools and sporting cascades, but again long bouldery sections towards the end detract from the overall enjoyment. In short, the Vinadia and its tributaries are a mixed bag. The sheer scale of the place means that the canyon cannot be ignored, but the descent cannot be wholeheartedly recommended.

ROUTE 78: PICCHIONIS

PICCHIONIS ★★★ ■ V4.A4.V

Rock	Limestone
Dimensions	Depth 428m (775m–347m); length 4500m
Ideal season	Summer
Time	Approach 0mins (Parking B); descent 5–7hrs (1hr–1hr 30mins to the Vinadia stream exit); return 0mins (Parking A)
Shuttle info	Parking A to Parking B – 13.8km (2hrs 30mins walk)
Tick rating	0
Gear	2x30m ropes; head-torch for dam escape route
Technical notes	Well-placed double P-hangars avoid the worst of the current (considerable, even in summer). Anchors in place for hand-lines and deviations. Current below the dam is usually pleasant – verify flow from Parking A.
Escapes	Obvious path after the confluence with the Vinadia stream. Escape may be possible at the dam via a long access tunnel (officially forbidden – emergencies only). There is a locked gate at the far end, but one of the bars has been missing for many years (a situation not guaranteed to last – be warned!).
Note	For the topo of the Vinadia canyon see Route 79

The aquatic but discontinuous arm of Vinadia.

 Dam mid-descent (no information)

PARKING A

From the SS52, take the turning to Vinadia a couple of kilometres east of Villa Santina. Park a 100m or so further on, in a lay-by on the far side of the bridge over the canyon.

GETTING FROM PARKING A TO B

By car
From the SS52, take a right to Lauco in Villa Santina. At Lauco climb through the village, signposted to Vinaio. At Vinaio follow signs to Buttea. Go 500m past the village and park just before the Torrente Picchions bridge.

On foot
Walk along the road to Villa Santina (30 miserable minutes). Take a right into Piazza Merato and go straight on through the large opening in the concrete wall, following signs for Troi di Lauco. Take the rising path which zigzags up to Lauco (1hr). In Lauco, go straight on at the church, heading east. Wind through the small streets to the back of the village, where there is a water fountain.

Take the road by the little shrine 10m away. Follow this to the end, then take a path signposted to Porteal (red and white stripes). At the top of the hill take a left at a house, along a vehicle track. Where it intercepts a tarmacked

CARNIA AND THE JULIAN ALPS

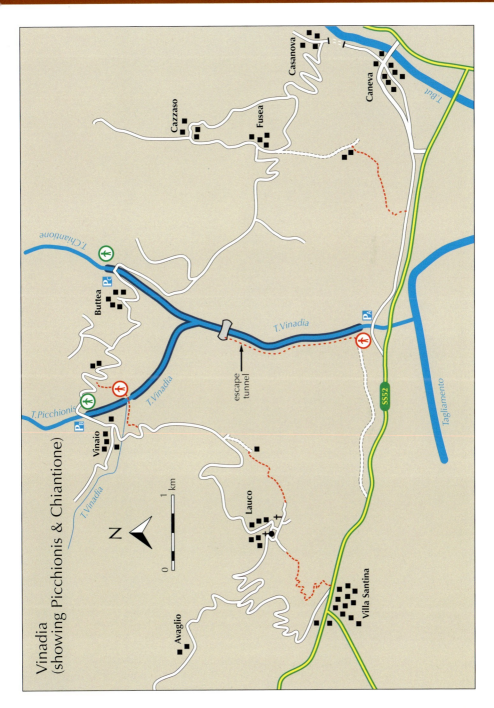

Vinadia (showing Picchionis & Chiantione)

ROUTE 78: PICCHIONIS

The end of Picchionis' first encased section (exit possible just around the corner)

CARNIA AND THE JULIAN ALPS

section, take a left to the main road. Walk 30mins along the road, taking a right through Vinaio (see above).

APPROACH FROM PARKING B
Access the river by a path on the left on the far side of the river.

DESCENT
The descent begins with four enclosed and aquatic pitches (maximum 20m) – beware of the current at the base of the second and third. Where the canyon opens out, it meets the Vinadia stream on the right. Exit is possible on the obvious path just beyond. Strip off a little neoprene for the bouldery walk downstream, then take a bracing dip in the deep pool of the impressive Forra del Vinadia – 50m long, 50m high, but only an arm's span across in places. A section of exciting via ferrata then starts, terminating in a wet 20m pitch, rigged out of the water with deviations. The canyon is then bouldery going to the dam, and passes the Chiantione inlet on the left.

Abseil off the dam. From here, most pitches have been rigged with a now rapidly decaying via ferrata. After an 8m pitch the canyon gets steadily more enclosed. A pretty section precedes the 25m pitch (the highest pitch after the dam). It is mostly bouldery streamway from here until the end, with two small pitches to punctuate the monotony.

ROUTE 79: CHIANTIONE

CHIANTIONE		★★★ ■ V5.A3.IV
Rock	Limestone	
Dimensions	Depth 453m (800m–347m); length 3700m	
Ideal season	Early to late summer	
Time	Approach 0mins (Parking C); descent 5–6hrs; return 0mins (Parking A)	
Shuttle info	Parking A to Parking C – 14km (2hrs walk)	
Tick rating	1	
Gear	2x60m ropes; head-torch for the escape route	
Technical notes	AIC rigging (good condition 2010). Minimal current in Chiantione. Current below dam usually pleasant – verify flow from Parking A.	
Escapes	May be possible at the dam via a long access tunnel (officially forbidden – emergencies only). There is a locked gate at the far end, but one of the bars has been missing for many years (a situation not guaranteed to last – be warned!).	
Note	For map see Route 78	

The spectacular but polluted arm of Vinadia.

 Dam mid-descent (no information)

PARKING A
As for Picchionis (see Route 78).

GETTING FROM PARKING A TO C

By car
Follow the road east, past the turning into Caneva. Just before the bridge over the River But, take a left towards Zuglio. The road enters a tunnel. Take the first left immediately after the tunnel ends (signposted 'Cazzaso' and 'Fusea'). The road climbs on hairpins to Fusea. Follow the road through Fusea, ignoring turnings to Cazzaso. Further on, take a left to Fornas/Buttea. Park by the bridge over the canyon.

On foot
The path is by no means obvious, and it is worth driving to the start first to ensure you can find it. From the parking, walk along the old road for 1.6km to an old stone marker post with a '1' on it (about 85m west of the 7km marker post). Head up the grassy slope directly from here into the trees, where the start of a very neglected path should be visible. It involves 45mins of steep climbing on a reasonably obvious but under-used path to a grassy clearing. Head through the clearing to a farm building (5mins) and take the track out to the main road. Take a left along the main road to the canyon.

CARNIA AND THE JULIAN ALPS

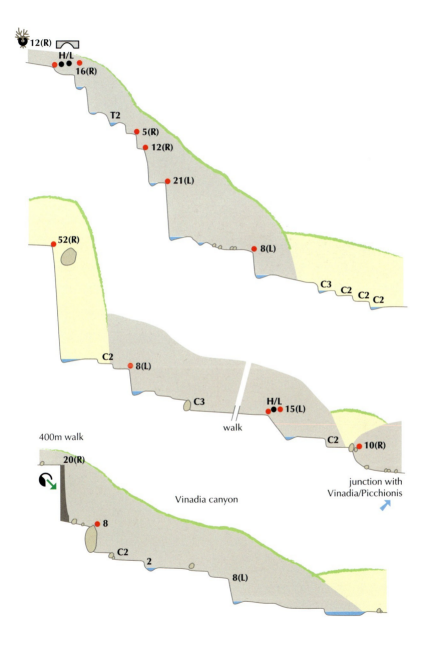

topo
continued
overleaf

ROUTE 79: CHIANTIONE

The base of the 52m pitch in Chiantione (photo: Simon Flower)

CARNIA AND THE JULIAN ALPS

Chiantione (continued)

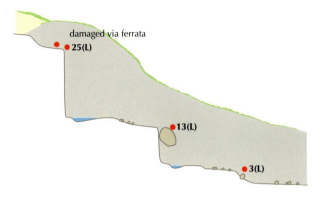

APPROACH FROM PARKING C
Upstream of the road, scramble down the bank on the true right of the river. Don't cross over the fence. The first belay is found on a tree down to the right.

DESCENT
The canyon begins immediately. A series of short pitches leads down to a long walking section in an imposing canyon passage. The canyon opens out a little for the 52m pitch. After this it is only two pitches to the junction with Vinadia. The canyon then widens considerably and the river increases greatly in size. It is a few hundred metres of largely uneventful streamway to the dam. See Route 78 for the description beyond the dam.

FIRST DESCENT
The Vinadia gorge was first explored in 1958 by a team of mountaineers led by Cirillo Floreanini (a K2 veteran). The team, which included Vittorio Lunari and Ignazio Piussi, was commissioned by a hydroelectric company to produce a survey of the canyon. The full descent took nearly a month, using a Himalayan-style approach involving fixed ropes, ladders and a small dinghy. Without neoprene, all effort was made to avoid the water, and any acquaintance with the stream was usually due to accidents, including the boat tipping over.

ROUTE 80: LA FOCE INFERIORE

LA FOCE INFERIORE

V4.A4.III

Rock	Limestone
Dimensions	Depth 95m (375m–280m); length 1000m
Ideal season	Summer
Time	Approach 10mins (Parking B); descent 1hr 30mins; return 2mins (Parking A)
Shuttle info	Parking A to Parking B – 3km (50mins road-walk; the alternative is hard to find)
Tick rating	0
Gear	2x10m ropes
Technical notes	Sufficient rigging on double hangars (positioning can be awkward for the inexperienced). Always aquatic, but usually non-threatening in summer.
Escapes	None – undertake in stable conditions only

La Foce is a beautifully encased and aquatic canyon, only 50cm wide in places. It is ideal for a lazy day, when the beautiful pools at the end provide an idyllic bathing opportunity. It is easily combined with Cosa (Route 81), only a short drive away.

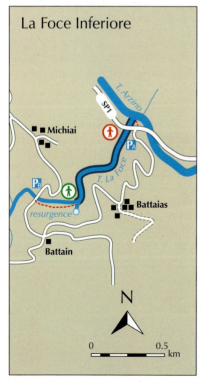

La Foce Inferiore

PARKING A

Take the SP1 south from Tolmezzo. Once through Reonis, look out for the turning to Prielungo. Park at the next turning a little further on, signposted 'Via Battaias' (space for one or two cars).

GETTING FROM PARKING A TO B

Follow Via Battaias through Battaias. At the top of the hill, the road crosses a bridge. Take an immediate right after this, which descends to the bridge over the canyon. Park on the other side of the bridge.

APPROACH FROM PARKING B

Walk down the path which skirts the right side of the canyon. Follow it all the way to the riverbed to where a stream (in fact a resurgence with some nice cave passage) enters on the right.

DESCENT

The descent begins as a boulder-hop down the river. The canyon walls then close in. From here it is aquatic going in a passage that becomes steadily narrower, down to 50cm wide in places. There are two short pitches (or climbs for the more confident).

CARNIA AND THE JULIAN ALPS

La Foce Inferiore is a superb canyon for beginners, current permitting

RETURN

Once under the road bridge the canyon widens out. Look for a good path on the right which leads back to the car at Parking A.

ROUTE 81: COSA

COSA ★★★ V2.A4.III

Rock	Limestone
Dimensions	Length 237m (510m–273m); length 4000m
Ideal season	Early to late summer
Time	Approach 0mins (Parking B); descent 3hrs–3hrs 30mins; return 15mins (Parking A)
Shuttle info	Parking A to Parking B – 9.5km (2hr road-walk)
Tick rating	0
Gear	2x15m ropes
Technical notes	Sufficient rigging, looking a bit dated now (2010). A couple of small jumps and easy climbs obligatory. Flow not threatening in summer.
Escapes	Only two evident (see descent description)

Torrente Cosa is a lengthy course in the rolling pre-alpine countryside west of Udine. Three pretty encased sections provide the attraction, which between them display all kinds of karst landforms, including caves, resurgences, sinks and rock arches. The descent is let down by its discontinuous nature and in particular a long and boring final part. Ideal in combination with La Foce Inferiore (Route 80), not too far away.

⚠ Passes through showcave property – discretion advised

Beautiful but brief – Cosa's cave-like section (photo: Simon Flower)

CARNIA AND THE JULIAN ALPS

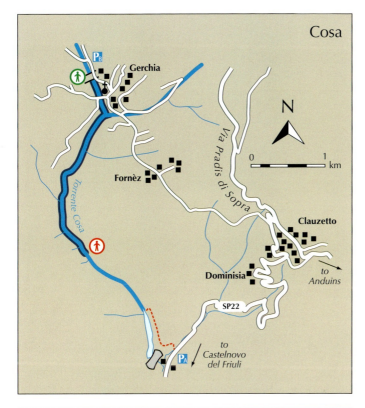

PARKING A

Torrente Cosa is surrounded by a confusing nest of roads – take a road map. From the SP1 south of Tolmezzo, take the turning into Via Battaias (see Route 80 for details). The road continues to climb along the Foce valley for 6.4km. At the top, bear left at a T-junction onto the SP55 (Via Pradis di Sopra), signposted to Clauzetto, into Orton. Continue along this road for about 3km. Ignore the turning to Anduins on a hairpin bend, then take a left (straight on) at the next junction a little further on, signposted to Spilimbergo (a right here, signposted to Fonte Pradis, leads to Parking B). The road enters Clauzetto. Descend through Clauzetto, ignoring all turnings as the road twists through the town. Follow any signs you might see for Castelnovo del Friulli or Spilimbergo. Descend all the way to the bottom of the hill (about 5km) and park about 100m before a restaurant in a large lay-by on the left. If you reach the dam you have gone too far.

GETTING FROM PARKING A TO B

Return to Clauzetto and follow signs for Fonte Pradis. Pass the show cave. At Gerchia, take the turning to Pielungo, then an immediate left behind the church (still following the signs for Fonte Pradis). Follow the road for 500m and park where the road splits (the left branch crosses the river).

ROUTE 81: COSA

Rock arches in Cosa (photo: Simon Flower)

APPROACH FROM PARKING B

Walk back down the road and clamber in at an old bridge which crosses over the river.

DESCENT

The canyon begins straight away, with a short encased section that ends in the open-air part of the show cave. Escape is possible here only if absolutely necessary. Exit the show cave by a short pitch from a boulder (anchors around to the right). A short length of bouldery streamway leads to the first exit (marked with a red spot on the left). Further on, a 7m pitch drops into a very pretty but brief cave-like part with two rock arches. After this the river opens out again for 15mins of boulder-hopping. A 12m pitch (partially down-climbable on the right, and the last 2–3m jumped with care) marks the beginning of the final encased part. Uninspiring to start, it soon becomes more clean washed, with little pools suited to jumping. Some 30–45mins of this and the canyon slowly fizzles out. Then the long march to the end begins.

RETURN

On arriving at the lake, look for a faint path on the left. The path climbs for 5–10mins to a blunt ridge crest. Descend the other side back to the road and Parking A.

ROUTE 82 : LEALE INFERIORE

LEALE INFERIORE   ★★★★    V4–5.A4.IV

Rock	Limestone
Dimensions	Depth 120m (320m–200m); length 750m + 450m walk downstream
Ideal season	Summer
Time	Approach 20–30mins (Parking B); descent 2hrs; return 20mins (Parking A)
Shuttle info	Parking A to Parking B – 4.5km (1hr walk)
Tick rating	1–2
Gear	2x20m ropes
Technical notes	Rigging sufficient on single and double anchors. Always aquatic. The current can be assessed to some extent at the ford, but the best place is in the canyon itself. For the first section, there should only be a small overflow into the siphon bypass passage. For the second section, the tributary entering on the left just prior to the first pitch should be little more than a splashy addition to the flow. If you struggle in the first section, do not commit to the second section.
Escapes	One, after the first section (see route description)

A superb little descent, spectacular and aquatic, demanding a head for high water and good rappelling skills. The canyon consists of two short encased sections, the second of which provides the crux. A large and slow-draining catchment area means this canyon requires a period of stable weather to come into condition – be prepared to bail out if water levels are too high.

 Water catchment upstream (low risk)

PARKING A

From Gemona di Friuli follow signs for Trasaghis, then Avasinis. Go through Avasinis (following signs for Tolmezzo/Alesso) and take an unsigned track about 400m past the last house on the left (about 200m before the bridge over Torrente Leale). Go up the track, ford the stream and park a few hundred metres further along in a wide clearing. Do not enter the private property immediately opposite the river crossing (or block its access).

GETTING FROM PARKING A TO B

By road
Go back through Avasinis and take a steep road (Via Novodet) on the right, signposted to Monte Prat. After about 3km there is a house and metal water fountain on the right. Either park just before this in a small lay-by or back at the 90° bend a couple of hundred metres down the hill.

On foot
Go back to Avasinis (1.3km), then take Via San Nicola to the paved square in Avasinis (Piazza 2 Maggio). Take Via V. del Bianco from the far right corner and

ROUTE 82 : LEALE INFERIORE

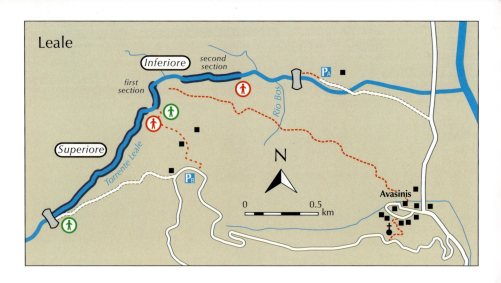

CARNIA AND THE JULIAN ALPS

A wet start to the second section – don't commit if this pitch is too wet

follow signs for 'Martiri 2 Maggio 1945', then 'Maina di Sant Antoni'. Climb on a cobbled path up to the road. It is another 2km from here.

APPROACH FROM PARKING B

Difficult to find, about 50m up from the 90° bend, there is a break in the trees marked with blobs of yellow paint. Follow the yellow markers initially through patchy woodland and grassy clearings. At a clearing overlooking the distant Lago dei Tre Comuni, the markers are easy to miss. Descend a little and skirt leftwards. Once in the trees the path is faint and at times non-existent – follow the yellow markers very carefully. The route passes a ruined stone building before descending further. The river is accessed via a steep gully which can be climbed to the left (care required) or abseiled from a tree (sling in situ).

LEALE SUPERIORE

Anyone who fails to find the way in could access the river via the water catchment upstream. Take the track to the right of the house with the metal water fountain (described above) and follow it for 1km to its end. From here a clear path gains the river in 5mins. Allow several hours for this upper section of river (not verified). Some jumps and toboggans are possible, but overall it is apparently rather boring and discontinuous.

ROUTE 82 : LEALE INFERIORE

Into the unknown – Leale's crux pitch

DESCENT

The canyon begins at a siphon passage, bypassed to the left through a pretty arched passage. An aquatic 5m abseil in the full flow of the stream follows. An 8m abseil/jump terminates the first section. A short march in open stream follows, where a tributary enters left (assess the flow here – see above). A 6m abseil signifies the start of the second section. Leave this rope in place while you inspect the next pitch, bearing in mind that this is the last chance to retreat before the 20m crux pitch, which is a little further on. Here the whole stream is funnelled into a narrow chute, and great care is needed to avoid the worst of it. The final 5m is probably safer jumped – watch for rocks. The canyon remains narrow, but comparatively fewer difficulties present themselves. The final pitch precedes a 150m swim, after which the canyon opens out.

The entire second section can be bypassed altogether if deemed too wet (route not verified). Immediately after the first section, head into the trees for 50m to pick up a vague track heading east. Follow this to where it intercepts Rio Bos. Follow Rio Bos back down to Torrente Leale, negotiating a 20m waterfall on the right.

RETURN

Follow the open riverbed down to the dam and jump off (8m). Follow a path on the left bank back to the car at Parking A.

ROUTE 83: LAVARIE

LAVARIE ★★★⯪ V4.A3.IV

Rock	Limestone
Dimensions	Depth 180m (450m–270m); length 300m
Ideal season	Early to late summer
Time	Approach 45mins (Parking A) or 5mins (Parking B); descent 2hrs; return 2mins (Parking A)
Shuttle info	Parking A to Parking B – 7.2km (45min walk)
Tick rating	0
Gear	2x40m ropes
Technical notes	AIC rigging (good condition 2010). Splashy and fun in summer.
Escapes	Possibly where the tributary comes in on the right about halfway down (not verified)

While by no means a classic, Rio Lavarie is a 'must do'. It is very brief – a sort of canyon in miniature – with a good variety of canyoning styles condensed into a couple of hours. The stream is splashy and entertaining, and the small catchment area may mean it is a possibility after rain.

Lavarie – great sport, no stress

ROUTE 83: LAVARIE

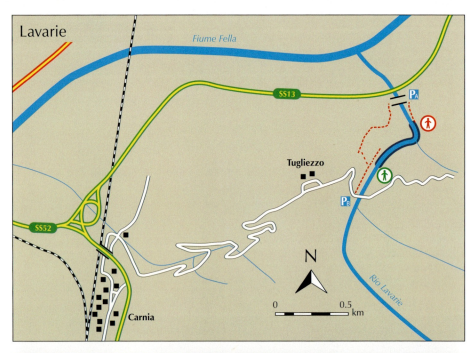

The top of the final 80m pitch

CARNIA AND THE JULIAN ALPS

PARKING A
From Tolmezzo follow the SS52 east and join the SS13 east towards Tarvisio. After 2km, park in the large lay-by at the 172km marker sign (**warning** tight turning off a fast road).

GETTING FROM PARKING A TO B
Go back along the SS13. About 200m beyond the Tolmezzo turning, take a right (signposted to Carnia). Take the first right and follow the road around, passing back underneath the SS13 to a crossroads. Go straight over (signposted Tugliezzo). The road climbs on hairpins to Tugliezzo (just a scattering of houses), after which it starts to descend again. The canyon is the first river the road crosses. Park just before it in the obvious lay-by. More parking is available on the far side of the river.

APPROACH FROM PARKING A
The approach path is difficult to follow and exposed in places. Cross the disused railway bridge. A concrete bunker is visible in the trees. Take an unmarked trail about 30–40m left of this. It climbs to two pylons, where it disappears. Keep heading directly up-slope. After about 50m another rising path is found. Follow this to a rock step, protected with a rusting metal cable (poor condition 2011). Above this the path follows a line of gullys and crests, always climbing steeply and often exposed. Near the top the path becomes less obvious again. Head for the ridge, where there is a good path. Follow this along. Where it deteriorates, head down about 50m to find a grassy vehicle track. Follow this left. The canyon begins where the track ends.

APPROACH FROM PARKING B
Take the track flanking the left bank of the river. After 5mins it turns into a path. Get in here (blue-on-white AIC marker).

DESCENT
The canyon consists of a series of nice enclosed pitches until the final 80m cascade. It is not clear from the pool preceding it that you are upon it, and there are re-belay anchors of all ages scattered all the way down it. It is probably better to stick to the newer rigging, which is not always easy to see from the top but is sensibly placed for trouble-free abseiling.

RETURN
From the right bank of the river head back to Parking A.

ROUTE 84: TRALBA INFERIORE

TRALBA INFERIORE ★★★★  V4.A3.IV

Alternative names	Rio Prealba, Rio Alba Affluente Sinistro, Forra dei Boscaioli (*boscaioli* = forest workers) – no consensus, as river not named on map
Rock	Limestone
Dimensions	Depth 344m (700m–356m); length 1700m + 1350m walk downstream
Ideal season	Summer
Time	Approach 1hr 15mins (Parking B); descent 3hrs 30mins; return 30mins (Parking A) or 1hr 30mins (Parking B, via Rio Alba)
Shuttle info	Parking A to Parking B – 8.8km (2hrs road-walk)
Tick rating	1–2
Gear	2x30m ropes
Technical notes	AIC rigging (good condition 2010). In summer the current entertains without causing any real problems (even when both dams are open), and most rigging is clear of danger.
Escapes	One, via Rio Alba (not always possible) – see description

Nestled in the Val Alba Natural Reserve the long, wild Rio Tralba offers some of north-east Italy's finest canyon scenery. Done in its entirety it is a full day out, with a very long walk-in and descent. Unfortunately its upper reaches (Tralba Superiore) are much drier and cannot be recommended. The route described here is the lower canyon only, a much more manageable excursion, whose first part is something quite special, with sculpted walls, deep green pools and a number of jumping possibilities. It is let down somewhat by its bouldery second half (for which it loses a star), but go on a sunny day and its open nature allows you to take in the stunning views. It is better started after midday, when the sun at last creeps into the recesses.

 Dams above both Tralba and Alba rivers

PARKING A

On the SS13 east from Tolmezzo, take the turning into Moggio-Udinese. Just before the village take a right (signposted Ovedasso). Drive for 2km and park by the bridge over the Rio Alba.

GETTING FROM PARKING A TO B

Follow the road back to the junction, then take a right into Moggio-Udinese. Take the right turn to Pontebba about 300m further on, then a right into Pradis after another 2.2km, following signs to 'Riserva Naturale della Val Alba'. A brief climb leads to a cluster of houses (Pradis). Continue through Pradis following signs for 'Riserva Naturale della Val Alba' and climb again. Where it levels out, pass a turning on the left and take the right immediately after (also signed 'Riserva Naturale della Val Alba'). Park after 1km on the first switch-back left.

CARNIA AND THE JULIAN ALPS

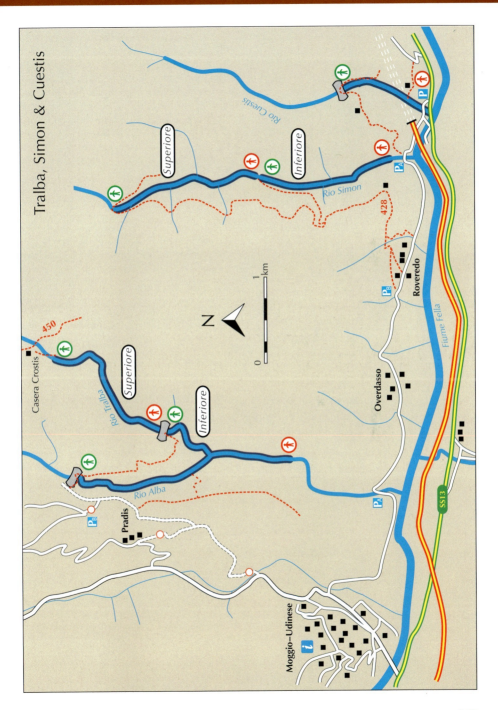

ROUTE 84: TRALBA INFERIORE

APPROACH FROM PARKING B

The access route is occasionally marked with blue-on-white AIC markers. Follow the track downhill. Five minutes after it swings back left, look out for a good path heading off down right into the trees. It is difficult to see when coming from this direction. This leads down to the dam over the Rio Alba (in normal summer conditions, do not worry if this is not capturing any of the flow). Cross over the dam and take a little path that ascends into the trees on the far side. The path then undulates across the hillside, exposed in places, to the dam over the Rio Tralba.

DESCENT

The canyon is instantly committing, with a 12m abseil from the left side. A beautiful section of canyon passage then follows, with a sequence of small pitches and possible jumps. It ends with two pitches that arrive back to back (25m and 30m; a 30m rope is recommended for the pull-through on the 25m pitch). The valley then opens out, and a long period of walking and boulder-hopping on sound rock begins (punctuated by a short pitch part-way down). The canyon closes down briefly for an 18m pitch just before the junction with Rio Alba. It is mostly open going from here, apart from two pitches in quick succession. The second pitch is in the full flow of water, but presents no real problems in 'normal' conditions.

RETURN TO PARKING A

Follow the open stream down. Exit right at the first bridge.

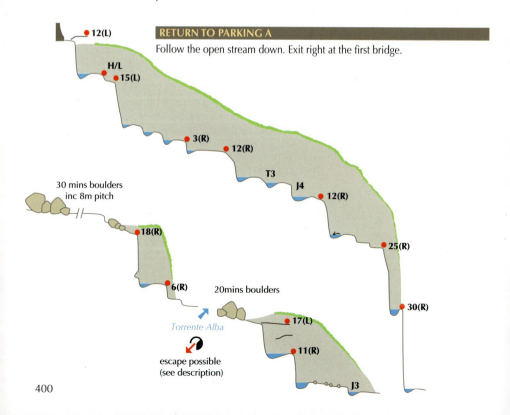

CARNIA AND THE JULIAN ALPS

A sculpted start to Tralba Inferiore (photo: Simon Flower)

RETURN TO PARKING B VIA RIO ALBA

It is possible to exit via Rio Alba via a steep, exposed and largely improvised route. At the confluence, head back upstream, up a couple of small climbs, as far as a 5m pitch. This pitch takes all the water in Rio Alba so probably would not be possible in high water or when the dam in Rio Alba is open. Continue up the stream for another 5–10mins until the grassy woodland on the left (true right) comes down to river level. Scramble steeply up the loose gravelly hillside – care required. Towards the top, things steepen. Search around for a way through the rocky bluffs, which is likely to involve a few exposed steps assisted by tree roots. The difficulties are brief though, and a good path exists along the ridge crest. Follow this right to a vehicle track, which climbs back up to the Rio Alba/Tralba approach track.

TRALBA SUPERIORE

Approach and descent not verified. Park 2km up the road from Parking B, where the road becomes a gravel track and off limits to traffic. Follow Path 428a. Take a right onto Path 450 (signed Casera Crostis) and cross over the Rio Alba. The path becomes steeper, passing over a col before descending to Casera Crostis, in a poor state. From here, enter the field on the right and pick up a faint path at the far side which descends to the river (2hrs 30mins). After an initial section of little interest, the canyon provides a few abseils in narrow passage as far as the poorly rigged 58m pitch. After this, it is mainly boulder-hopping until the end. The canyon is mainly dry until near the end, where there are some curious ancient wooden dams. Take a bolting kit (the canyon is very sparsely rigged) and allow 5hrs for the descent.

ROUTE 84A: ALBA

ALBA  V3.A1.III

A short, easy and at times pretty canyon, but one that lacks any real entertainment value.

After the junction with Rio Alba. This pool is dry when both dams are closed (photo: Euan Major)

ROUTE 85: SIMON INFERIORE

SIMON INFERIORE  ★★★★ V4.A4.V

Rock	Limestone
Dimensions	Depth 374m (720m–346m); length 1600m + 500m walk downstream
Ideal season	Summer
Time	Approach 1hr (Parking B); descent 2hrs 30mins–3hrs; return 5mins (Parking A)
Shuttle info	Parking A to Parking B – 2km (30mins road-walk)
Tick rating	2
Gear	2x40m ropes
Technical notes	AIC rigging (good condition 2010). Considerable current, but rigged to avoid danger (in normal summer conditions).
Escapes	Unlikely given steepness of valley
Note	For map see Route 84

Rio Simon is one of the longest and most dramatic canyons of north-east Italy, renowned among canyoning communities all over Europe for its stunning canyon scenery. But for all its reputation, the canyoning is actually quite discontinuous. Memorable passages are usually brief and separated by often lengthy stretches of open streamway. Additionally, sensible rigging means that the lively river is seldom close enough to get acquainted. It tantalises but does not quite deliver. This is particularly true of the upper (Superiore) part, where an extra 90mins walk up the hill is rewarded with near enough 90mins walking back down it. For the canyoner looking for sport, Simon Superiore has little to recommend it. Fortunately the lower canyon can be accessed directly, and it is this descent which is described in detail here.

It is not worth doing this route unless you intend to meet a more experienced team doing Rio Tralba. It consists of four pitches, rigged out of the water. Allow 2hrs for the descent. Maximum pitch 18m.

PARKING A

Follow the SS13 east from Tolmezzo. Pass the Moggio-Udinese junction and after a short tunnel section take a left turn (signposted Roveredo). After a few hundred metres, cross the bridge over Rio Simon and park in the small lay-by.

GETTING FROM PARKING A TO B

If needed, park beyond Roveredo, where Path 428 starts behind a little wall (red-and-white markers).

APPROACH FROM PARKING A

Follow the road to Roveredo. After about 1.2km, take a path marked with the number 70 and red spots. This climbs steeply to a pylon. Just before the pylon a much smaller path heads off – watch out for AIC markers (blue spot on white background). Alternatively, follow the road through Roveredo, looking for a

ROUTE 85: SIMON INFERIORE

The 37m pitch into the final sombre section

The typical green pools of Rio Simon

CARNIA AND THE JULIAN ALPS

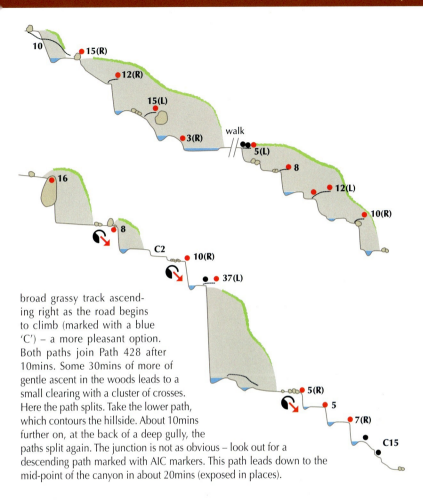

broad grassy track ascending right as the road begins to climb (marked with a blue 'C') – a more pleasant option. Both paths join Path 428 after 10mins. Some 30mins of more of gentle ascent in the woods leads to a small clearing with a cluster of crosses. Here the path splits. Take the lower path, which contours the hillside. About 10mins further on, at the back of a deep gully, the paths split again. The junction is not as obvious – look out for a descending path marked with AIC markers. This path leads down to the mid-point of the canyon in about 20mins (exposed in places).

APPROACH FROM PARKING B
Take Path 428 up the hill, then follow the description above.

DESCENT
The first waterfall can be bypassed right, after which the canyon begins in earnest with two nice encased parts, each with a number of short, well-rigged pitches (maximum 16m). Things then become a little less continuous, while remaining pleasant. The final part begins with a 37m pitch into sombre canyon passage, the blanched white limestone replaced by steel grey. The canyon soon opens out again, then it's only three or four more pitches to the end. The final obstacle is an inclined ramp – down-climbable but best descended on rope as it is often slippery. Walk down the river to the bridge (path on the right).

ROUTE 85A: SIMON SUPERIORE

SIMON SUPERIORE ★★↷  V3.A3.IV

This lengthy addition to the classic route is pretty, but lacks sporting interest.

To access, start as for Route 85, but rather than following the AIC markers down the gully, continue along the main path. From here it takes a tiring and undulating course across the hillside, overgrown and exposed in places. Where the river finally comes up to meet the path, get in when possible. The descent consists of two short enclosed sections (only the second of which inspires), then a long period of walking and boulder-hopping. A little string of pretty pitches can be bypassed without the need of rope. Maximum pitch 26m (2x30m ropes needed), well rigged when needed.

Simon Superiore – pretty but not especially sporting

ROUTE 86: CUESTIS

CUESTIS ★★★★ V5.A3.IV

Rock	Limestone
Dimensions	Depth 400m (750m–350m); length 1350m
Ideal season	Early to late summer
Time	Approach 1hr; descent 3–4hrs; return 10mins
Shuttle info	Optional – park by the bridge at the end of the canyon (700m)
Tick rating	1
Gear	2x60m ropes – after shrinkage (a 40m rope also useful); wetsuit not always needed
Technical notes	AIC rigging (good condition 2010). Minimal flow in summer. Avoid when dry (verify from the bridge at the end). Dangerous in high water.
Escapes	After the first series of short pitches, and after the 70m pitch
Note	For map see Route 84.

Rio Cuestis is one of the few canyons in the area that is better done after rain. A long and uninspiring start is well compensated for by the beautiful and varied canyoning that follows it. It is not at all aquatic – in fact, it is frequently dry (when it loses a star). But what it lacks in this respect it makes up for in cave-like scenery and a spectacular finale, where a series of vertiginous open pitches gives sweeping views over the Fella valley. The excellent rigging takes the edge off the exposure (well, sort of).

PARKING
Park as for Rio Simon Parking A (see Route 85).

APPROACH
Cross back over Rio Simon and take an obvious track marked with red and white stripes just around the corner. This climbs steeply on the Rio Simon side of the hill for around 50mins, before crossing into the Cuestis valley, where the path deteriorates a little. From here it contours gently around to the starting point by a concrete water capture.

DESCENT
The canyon begins with a few pretty but lacklustre pitches (maximum 23m; escape possible just after). A long walking section in bouldery streamway then ensues. After 30mins of this, the canyon finally begins in earnest. The walls close in and the boulders disappear. The canyon becomes distinctly cave-like for 100m or so (a few short climbs or abseils in dry conditions) before opening out slightly for a few short, well-sculpted pitches. After a rock arch, the canyon becomes more vertically developed, with pitches of 16, 13 and 21m, before the final dramatic 70m pitch. This is best split 18m down at a ledge beneath an overhang (space for two people; 40m rope recommended). There are good anchors here, but the rope joining them may well be worn. The abseil from here can be deviated 5m and 10m down to avoid the flow of water. A derelict

ROUTE 86: CUESTIS

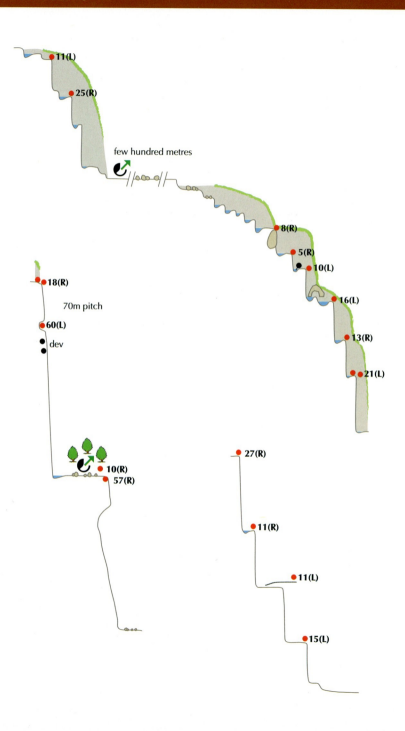

The vertiginous 70m pitch

building at the base of the pitch signifies an escape route left. The canyon then widens out dramatically, offering a final few pitches in a vast amphitheatre. The first of these is an airy 57m free-hang. The anchors are situated over the edge on the right and must be reached by a short abseil from anchors set back on the wall behind. After this, it's just a few short uninspiring pitches to the end.

RETURN

Scramble up to the road at the second bridge and follow the road back to the car (10mins).

ROUTE 86: CUESTIS

An exposed start to the final pitch series of Cuestis

RIO NERO

It seems surprising, given its ease of access, that Rio Nero (or Cerni Potok) was only relatively recently explored. While not having the imposing gorge scenery of some its neighbours, it has a wonderful wild feel to it, with abundant, crystal-clear waters and a forested setting. Points of interest are quite widely spaced, but the bouldery walking sections separating them come as welcome opportunities to rewarm – the water is bitingly cold, especially in Nero Superiore.

PARKING
From Tolmezzo follow the SS52 east and join the SS13 east towards Tarvisio. Turn off at Resiutta and follow the road into the village. Cross over the river and take a right up Val Resia. Follow this road for 4km to the first house by the road on the left (marked 'Case Oblase' on the Tobacco maps). Park in the lay-by just before it.

APPROACH
Thrash down the embankment and ford the River Resia where sensible. On the far bank, head for the tree-line at a point roughly where the telephone wires enter it. A track on the right may be visible as you approach, which will ease things, but otherwise it is a couple more minutes of thrashing through vegetation. On reaching the obvious Path 703 (marked with red and white stripes), turn right and cross the bridge over the river. Take a left on the far bank. The path can be followed all the way to the top of the canyon (following signs to 'C.ra Nero'). A wooden bridge over the canyon marks the top of the Nero Inferiore. To reach Nero Superiore, follow the path up a slope, cross over a tributary, then enter the woods. The path initially climbs. Where it starts to descend, look out for a small path right heading down to the river, shortly after a crossing over a dry gully.

ROUTE 87: RIO NERO SUPERIORE

RIO NERO SUPERIORE

★★★✦   V4.A3.III

Alternative name	Cerni Potok Superiore
Rock	Limestone
Dimensions	Depth 100m (700m–600m); length 700m
Ideal season	Early to late summer
Time	Approach 1hr 30mins; descent 1hr 30mins; return 40mins
Shuttle info	N/A
Tick rating	1
Gear	2x20m ropes; slings or a length of cord
Technical notes	Well-placed rigging, usually dual thru-bolts equalised with cord (2010). Current unlikely to cause too many problems in summer. Ice-cold water.
Escapes	After first encasement, otherwise improvised escapes only

Nero Superiore's cold but enticing opening sequence is let down somewhat by a laborious second half.

One of Nero Superiore's icy pools

ROUTE 87: RIO NERO SUPERIORE

The canyon begins strongly with a beautiful encased section, consisting of a little jump and an aquatic 16m pitch (escape right possible here). An entertaining 16m pitch and a 5m jump follow, but after that interest starts to wane. Walking and boulders (with the odd down-climb and jump) stand between here and the bridge.

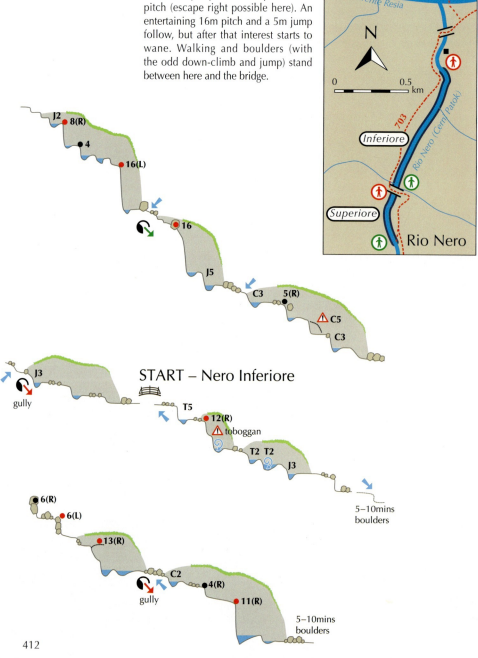

ROUTE 88: RIO NERO INFERIORE

RIO NERO INFERIORE   ★★★★    V4.A4.IV

Alternative name	Cerni Potok Inferiore
Rock	Limestone
Dimensions	Depth 240m (600m–360m); length 1300m
Ideal season	Summer
Time	Approach 1hr; descent 2hrs 30mins; return 10mins
Shuttle info	N/A
Tick rating	1
Gear	2x15m ropes – 1x20m rope useful for pull-through; slings or cord
Technical notes	Well-placed rigging, usually dual thru-bolts equalised with cord (2010). A few awkward, unrigged climbs and jumps. Significant stream even in summer, augmented by several inlets. A few pools could be problematic.
Escapes	Improvised escapes only
Note	For map and topo see Route 87

The lower canyon is more aquatic and technical, but there are rewards at every stage.

Toboggan in Nero Inferiore – avoid the overhang on the right

ROUTE 88: RIO NERO INFERIORE

Jumping into a narrow stretch

After a brief period of walking and boulder-hopping, the lower canyon begins in earnest, with two toboggans and an encased, clean-washed section. On the second toboggan, steer clear of the overhang seen from above – the water pummels the far wall here and will drag canyoners under. The encased section is short but stunning, with three aquatic 2–3m steps (again, watch for the current in the pools). The canyon then widens, and a long march and boulder-hop ensue. Two very wet pitches of 13m and 11m, separated by more open canyon, are the only two features of note before the end (a 20m rope will be needed for a comfortable pull-through).

RETURN

Follow the bouldery river downstream for 5–10mins. Where it levels out, step left onto the approach path and reverse the walk-in.

ROUTE 89: BRUSSINE

BRUSSINE ★★★↙ ■ V4.A3.III

Alternative name	Rio Le Macile
Rock	Limestone
Dimensions	Depth 250m (600m–350m); length 1200m
Ideal season	Summer
Time	Approach 30mins; descent 2hrs 30mins; return 20mins
Shuttle info	N/A
Tick rating	1
Gear	2x60m ropes – after shrinkage
Technical notes	Sufficient rigging, mostly on double 10mm thru-bolts, equalised with rope (2010). Occasional single-point anchor on short pitches. A small catchment means low flow in summer.
Escapes	Before the 57m waterfall (not verified but seems likely)

Apart from its slightly irksome beginnings, Rio Brussine offers a pleasant string of splashy pitches in pretty canyon passage. The water is wonderfully clear, and the pools are often deep and inviting. It would be excellent for aspiring beginners if it wasn't for the vertiginous 60m pitch at the end. Better done in the afternoon, when the sun finally appears from behind the hills.

⚠ **Ensure the River Fella is not in flood – it has to be forded to get back to the road**

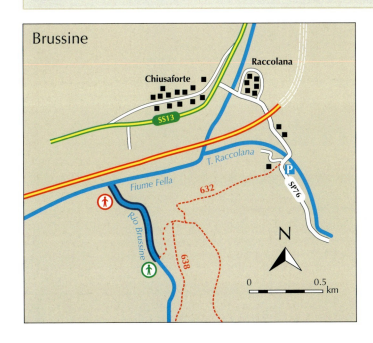

ROUTE 89: BRUSSINE

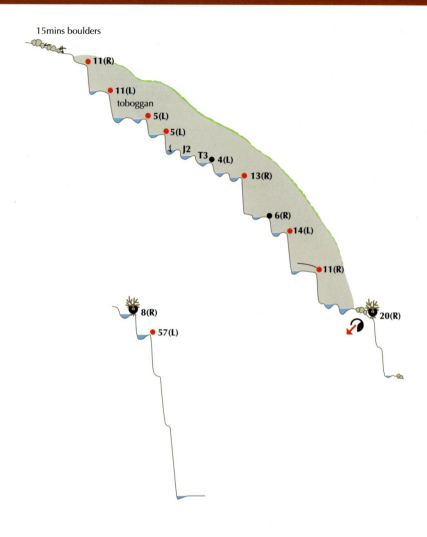

PARKING

From Chiusaforte on the SS13, take the SP76 over the River Fella (signposted to Sella Nevea). Pass through Raccolana and cross the bridge over the Raccolana river. Some 10m after the bridge, take a hidden left down a track (signposted 'Localita San Floriano', but only from the other direction). Park by the disused building.

APPROACH

About 20m from the bridge, take Path 632, marked with red and white stripes. The path climbs, then splits after 25mins. Take Path 638 (signposted to 'Sella

CARNIA AND THE JULIAN ALPS

In Brussine's initial encased section (photo: Simon Flower)

Sagata' and 'Prato di Resia'). A few minutes further on, just before an electricity pylon, take a path off right. Initially faint, it quickly improves and contours the hillside to the river bed (marked with red spots).

DESCENT

The canyon begins with 15mins of scrambling over slippery boulders. Suddenly the walls close in and the canyon starts. An 11m pitch precedes an excellent toboggan, after which the pitches continue in quick succession (maximum 14m). One or two of these can be jumped with care. The canyon opens out as it approaches the main valley. Pitches of 20m and 8m precede the big cascade – 57 panoramic metres to the valley floor.

RETURN

Ford the Fella where sensible to do so. This has to be done twice to get back to the same side of the river. Where the river splits, follow the Raccolana river (the right-hand branch) to where it is possible to escape right onto a track. Follow the track past an electricity substation back to the car.

ROUTE 90: MLINARICA

MLINARICA	★★★★⤴ ■ V4.A4.IV
Alternative name	Sometimes (mistakenly) spelt Milnarica
Rock	Limestone
Dimensions	Depth 325m (1100m–775m); length 1100m
Ideal season	Summer
Location	Slovenia
Time	Approach 10mins (Parking B); descent 3hrs–3hrs 30mins; return 5mins (Parking A)
Shuttle info	Parking A to Parking B – 4km (40–50mins walk)
Tick rating	0
Gear	2x55m ropes
Technical notes	Excellent rigging on double P-hangars or 10mm thru-bolts and chains (2010). Hand-lines in situ. Flow a threat only in lower canyon, but rigging mostly clear of danger. A storm in here would be disastrous.
Escapes	To the right before the 50m pitch (the path passes through private property). Improvised escapes possible between the two enclosed parts.
Access restrictions	In Triglav National Park (see Warning box below)

Any canyoning guidebook on the Julian Alps would be deficient without inclusion of this canyon, arguably the finest outing in Slovenia. Its setting in the spectacular Soça valley is almost worth the drive alone. That said, for the first half of the descent you'd be forgiven for wondering why you'd been dragged all this way. Pretty yes, but nothing special...Then, all of a sudden, one giant boulder changes everything. It sits wedged across a 50m defile, providing a spectacular free-hanging abseil into some of the most atmospheric canyon passages anywhere in the Alps.

⚠ **An enormous landslide in 2011 rendered everything beyond the 50m pitch unstable and dangerous. Additionally, the Triglav National Park authorities declared canyons in the national park off limits to canyoners. Do not descend without first seeking up-to-date information. The AIC and www.descente-canyon.com forum pages are a good place to start.**

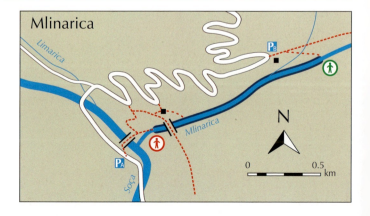

CARNIA AND THE JULIAN ALPS

PARKING A

This is a 1hr 30min drive from Tolmezzo. Make sure your car-hire agreement allows you entry to Slovenia. The best route from Tolmezzo is to take the A23 to Tarvisio, then hop over the border to Kranjska Gora on the SS54. From here, take the road south over the Moistrocca pass. The hairpin turns are numbered on the far side. Follow the road to the bottom of the hill. Pass the turning to the Izmir Soča just after turn 49 (the source of the Soča river – an interesting side-trip in its own right) and cross the Limarica and Soča rivers. Park in a lay-by on the left about 500m further on, just before a yellow sign announces your arrival in Trenta (look out for a tourist path, which starts from the lay-by). If you cross the Soča river a second time you've gone 250m too far.

GETTING FROM PARKING A TO B

By car
Go back up the hill and place one car at hairpin number 38, at 1080m altitude, by a large disused building.

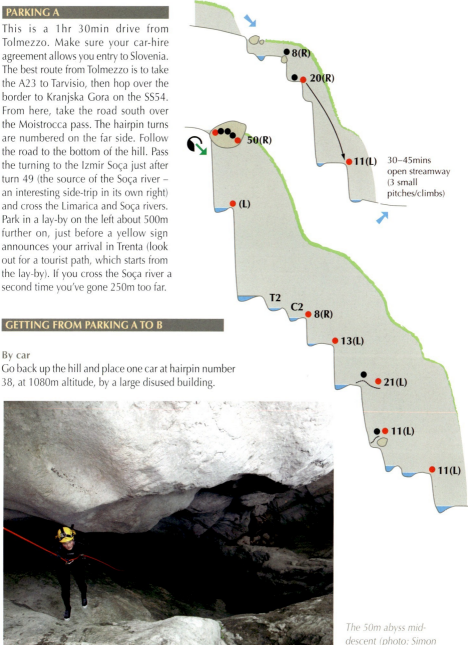

The 50m abyss mid-descent (photo: Simon Flower)

ROUTE 90: MLINARICA

Emerging from Mlinarica's cave-like interior (photo: Simon Flower)

On foot
Take the tourist path over the Soča river. Take a left to Kugyev Spomenik. This climbs to a large statue overlooking the valley. Take a left back towards the road. Just before crossing over a wooden bridge, take a right into the trees. Climb for a few minutes and take a left where the path splits (going right leads to an impressive vantage point over the gorge). Climb on a good path to a clearing with a house. Two paths lead off here. To reach Parking B, continue straight up on a good path back to the road, then follow the road up. Another path in the far right corner of the field leads to the canyon just before the 50m pitch, but is on private property and should be avoided.

APPROACH FROM PARKING B
Follow the good track by the side of the house. It quickly turns into a path and contours around to meet the river.

DESCENT
The first encased section begins immediately. It is short, with only three abseils (maximum 20m). About 30–45mins in open sunny streamway then begins. This is mostly boulder-hopping, but a few short pitches and down-climbs spice things up a bit. An enormous boulder in the stream puts a stop to this. The 50m pitch beyond can either be descended in the active stream to the left (re-belay at a pool perched halfway down – danger of damaged rigging) or done in one, following a vertiginous traverse around to the right. This is the more usual approach, although access to the pitch-head is awkward, made no easier by the sheer exposure. Five more abseils follow (maximum 21m), rigged to avoid most of the water (look out for hand-lines). Unfortunately it is over too soon and you're basking in the sunshine again by the tourist path with its spectators. Follow this back to the road.

APPENDIX A: CANYON SUMMARY TABLE

Area	Route no	Canyon	Part	Star rating	Overall difficulty	Approach (with/without shuttle)	Descent	Return	Max pitch (Rope length after shrinkage)	Season (**early**/**mid**/**late** summer)	Dam (*=info line available)
Val d'Ossola											
	1	Massaschluct		3.5	Red	20mins/2hrs	4–6hrs	25mins	25 (2x35)	E M L	Yes – high risk
	2	Gondo		4	Blue-red	0mins/20mins	1hr30–2hrs	3mins	27m (2x30m)	M L	Yes – no info
	3	Rasiga	Superiore	4.5	Red	30mins/1hr30–2hrs	6hrs	15mins	26m (2x30m)	E M L	Yes – low risk
	3a	Rasiga	Inferiore	2.5	Red	20mins	1hr30	15mins	70m (2x50m)	E M L	Yes – low risk
	4	Variola Superiore		4	Red	1hr	4–5hrs	30mins	27m (2x30m)	E M L	Yes – low risk
	5	Mondelli	Part 2	4.5	Blue	10mins	2hrs	10mins	20m (2x30m)	M L	No
	5a	Mondelli	Part 1	3	Blue	30mins	1hr	10mins	30m (2x40m)	M L	No
	6	Mondelli	Part 3	3.5	Red	10mins/40mins	4hrs	0mins	60m (2x40m + 15m prusik rope)	M L	No
	7	Bianca		3.5	Blue	0mins/30mins	2hrs	0mins	90m (2x50m)	E M L	Yes – low risk
	7a	Segnara		2.5	Green-blue	2mins	2hrs	20mins	30m (2x40m)	M L	Mid-descent – low risk
	8	Toce		3.5	Red-black	30mins	3–4hrs	20–30mins	18m (2x20m)	M L	Yes – dangerous
	9	Rio d'Alba		3	Red-black	1hr30	5–7hrs	30mins	250m (2x65m)	E M L	No
	10	Antolina		3.5	Blue-red	30mins/50mins	3–4hrs	5mins	50m (2x55m)	E M L	Yes – low risk
	11	Isorno Finale		4.5	Blue	20mins/9,1km	1hr30	2mins	28m (2x35m)	E M L	Yes – low risk*
	12	Antoliva		3	Blue	45mins	3–4hrs	2mins	22m (2x25m)	E M L	Yes – low risk
	13	Ogliana di Quarata		4	Red	1hr30	4–5hrs	0mins	50m (2x35m)	M L	No
	13a	Menta Inferiore		3	Blue	2hrs	1hr30		41m (2x45m)	E M L	No
	14	Ogliana di Beura – Finale		3.5	Blue-red	20mins	1hr–1hr30	10mins	20m (2x25m)	M L	No
	15	Marona		3.5	Blue-red	1hr15	3–4hrs	45mins	45m (2x30m)	E M L	No

CANYONING IN THE ALPS

Area	Route no	Canyon	Part	Star rating	Overall difficulty	Approach (with/ without shuttle)	Descent	Return	Max pitch (Rope length after shrinkage)	Season (early/mid/late summer)	Dam (*=info line available)
Ticino											
	16	Serenello		3	Green-blue	20mins	1–2hrs	5mins	40m (2x45m)	E M L	No
	17	Bignasco		3.5	Red	10mins/1hr	3–4hrs	2mins	83m (2x85m)	E M L	No
	18	Sponde		3.5	Red-black	1hr30/1hr50	6hrs	2mins	105m (2x110m)	E M L	No
	19	Giumaglio		3.5	Red	30mins	2–3hrs	5mins	37m (2x40m)	E M L	Yes – low risk*
	20	Salto		4	Red	1hr20	6hrs	0mins	65m (2x65)	E M L	Yes – low risk*
	21	Gei Inferiore		3.5	Blue-red	30mins	2–3hrs	2mins	60m (2x50m)	E M L	No
	22	Grande Inf.		3.5	Blue	30mins	2–3hrs	2mins	27m (2x30m)	E M L	No
	23	Loco Inf.		3.5	Red	5mins	1hr30–2hrs	30mins	55m (2x60m)	E M L	No
	24	Ticinetto Inf.		4	Red	0mins	1hr30–2hrs30	15mins	60m (2x40m)	E M L	Yes – low risk*
	25	Barougia		3	Green-blue	0mins	1–2hrs	15mins	32m (2x35m)	E M L	No
	26	Malvaglia Inf.		3	Blue-red	10mins/55mins	2–3hrs	2mins	80m (2x45m)	E M L	Yes – low risk*
	27	Combra		3.5	Blue-red	25mins	1hr30 – 2hrs	5–10mins	22m (2x25m)	M L	No
	28	Pontirone	Superiore	3.5	Red	0mins/1hr30	3–4hrs	20mins	30m (2x35m)	E M L	Yes – low risk*
	29	Pontirone	Inferiore	5	Red	30mins	1hr–1hr30	0mins	40m (2x45m)	E M L	Yes – low risk*
	30	Iragna	Superiore	4	Red	15mins/1hr15	2–4hrs	20mins	32m (2x35m)	E M L	No
	31	Iragna	Inferiore	4	Blue-red	30mins	3–4hrs	2mins	40m (2x45m)	E M L	No
	32	Lodrino	Intermedio	4	Red	30mins	1hr–1hr30	15mins	45m (2x50m)	M L	No
	33	Lodrino	Inferiore	5	Red-black	10mins/40mins	3hr–3hrs30	2mins	45m (2x50m)	M L	No
	34	Osogna	Intermedio	3.5	Red	1hr30	4–5hrs	15mins	34m (2x35m)	E M L	Yes – low risk*
	34a	Osogna	Superiore	2.5	Green-blue	2hrs	2hrs	1hr	40m (2x40m)	E M L	Yes – low risk*
	35	Osogna	Inferiore	4.5	Red	15mins	2hrs	5mins	50m (2x60m)	E M L	Yes – low risk*
	36	Cresciano	Superiore	4	Red	50mins/1hr45	4–6hrs	15mins	35m (2x40m)	E M L (after rain)	Yes – low risk*
	37	Cresciano	Inferiore	4.5	Blue	30mins	1hr30–3hrs	2mins	27m (2x30m)	E M L	Yes – low risk*

422

APPENDIX A: CANYON SUMMARY TABLE

Lake Como

#	Name	Variant	Grade	Water	Approach	Descent	Return	Biggest rappel	Equipment	Escape
38	Bodengo	Part 2	4	Blue-red	0mins/20mins	2-3hrs	10mins	35m (2x40m)	E M L	Yes – low risk
38a	Bodengo	Part 1	3	Green–blue	0mins/10mins	30mins	0mins	27m (2x30m)	E M L	Yes – low risk
39	Bodengo	Part 3	4.5	Red	5mins/1hr30	5-6hrs	0mins	60m (2x40m)	M L	Yes – low risk
40	Pilotera		3	Blue	30mins/1hr30	2-3hs	5–10mins	30m (2x25m)	E M L	Yes – low risk
41	Mengasca		3.5	Red	1hr–1hr30/1hr30–2hrs	3-4hrs	5mins	56m (2x50m)	E M L	No
42	Casenda		3	Red	10mins/1hr40	5hrs	5mins	70m (2x50m)	E M L	Mid-descent – low risk
43	Bares		4.5	Red-black	2hrs	6-8hrs	30mins	28m (2x30m)	M L	No
44	Borgo		3	Red	1hr15	3-4hrs	5mins	16m (2x20m)	M L	No
45	Perlana Inferiore		3.5	Green–blue	40mins	2-3hrs	10mins	13m (2x15m)	E M L	No
46	Bondasca		4	Red	0mins/30mins	3hrs	0mins		M L	Yes – medium risk*
46a	Drögh Grand		2	Green–blue	10mins	1hr	10mins	19m (2x25m)	E M L	No
47	Lesina	Dam open	3.5	Red-black	1hr30–2hrs	2hrs	0mins	17m (2x20m)	M L	Yes – no info
		Dam closed	3	Green–blue		1hr30			E M L	
48	Ferro		4	Red	30mins	2-3hrs	5mins	55m (2x50m)	M L	No
49	Cormor		5	Red	2mins/1hr30	4-5hrs	15mins	27m (2x30m)	E M L	Yes – low risk*
50	Lanterna	Scerscen	3.5	Red	30mins	2-3hrs	10mins	18m (2x20m)	M L	Yes – no info
51	Lanterna	Brutta	3.5	Blue-red	0mins/40–50mins	2-3hrs	5mins	25m (2x30m)	M L	Yes – no info
52	Esino Inferiore		3	Green	20mins	1hr	5mins	9m (2x10m)	E M L	No
53	Boazzo		3.5	Blue-red	10mins/1hr30	3hrs	10mins	20m (2x25m)	E M L	Mid-descent – low risk

CANYONING IN THE ALPS

Area	Route no	Canyon	Part	Star rating	Overall difficulty	Approach (with/without shuttle)	Descent	Return	Max pitch (Rope length after shrinkage)	Season (**early**/**mid**/**late** summer)	Dam (*=info line available)
Dolomites	54	Grigno		4.5	Black	15mins/1hr30	4hrs	15mins	25m (2x35m)	E M L	Yes – no info
	55	Soffia		4.5	Blue–red	1h	4hrs30	2mins	38m (2x40m)	E M L	No
	56	Forti		4	Red	2hrs30–3hrs	3–4hrs	45mins	48m (2x50m)	E M L	No
	57	Pisson (+/– Soffia)		4.5	Red–black	1hr30	2hrs (4hrs)	20mins (2mins)	105m (2x50m)	E M L	No
	58	Clusa	Superiore	4.5	Red	1hr30	3hrs30–5hrs	30mins	35m (2x40m)	E M L	No
	59	Clusa	Inferiore	5	Black	40mins	2–3hrs	5mins	27m (2x30m)	M L	Yes – no info, but likely risky
	60	Mus	Inferiore	4	Red	45mins/1hr15	3hrs	5mins	26m (2x30m)	E M L	No
	60a	Mus	Superiore	2.5	Red	2hrs–2hrs30/2.3km RW	2hrs	30mins	63m (2x45m)	E M L	No
	61	Fogarè	Superiore	3	Red	2hr30–3hrs	2hrs–2hrs30	30mins	30m (2x35m)	E M L	No
	62	Fogarè	Inferiore	4	Blue–red	40mins	2hrs–2hrs30	10mins	24m (2x25m)	E M L	No
	63	Maor		4	Green	0mins/3km RW	2hrs–2hrs30	30–60mins	12m (2x15m)	E M L	No
	64	Maggiore		3–3.5	Blue	1min/6km RW	4hrs30	0mins	25m (2x25m ropes)	E M L	No
	65	Tovanella		4	Blue–red	15mins	1hr30	0mins	19m (2x25)	E M L	No
	66	Zemola		5	Red	20–30mins/1hr–1hr15	4hrs	15mins	17m (2x20m)	M L	No
	67	Pezzeda	Eastern tributary	3	Red	3hr	3–5hrs	30mins	13m (2x20m)	E M L	No
	68	Ciorosolin		3	Red	1hr	2hrs30–4hrs	5mins	45m (2x50m)	E M L	No
	69	Torrente Chiadola		3	Green	2mins	45mins	5mins	15m (2x15m)	E M L	Yes – low risk
	70	Ciolesan		3.5	Blue	45mins	2hrs	10mins	18m (2x20m)	E M L	No
	71	Alba-Molassa		3	Green	0mins	1hr–1hr30	30mins	n/a	E M L	Yes – no info

APPENDIX A: CANYON SUMMARY TABLE

Carnia and the Julian Alps											
	72	Rötenbach	Lower	3.5	Red	20mins/2.6km RW	2–3hrs	10mins	33m (2x35m)	E M L	No
	72a	Rötenbach	Upper	2.5	Red	45mins–1hr15/2.6km RW	1hr30–2hrs	45mins	38 (2x45m)	E M L	No
	73	Frauenbach		3.5	Blue–red	40mins	3–4hrs	5mins	50m (2x30m)	E M L	Yes – no info
	74	Novarza and Lumiei	Novarza	3	Blue–red	20mins/0.8km RW	2hrs30–3hrs	15mins	50m (2x40m)	E M L	Yes – no info
	75	Novarza and Lumiei	Lumiei	3.5	Green–blue	10mins/3.2km RW	2hrs	15mins	16m (2x20m)	E M L	Yes – no info
	76	Rio Negro		3.5	Red–black	1hr40	2–3hrs	40mins	18m (2x20m)	M L	No
	77	Viellia	Part 1	3	Red	2hr30	2–3hrs		55m (2x40m)	E M L	No
		Viellia	Part 2	4	Blue–red	1hr50	1hr30		35m (2x25m)	M L	No
		Viellia	Part 3	4	Blue	1hr30	1hr30		23m (2x25m)	E M L	No
		Viellia	Part 4	4.5	Red–black	1hr	3–4hrs	15mins	20m (2x25m)	M L	No
	78	Vinadia	Picchionis	3	Red	0mins/2hrs30	5–7hrs	0mins	25m (2x30m)	E M L	Mid-descent – no info
	79	Vinadia	Chiantione	3	Red	0mins/2hrs	5–6hrs	0mins	52m (2x60m)	E M L	Mid-descent – no info
	80	La Foce Inferiore		3.5	Green–blue	10mins/3km RW	1hr30	2mins	7m (2x10m)	E M L	No
	81	Cosa		3	Green–blue	0mins/9.5km RW	3hrs–3hrs30	15mins	12m (2x15m)	E M L	No
	82	Leale Inferiore		4	Red	20–30mins/1hr30	2hrs	20mins	20m (2x20m)	E M L	Yes – low risk
	83	Lavarie		3.5	Blue–red	5mins/45mins	2hrs	2mins	80m (2x40m)	E M L	No
	84	Tralba Inferiore		4	Blue–red	1hr15/8.8km RW	3hrs30	30mins	30m (2x30m)	E M L	Yes – no info
	84a	Alba		2.5	Green	25mins/8.8km RW	2hrs	30mins	18m (2x20m)	E M L	Yes – no info

CANYONING IN THE ALPS

Area	Route no	Canyon	Part	Star rating	Overall difficulty	Approach (with/without shuttle)	Descent	Return	Max pitch (Rope length after shrinkage)	Season (early/**mid**/late summer)	Dam
Carnia and the Julian Alps *(continued)*	85	Simon	Inferiore	4	Blue–red	1hr/2km RW	2hrs30–3hrs	5mins	26m (2x30m)	E **M** L	No
	85a	Simon	Superiore	2.5	Blue–red	2hrs30/2km RW	1hr30–2hrs	45mins	37m (2x40m)	E **M** L	No
	86	Cuestis		4	Red	1hr	3–4hrs	10mins	70m (2x60m)	E **M** L	Yes – low risk
	87	Rio Nero	Superiore	3.5	Blue–red	1hr30	1hr30	40mins	16m (2x20m)	E **M** L	No
	88	Rio Nero	Inferiore	4	Red	1hr	2hrs30	10mins	13m (2x20m)	E **M** L	No
	89	Brussine		3.5	Blue	30mins	2hrs30	20mins	57m (2x60m)	E **M** L	No
	90	Mlinarica		4.5	Red	10mins/50–60mins	3hrs–3hrs30	5mins	50m (2x55m)	E **M** L	No

426

The sombre passage beneath the road (Route 66)

APPENDIX B: FURTHER INFORMATION AND RESOURCES

Information on the web
For information on many aspects of canyoning, including brief descriptions of most canyons in Europe, see www.descente-canyon.com (in French). The Spanish and German equivalents are www.barranquismo.net and www.deutschercanyoningverein.de (subscription fee at the time of writing). The forum pages of descente-canyon and the Associazione Italiana Canyoning website (www.aic-canyoning.it) are the best places to learn of new descents and developments. Other useful sites for Italian and Swiss canyons are www.cicarudeclan.com (mainly Italian, but some English translations), www.x-gatt.com (Italian only), www.swisscanyon.ch (in Italian, German and French) and www.schlucht.ch (in German, with occasional translations into French, Italian and English). For Austrian canyons, there is also http://canyon.carto.net.

Foreign language guidebooks
This guidebook details only the finest canyons in northern Italy and Switzerland. A more complete picture can be gained by referring to foreign-language guidebooks. The following are recommended.

Canyoning Alpi Giulie and Canyoning Slovenia, both by Franco Longo, are available from the author at www.canyoningalpigiulie.blogspot.com

Canyoning in Lombardia, by Pascal van Duin (Edizioni TopCanyon)

Canyoning in Switzerland 2, by Franz Baumgartner, Andreas Brunner and Daniel Zimmermann (Eigenverlag)

Canyoning nelle Alpi Occidentali, by Daniele Geuna and Dino Ruotolo (Versante Sud)

Canyoning Nord Italia, by Pascal van Duin (Edizioni TopCanyon)

Canyons du Haut Piémont Italien – Val d'Ossola, by Speleo Club de la Vallée de la Vis, Club Omni Sport Perrier and Speleo-Club Vacances du CAF – Briancon (out of print)

Canyons Slovènes, by Franck Jourdan and Jean-Francois Fiorina (Association Corse-Canyon)

Eldorado Ticino, by Anna and Luca Nizzola (SwissCanyon) (in English)

Gole & Canyons Vol 2: Italia Nord-Est, by Maurizio Biondi, Francesco Cacace and Roberto Schenone (Associazione Italiana Canyoning)

Gole & Canyons Vol 3: Italia Nord-Ovest, by Francesco Cacace, Roberto Jarre, Dino Ruotolo and Roberto Schenone (Associazione Italiana Canyoning)

Grand Canyons, by Timo Stammwitz

Le Tour de l'Europe en Canyon Vol 1, by Caracal et les Sancho Panza (Association Promotion Projets Canyon)

Schluchten-Canyon: Die besten Schluchten in Kärnten, Friaul und Slowenien, by Alfred Wieser, Franz Karger, Reinhard Ranner and Ingo Neumann (Edition Neumann)

These books are not on sale in the UK. The best websites for buying them are www.descente-canyon.com, www.expe.fr (also a good source of canyoning equipment), www.amazon.fr and www.amazon.it.

Canyoning techniques
Information on canyoning techniques can be found on various websites, including www.murdeau.org and the forum pages of www.descente-canyon.com, www.aic-canyoning.it (AIC) and www.canyoneering.net (the American Canyoneering Association). Alternatively, get hold of the techniques bible – *Canyonisme: Manuel Technique*, by FFS/FFME (in French, available from the shops and websites detailed above).

APPENDIX B: FURTHER INFORMATION AND RESOURCES

Peering into Grigno's fearsome depths (Route 54)

UK caving shops

See 'Equipment and Clothing' in the Introduction. Some gear can be obtained in the UK from climbing and general outdoor shops (too numerous to list here). Caving shops may be a better source for more canyon-specific items (although equipment may still have to be ordered in). The websites of the main caving suppliers in the UK are listed below:

www.caveclimb.com
www.inglesport.com
www.berniescafe.co.uk
www.caving-supplies.co.uk
www.hitchnhike.co.uk
www.upandunder.co.uk
www.starlessriver.com

Via ferrata and climbing

Ideas are given for rest-day activities in each chapter. With regard to climbing and via ferrata (or klettersteig), no English-language guidebooks exist that wholly cover the areas described in this guide. Although Cicerone's *Via Ferratas of the Italian Dolomites Vol 2* covers a handful of routes in the south-eastern Dolomites, for the most part it is necessary to refer to foreign-language publications. A good starting point for via ferrata is *Klettersteigatlas Alpen*, by Paul Werner and Iris Kürschner, which gives brief descriptions (in German) of 729 via ferrata and protected paths all over the Alps. Another useful resource is www.klettersteig.de, which contains route descriptions of many via ferrata in the region and provides links to various other German-language guidebooks. All these guidebooks are available from www.amazon.de.

Details of climbing possibilities are given in each chapter, but good places to start are www.worldtopo.com, www.planetmountain.com and the 'logbooks' pages of www.UKclimbing.com. Local gear shops can also be a goldmine of information.

429

APPENDIX C: CAMPSITES

VAL D'OSSOLA
Camping Rio Buscagna
Località Pedemonte, Alpe Devero
Tel +39 0349 1098585; mob. 0334 2311546
www.riobuscagna.com

Campeggio Cistella
(15mins drive from Crodo, but not well signposted and very difficult to find)
Località Quartarone, 9
Tel +39 0324 61493
www.campeggiocistella.it

Villagio Yolki Palki
Località La Gomba, near Bognanco
Tel +39 0324 234245
www.yolkipalki.it

Campeggio La Pineta
Via Pittor Belcastro 13 (SS337), Santa Maria Maggiore
Tel +39 0324 94123
www.campeggiopineta.it

Campeggio Ristorante Hermitage
Via Melezzo-Siberia 43, Craveggia
Tel +39 0324 98073
www.campinghermitage.it

Campeggio Monte Rosa
Località San Carlo, near Bannio Anzino
Tel +39 0324 828971
www.campingmonterosa.it

Campeggio Sporting Center
Località Testa, Macugnaga
Tel +39 0324 65489
www.sportingcentermacugnaga.com

Camping Geschina
Geschinastrasse 41, Brig, Switzerland
Tel +41 (0) 27 9230688
www.geschina.ch

Camping Tropic
3911 Ried-Brig
Tel +41 (0) 27 9232537
www.tropic-musik-bar.ch

By Lake Mergozzo
Campeggio Lago delle Fate
Via Pallanza, Mergozzo
Tel +39 0323 80326
www.lagodellefate.com

Campeggio Continental
Via 42 Martiri, near Fondotoce
Tel +39 0323 496300
www.campingcontinental.com

Campeggio La Quiete
Via Turati, near Fondotoce
Tel +39 0323 496013
www.campinglaquiete.it

There are further campsites along the shores of Lake Maggiore.

TICINO

Valle Maggia area
TCS Camping Bella Riva (4 star)
Gordevio
Tel +41 (0) 91 7531444
www.reisen-tcs.ch

Campeggio Piccolo Paradiso (4 star)
Avegno
Tel +41 (0) 91 7961581 or 7562377; mob +41 (0) 079 2128776
www.piccolo-paradiso.ch

Camping Riposo (2 star)
Via Arbigo 21, Losone
Tel +41 (0) 91 7921204
www.campingriposo.ch

APPENDIX C: CAMPSITES

Camping Zandone (3 star)
Via Arbigo, Losone
Tel +41 (0) 91 7916563
www.campingzandone.ch

Magadino Plain
Camping Bellavista (2 star)
Vira
Tel +41 (0) 91 7951477
www.campingbellavista.ch

Camping Riarena (4 star)
Cugnasco
Tel +41 (0) 91 8591688
www.camping-riarena.ch

Camping Isola (4 star)
Gudo
Tel +41 (0) 91 8593244
www.camping-isola.ch

Camping La Serta (1 star)
Gudo
Tel +41 (0) 91 8591155

Camping Joghi e Bubu (2 star)
Via ai Lischedi, Cadenazzo
Tel +41 (0) 91 8572541
campingjoghiebubu@ticino.com

Valle Leventina/Valle di Blenio
TCS Camping Bosco di Molinasco (4 star)
Via San Gottardo 131, Bellinzona
Tel +41 (0) 91 8291118
www.campingtcs.ch

Camping Al Censo (4 star)
Claro
Tel +41 (0) 91 8631753
www.alcenso.ch

Camping Acquarossa (2 star)
Acquarossa
Tel +41 (0) 91 8711603; mob 079 4443506
www.camping-acquarossa.ch

LAKE COMO

Campsites away from the lake shore
Camping Lo Scoiattolo
Località Bregolana, San Martino
Tel +39 0342 64107; mob+39 (0) 338 3914742
www.campingloscoiattolo.it

Camping Sasso Remenno
Località Sasso Remenno, Val Masina
Tel/fax +39 0342 640059; mob+39 (0) 339 5225181
www.campingsassoremenno.com

'Ground Jack' Agricampeggio
(formerly Camping Paradiso)
Val di Mello
Tel +39 0342 672056; mob+39 (0) 335 6746347
www.groundjack.it

Camping Acquafraggia
Borgonuovo (5km east of Chiavenna)
Tel/fax +39 0343 36755
www.campingacquafraggia.com

Camping Villaggio le Rocce Rosse
Via Provinciale Sud, 1 – Taceno
Tel +39 0341 880160
info@roccerosse.com

Campeggio La Fasana
Via Provinciale Bindo, Cortenova
Tel +39 0341 901447

Camping El Ranchero
Via Nazionale 211, Novate Mezzola
Tel/fax +39 0343 44169
www.elranchero.it

Campodolcina Camping
Via per Starleggia 2, Campodolcino
Tel +39 0343 50097
www.campodolcinocamping.it

Camping Bondo (Switzerland)
Tel +41 (0) 81 8221558 or 8322381 or 8221653
www.camping-bondo.ch

CANYONING IN THE ALPS

THE BELLUNO AND FRIULI DOLOMITES
Camping International di Cologna
Loc. Cologna, Vallesella di Cadore
(near Pieve di Cadore)
Tel +39 0435 72135 (June–Sept)
www.campingcologna.com

Park Camping Nevegal
Via Nevegal 347, Belluno
Tel +39 0437 908143
camping.nevegal@tin.it

Camping Sarathei
Viale al Lago 13, Farra d'Alpago
Tel +39 0437 46996 or 454937
www.sarathei.it

Camping Al Lago
Via Campagna 14, Arsiè
Tel +39 0439 58540
www.campingallago.bl.it

Camping Gajole
Località Soravigo, Arsiè
Tel +39 0439 58505
www.campinggajole.it

Campeggio Orsera Val Canzoi
Via Val Canzoi, 9 – Loc. Soranzen, Cesiomaggiore
Tel +39 0439 43722
orsera.valcanzoi@gmail.it

Area Camper Vincheto
Via Casonetto 158/C, Feltre
Tel +39 0439 81687; mob +39 (0) 328 3539292
www.areacampervincheto.it

Camping Bresin
A few km north of Cimolais (quiet, toilets only)
Mob +39 (0) 335 5269762

Campeggio San Francesco
Località Ribe, Barcis (on the SS251)
Tel +39 0427 76366
www.campingbarcis.it

CARNIA AND THE JULIAN ALPS
Camping ai Pioppi
Via Bersaglio 118, Gemona Del Friuli
Tel +39 0432 981276
www.aipioppi.it

Camping Lago dei Trei Comuni
Via Tolmezzo 52, Alesso – Trasaghis
Tel +39 0432 979464
www.campinglagodeitrecomuni.com

Camping Val del Lago
Via Tolmezzo, Alesso – Trasaghis
Tel +39 0348 2431337; mob +39 (0) 331 6199953
www.valdellago.it

Campeggio Spin
Via Vidrina di Chialina 31, Ovaro – Zoncolan
Tel +39 0433 67047; mob +39 (0) 349 5446591

Campeggio Valtramontina
Tramonti di Sotto
Tel +39 0427 869004; mob +39 (0) 333 6262164
www.camptramontina.com

Camping Seeweise
Tristachersee 2, 9900 Lienz
Tel +43 (0) 4852 69767
www.campingtirol.com

Dolomiten Camping Almacherhof
Almach 4, A-9900 Lienz
Tel +43 (0) 4852 62317
www.almacherhof.at

Camping Falken
Falconweg 7, A-9900 Lienz
Tel +43 (0) 664 4107973
www.camping-falken.com

Camping Oberdrauburg
Marktstrasse 1, 9781 Oberdrauburg
Tel +43 (0) 4710 2210
http:/camping.oberdrauburg.info

Camping Trenta, Sergej Bolcina
Trenta 60a, 5232 Soça
Tel +386 (0) 31 615966

APPENDIX D: TOURIST INFORMATION OFFICES

VAL D'OSSOLA
Ossola Tourist Information
www.prodomodossola.it
www.distrettolaghi.it

Bognanco
Piazzale Giannini 2
Tel +39 0324 234127
bognanco@distrettolaghi.it

Crodo
Località Bagni
Tel +39 0324 600005 or 618831
iataltaossola@libero.it
crodo@distrettolaghi.it

Domodossola
Piazza Matteotti (in the International Station)
Tel +39 0324 248265
info@prodomodossola.it
prodomodossola@distrettolaghi.it

Macugagna
Piazza Municipio 6
Tel +39 0324 65119
macugnaga@distrettolaghi.it

Malesco
Via Trabucchi 2
Tel +39 0324 929901
malesco@distrettolaghi.it

Mergozzo
Via Roma 20
Tel +39 0323 800935
mergozzo@distrettolaghi.it

Santa Maria Maggiore
Piazza Risorgimento 10
Tel +39 0324 95091
info@comune.santamariamaggiore.vb.it
santamariamaggiore@distrettolaghi.it

TICINO
Ticino Tourist Board
www.ticino.ch

Bellinzona
Palazzo Civico – Casella Postale 1419
Tel +41 (0) 91 8252131
www.bellinzonaturismo.ch

Biasca
Contrada Cavalier Pellanda 4
Tel +41 (0) 91 8623327
www.biascaturismo.ch

Maggia
Tel +41 (0) 91 7551885
www.vallemaggia.ch

Olivone
Tel +41 (0) 91 8721487
www.blenioturismo.ch

Tenero
Via ai Giardini
Tel +41 (0) 91 7451661
www.tenero-tourism.ch

LAKE COMO

For an area so heavily dependent on tourism, tourist information seems a little fragmented and inaccessible, with no single umbrella organisation. Try the following.

Como province
www.lakecomo.it
www.gravedona.it

Lecco province
www.turismo.provincia.lecco.it

Lombardia
www.turismo.regione.lombardia.it

Sondrio province
www.provincia.so.it/turismo
www.portedivaltellina.it
www.valtellina.it
www.valmasino-online.eu
www.sondrioevalmalenco.it

CANYONING IN THE ALPS

Campodolcino
Via Don Romeo Ballerini, 2
Tel +39 0343 50611
infocampodolcino@provincia.so.it

Chiavenna
Via Vittorio Emanuele II, 2
Tel +39 0343 33442
infochiavenna@provincia.so.it

Chiesa in Valmalenco
Località Vassalini
Tel +39 0342 451150
info@sondrioevalmalenco.it

Domaso
Via Roma
Tel +39 0344 96322
ufficioturistico@comunedomaso.it

Dongo (info point)
Palazzo Manzi
Tel/fax +39 0344 82572

Gravedona
Piazza Trieste
Tel/fax +39 0344 85005
turismo.gravedona@gmail.com

Lecco
Via Nazario Sauro 6, Lecco
Tel +39 0341 295720 or 295721
www.turismo.provincia.lecco.it
info.turismo@provincia.lecco.it

Lenno
Piazza XI Febbraio
Tel +39 0344 5583417

Menaggio
Piazza Garibaldi 8
Tel/fax +39 0344 32924

Morbegno (Valgerola – Valmasino – Valtartano)
Piazza M. Bossi 7/8, Morbegno
Tel +39 0342 601140
info@portedivaltellina.it

Piantedo (info point) (on the SS38 at the entrance to Valtellina)
Tel +39 0342 683470
info@valtellina.it

Sondrio and Valmalenco
Via Tonale 13, Sondrio
Tel +39 0342 451150 or 219246
info@sondrioevalmalenco.it

Sorico
Piazza Cesare Battisti, 2
Tel +39 0341 940393
info@northlakecomo.com

Val Masino (seasonal)
Via Roma 2 (c/o Municipio) (just south of San Martino)
Tel +39 0342 641117; mob +39 (0) 338 1762312
info@valmasino-online.eu

THE BELLUNO AND FRIULI DOLOMITES
Tourist Information Dolomites
www.infodolomiti.it

Tourist information Pordenone
www.prolococellinameduna.it
www.turismofvg.it

Agordo
Via XXVII Aprile 5/a
Tel +39 0437 62105
agordo@infodolomiti.it

Belluno (main office)
Piazza Duomo 2
Tel +39 0437 940083
mail@infodolomiti.it

Farra d'Alpago
Viale al Lago
Tel +39 0437 46448 (seasonal)
farra@infodolomiti.it

Feltre
Piazza Trento-Trieste 9
Tel +39 0439 2540; fax +39 0439 2839
feltre@infodolomiti.it

Limana
Via Roma 90
Tel +39 0437 966120
comune_limana@infodolomiti.it

APPENDIX D: TOURIST INFORMATION OFFICES

Longarone
Piazza Gonzaga 1
Tel +39 0437 770119
proloco_longarone@infodolomiti.it

Mel
Piazza Papa Luciani c/o Municipio
Tel +39 0437 544294
comune_mel@infodolomiti.it

Pieve di Cadore
Piazza Municipio 17
Tel +39 0435 31644
pievedicadore@infodolomiti.it

Ponte nelle Alpe
Piazzetta al Bivio 14
Tel +39 0437 981792
proloco_pontenellealpi@infodolomiti.it

Puos d'Alpago
Piazza Papa Luciani 7
Tel/fax +39 (0) 437 454650
proloco_puosdalpago@infodolomiti.it

Tambre
Piazza 11 Gennaio 1945, 1
Tel +39 0437 49277
alpago@infodolomiti.it

Ovaro
Via Caduti 2 Maggio, 197
Tel +39 0433 67223
info.ovaro@turismo.fvg.it

Paluzza
Piazza XXI–XXII luglio 7
Tel +39 0433 775344
info.paluzza@turismo.fvg.it

Tarvisio
Via Roma 14
Tel +39 0428 2135
info.tarvisio@turismo.fvg.it

Tolmezzo (centre)
Via della Vittoria 4
Tel +39 0433 44898
info.tolmezzo@turismo.fvg.it

Villa Santina
Piazza Venezia 1
Tel +39 0433 74040
turismovilla@tiscali.it

CARNIA AND THE JULIAN ALPS
Friuli-Venezia-Giulia Tourist Board
www.turismofvg.it

Ampezzo
Piazza zona libera 1944, 5
Tel +39 0433 80758
info.ampezzo@turismo.fvg.it

Arta Terme
Via Umberto I°, 15
Tel +39 0433 929290
info.artaterme@turismo.fvg.it

Lienz
Europaplatz 1
Tel +43 (0) 50 212400
www.lienzerdolomiten.info

APPENDIX E: GLOSSARY OF TECHNICAL TERMS

This glossary is intended for those who are not from a caving background. Basic knowledge of climbing terminology is assumed.

Anchor/bolt	A generic term for mechanically placed protection
Thru-bolt	A type of bolt drilled into the rock, one end of which protrudes. A nut is then screwed on to this to secure a hangar in place.
Spit or expansion-bolt	A metal sheath (or spit) is drilled into the rock, secured in place by expansion. A bolt is then screwed into it, which clamps a hangar in place. They may either be 8mm or 10mm in diameter.
P-hangar	A long P-shaped anchor, held in place by resin. Only the metal ring at the tip protrudes from the rock. These take longer to place than thru-bolts or expansion-bolts, but are thought to be much stronger and longer lasting.
Maillon or Maillon-rapide	A metal ring with a screw gate. It performs the job of a karabiner but is much smaller. Its strength relies on the gate being fully done up.
Hand-line	A rope to aid a down-climb or protect access to the main anchors at pitch-heads
Re-belay	A pitch that is too high or awkward to descend in one abseil must be split into a number of smaller stages. The re-belay is the point at which the intermediate anchors are found.
Deviation	A sling or anchor situated part-way down a pitch that, when clipped, deviates the path of an abseil away from the flow of water (or other obstacle)
Guide-line	A taut rope running the entire length of the pitch that, when clipped, directs an abseil away from the flow of water
Sump	An underwater passage. These are very rare in canyons, and usually very brief or avoidable.
Siphon	A potentially lethal canyoning hazard, usually found among boulders in a fast-flowing stream. The gaps between boulders create strong currents which can suck body parts in, trapping people under water. There is often some confusion over the terms 'sump' and 'siphon' when interpreting foreign-language canyoning guides, as the same word is used for both in Italian and in French (*sifòn* and *sifone* respectively).

Emerging from the cave section (Route 55)

APPENDIX F: FIRST DESCENTS

Canyoning history is unfortunately not very well documented. The following is list of first descents, where known.

VAL D' OSSOLA
In the early 1990s, visiting French cavers from Speleo Club de la Vallée de la Vis, Club Omni Sport Perrier and Speleo-Club Vacances du CAF made the first descents of Antolina, Bianca, Rio di Menta and Ogliana di Quarata, Mondelli, Rasiga, Toce and Variola (among others).

TICINO
Cresciano Superiore K Bühler, A Brunner, P Lauber, D Zimmermann, October 1997
Gei Inferiore A Brunner, P Graf
Malvaglia Inferiore M Vogel et al, 1997
Osogna Superiore L Nizzola
Pontirone Superiore possibly A Brunner, D Zimmermann, 1997
Serenello A Brunner, Eva Tiepner
Sponde L Nizzola et al

LAKE COMO
Borgo F Giacomelli, R and C Rossi, 2001
Val Bodengo *Bodengo 1* R Alemann, L Blattler, 1997; *Bodengo 2* P van Duin, L Rucci, 1996; *Bodengo 3* F Giacomelli, R Rossi, F Gallegioni, 1997; P van Duin, L Rucci, 1996
Bares P van Duin, G Monti, C Gianetti, A Colombo, 30 June 2002 and 27 July 2002
Boazzo G Beltrami, P Cortenova, A Boggiali, S Maggi (Gruppo Speleologico Lecchese), July 1981
Bondasca L Blattler, R Alemann, 1999
Casenda *Inferiore* P van Duin, M Gentili 3 Sept 1994; *first complete descent* P van Duin, M Crottogini, A Colombo, G Monti, 25 Aug 2001
Cormor P van Duin, M Crottogini, A Colombo 2 Sept 2001; *partial descent* P Merizzi, M Sala, L Maspes, M Tonni, N Parolini, P van Duin, F Brusamarello, 22/28 Aug 2001
Esino Inferiore D Basola et al, late 1980s
Ferro P van Duin, C Gianatti, 26 July 1997
Lanterna (Val Brutta) First explored as an ice-climb during the winter
Lanterna (Valle di Scerscen) P van Duin, C Tonini, M Zuin, E Ferrari, 27 Sept 2002
Lesina P van Duin, P Covelli, 11 Aug 1998
Mengasca P van Duin, L Rucci, 21 Aug 1996
Perlana Inferiore D Basola, Donini, M Filipazzi, M Miragoli (Gruppo Grotte Milano), 1995; *final cascades* P van Duin, G Monti, 2004
Pilotera F Giacomelli, F Gallegioni, R Rossi, C Zani, 1998

APPENDIX F: FIRST DESCENTS

The 45m pitch (Route 32)

DOLOMITES

Clusa GP Bianucci, S Matteoli, M Menicucci, M Sivelli, Aug 1987
Grigno *initial exploration* Gruppo Speleologico Gaetano Chierici di Reggio Emilia (GSPGC) in 1983/4, but abandoned owing to its length and difficulty; *first descent* E Bagni (student caver) and M Salvi, M Picciati, G Gavazzoli from Reggio Emilia, July 1985
Pezzeda A Kaiser, L Piccini, M Sivelli, 5 Sept 1992. Eastern tributary: P van Duin 31 July 2008
Pissa G Antonini, L Piccini, A Kaiser, M Menicucci and others, summer 1994
La Soffia *partial descent* S Martinuzzi, I Panicucci, A Sivelli, M Sivelli, Aug 1985; *full descent* S de Benedet et al, Aug 1986
Zemola GP Carrieri, S Martinucci, I Panicucci, A Sivelli, M Vianelli, Aug 1986

CARNIA AND THE JULIAN ALPS

Brussine F Longo, N Terenzani, 3 June 2009
Chiantione I Panicucci, M Sivelli, Aug 1986
Ciorosolin A Kaiser, L Piccini 6 Sept 1992
Cosa D Marini and other cavers from Trieste, summer 1959
Cuestis M Biondi, R Siegl, G Pizzorni, R Perotto, R Recchioni, JC Vaternel, 5 Aug 2004
Leale PP Pedrini, A De Rovere and R Del Fabbro, 16 July 2010
Rio Negro P van Duin *et al*, 15 July 2010
Nero (Cerni Potok) P Toffoletti and cavers from Cividale, 2004
Rötenbach W Stich, W Baumgarten, L Grasmück
Simon A Kaiser, A Lombardi, M Taverniti (Gruppo speleologico Pipistrelli di Fiesole), August 1993
Tralba A Kaiser, A Lombardi, M Taverniti (Gruppo speleologico Pipistrelli di Fiesole) 2 August 1993
Viellia P van Duin and G Monti descended on 21/22 Aug 2008 and found the first 10 and the last 2 pitches rigged. The canyon's upper reaches were first descended in 2004 by Gruppo Speleologico Carnico (Kristian Muser *et al*), while the final part was done by local guides P Pedrini and E Rizzotti in 2006.
Vinadia C Floreanini *et al*, 1958 (see route description for more details)

ROUTE INDEX

Alba (Carnia) 402	Cresciano 187	Nala 177
Alba (Dolomites) 338	Cuestis. 407	Negro 366
Alba (Ossola). 88	Dagliano 70	Nero 410
Alba Affluente Sinistro 398	Darengo 206	Novarza 360
Arabianca 69	Drögh Grand. 240	Ogliana di Quarata 104
Antolina 93	Esino Inferiore 258	Ogliana di Buera 110
Antoliva. 101	Ferro 243	Orino 153
Apocalypse Now 273	La Foce Inferiore 386	Orrido di Arvera 85
Avera, Orrido di 85	Fogarè 302	Orrido di Vezio 258
Bares. 224	Forti. 284	Osogna 177
Barougia 151	Frauenbach 354	Perlana 232
Beura, Ogliana di 110	Gei Inferiore 140	Pezzeda. 325
Bianca. 81	Giumaglio. 132	Picchionis 378
Bignasco 125	Gondo. 60	Pilotera 212
Boazzo 260	Grande 142	Pissa 319
Bodengo 202	Grigno. 273	Pisson 286
Boggera. 187	Grosswasser 60	Pontirone, Val 159
Boggia. 202	Iragna 165	Prealba 398
Bondasca. 236	Isorno Finale 97	Quarata, Ogliana di. 104
Bordione 145	Lanterna 251	Rasiga 63
Borgo 206	Lavarie. 395	Rötenbach. 349
Boscaioli, Forra dei 398	Leale 391	Rovine. 110
Brussine. 415	Lesina 241	Salto 135
Brutta 255	Lesgiüna 159	Scerscen 252
Caldone. 260	Loco 145	Segnara 84
Casenda 219	Lodrino 173	Serenello 123
Cerosolin. 330	Lumiei 364	Sernel 123
Cerni Potok 411	Macile, Rio Le 415	Simon 403
Chiadola 333	Maggiore. 313	Soffia 279
Chiantione. 382	Malvaglia Inferiore 153	Sponde 125
Chignolasc 125	Maor 310	Ticinetto Inferiore 148
Ciadula 333	Marona 112	Toce 85
Ciarfule 333	Massaschluct. 56	Tovanella. 317
Ciolesan 335	Mengasca 215	Tralba 398
Ciorosolin. 330	Menta 109	Variola. 70
Clusa. 289	Mlinarica. 418	Vezio, Orrido di 258
Combra. 156	Molassa. 402	Viellia 370
Cormor 247	Mondelli 73	Vinadia 377
Cosa 388	Mus. 298	Zemola 321

A rare enclosed section (Route 67)

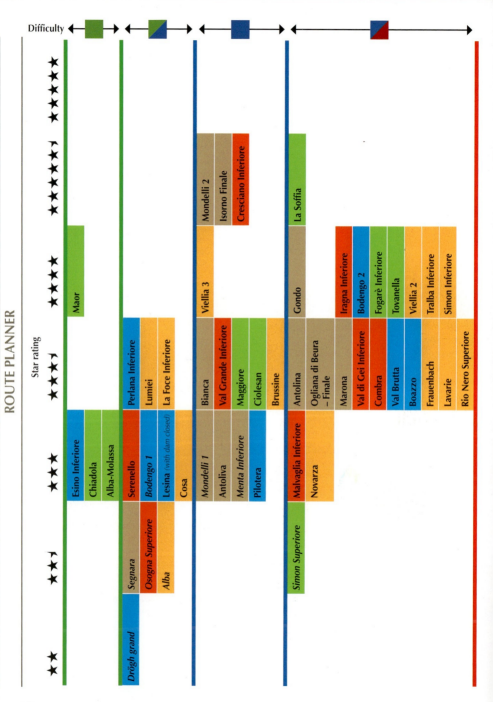

ROUTE PLANNER

Rasiga Inferiore	Casenda	Massaschluct	Variola Superiore	Rasiga Superiore	Pontirone Inferiore	Lodrino Inferiore	Clusa Inferiore
Mus Superiore	Borgo	Mondelli 3	Ogliana di Quarata	Bodengo 3	Cormor		
Röitenbach (upper)	Fogarè Superiore	Bignasco	Salto	Clusa Superiore	Zemola	Bares	Grigno
	Pezzeda	Giumaglio	Ticinetto Inferiore	Mlinariça		Pisson	
	Ciorosolin	Loco Inferiore	Iragna Superiore			Viellia 4	
	Viellia 1	Pontirone Superiore	Lodrino Intermedio				
	Vinadia (Picchionis)	Osogna Intermedio	Cresciano Superiore				
	Vinadia (Chiantione)	Mengasca	Bondasca				
		Scerscen	Ferro			Toce	
		Röitenbach (lower)	Forti			Sponde	
			Mus Inferiore			Lesina (dam open)	
			Leale Inferiore			Negro	
			Cuestis				
			Rio Nero Inferiore				
						Rio d'Alba	

Val d'Ossola
Ticino
Lake Como
Dolomites
Carnia and the Julian Alps

Italics = Minor route (labelled 'a' in text)

LISTING OF CICERONE GUIDES

INTERNATIONAL CHALLENGES, COLLECTIONS AND ACTIVITIES
Canyoning
Europe's High Points
The Via Francigena (Canterbury to Rome): Part 1

TECHNIQUES
Geocaching in the UK
Indoor Climbing
Lightweight Camping
Map and Compass
Mountain Weather
Moveable Feasts
Outdoor Photography
Polar Exploration
Rock Climbing
Sport Climbing
The Book of the Bivvy
The Hillwalker's Guide to Mountaineering
The Hillwalker's Manual

MINI GUIDES
Avalanche!
Navigating with a GPS
Navigation
Pocket First Aid and Wilderness Medicine
Snow

EUROPEAN CYCLING
Cycle Touring in France
Cycle Touring in Ireland
Cycle Touring in Spain
Cycle Touring in Switzerland
Cycling in the French Alps
Cycling the Canal du Midi
Cycling the River Loire
The Danube Cycleway
The Grand Traverse of the Massif Central
The Way of St James

AFRICA
Climbing in the Moroccan Anti-Atlas
Kilimanjaro
Mountaineering in the Moroccan High Atlas
The High Atlas
Trekking in the Atlas Mountains
Walking in the Drakensberg

ALPS – CROSS-BORDER ROUTES
100 Hut Walks in the Alps
Across the Eastern Alps: E5
Alpine Points of View
Alpine Ski Mountaineering
 1 Western Alps
 2 Central and Eastern Alps
Chamonix to Zermatt
Snowshoeing
Tour of Mont Blanc
Tour of Monte Rosa
Tour of the Matterhorn
Trekking in the Alps
Walking in the Alps
Walks and Treks in the Maritime Alps

PYRENEES AND FRANCE/SPAIN CROSS-BORDER ROUTES
Rock Climbs in The Pyrenees
The GR10 Trail
The Mountains of Andorra
The Pyrenean Haute Route
The Pyrenees
The Way of St James
 France & Spain
Through the Spanish Pyrenees: GR11
Walks and Climbs in the Pyrenees

AUSTRIA
The Adlerweg
Trekking in Austria's Hohe Tauern
Trekking in the Stubai Alps
Trekking in the Zillertal Alps
Walking in Austria

EASTERN EUROPE
The High Tatras
The Mountains of Romania
Walking in Bulgaria's National Parks
Walking in Hungary

FRANCE
Chamonix Mountain Adventures
Ecrins National Park
GR20: Corsica
Mont Blanc Walks
Mountain Adventures in the Maurienne
The Cathar Way
The GR5 Trail
The Robert Louis Stevenson Trail
Tour of the Oisans: The GR54
Tour of the Queyras

Tour of the Vanoise
Trekking in the Vosges and Jura
Vanoise Ski Touring
Walking in Provence
Walking in the Cathar Region
Walking in the Cevennes
Walking in the Dordogne
Walking in the Haute Savoie
  North & South
Walking in the Languedoc
Walking in the Tarentaise and Beaufortain Alps
Walking on Corsica

GERMANY
Germany's Romantic Road
Walking in the Bavarian Alps
Walking in the Harz Mountains
Walking the River Rhine Trail

HIMALAYA
Bhutan
Everest: A Trekker's Guide
Garhwal and Kumaon: A Trekker's and Visitor's
  Guide
Kangchenjunga: A Trekker's Guide
Langtang with Gosainkund and Helambu: A
  Trekker's Guide
Manaslu: A Trekker's Guide
The Mount Kailash Trek
Trekking in Ladakh

IRELAND
Irish Coastal Walks
The Irish Coast to Coast Walk
The Mountains of Ireland

ITALY
Gran Paradiso
Italy's Sibillini National Park
Shorter Walks in the Dolomites
Through the Italian Alps
Trekking in the Apennines
Trekking in the Dolomites
Via Ferratas of the Italian Dolomites: Vols 1 & 2
Walking in Abruzzo
Walking in Sardinia
Walking in Sicily
Walking in the Central Italian Alps
Walking in the Dolomites
Walking in Tuscany
Walking on the Amalfi Coast
Walking the Italian Lakes

MEDITERRANEAN
Jordan – Walks, Treks, Caves, Climbs and
  Canyons
The Ala Dag
The High Mountains of Crete
The Mountains of Greece
Treks and Climbs in Wadi Rum, Jordan
Walking in Malta
Western Crete

NORTH AMERICA
British Columbia
The Grand Canyon
The John Muir Trail
The Pacific Crest Trail

SOUTH AMERICA
Aconcagua and the Southern Andes
Hiking and Biking Peru's Inca Trails
Torres del Paine

SCANDINAVIA & ICELAND
Trekking in Greenland
Walking and Trekking in Iceland
Walking in Norway

SLOVENIA, CROATIA AND MONTENEGRO
The Julian Alps of Slovenia
The Mountains of Montenegro
Trekking in Slovenia
Walking in Croatia

SPAIN AND PORTUGAL
Costa Blanca: West
Mountain Walking in Southern Catalunya
The Mountains of Central Spain
Trekking through Mallorca
Walking in Madeira
Walking in Mallorca
Walking in the Algarve
Walking in the Canary Islands: East
Walking in the Cordillera Cantabrica
Walking in the Sierra Nevada
Walking on La Gomera and El Hierro
Walking on La Palma
Walking on Tenerife
Walks and Climbs in the Picos de Europa

SWITZERLAND
Alpine Pass Route
Canyoning in the Alps
Central Switzerland
The Bernese Alps

The Swiss Alps
Tour of the Jungfrau Region
Walking in the Valais
Walking in Ticino
Walks in the Engadine

BRITISH ISLES CHALLENGES, COLLECTIONS AND ACTIVITIES
The End to End Trail
The Mountains of England and Wales
  1 Wales & 2 England
The National Trails
The Relative Hills of Britain
The Ridges of England, Wales and Ireland
The UK Trailwalker's Handbook
The UK's County Tops
Three Peaks, Ten Tors

MOUNTAIN LITERATURE
Unjustifiable Risk?

UK CYCLING
Border Country Cycle Routes
Cycling in the Hebrides
Cycling in the Peak District
Cycling the Pennine Bridleway
Mountain Biking in the Lake District
Mountain Biking in the Yorkshire Dales
Mountain Biking on the South Downs
The C2C Cycle Route
The End to End Cycle Route
The Lancashire Cycleway

SCOTLAND
Backpacker's Britain
  Central and Southern Scottish Highlands
  Northern Scotland
Ben Nevis and Glen Coe
Great Mountain Days in Scotland
North to the Cape
Not the West Highland Way
Scotland's Best Small Mountains
Scotland's Far West
Scotland's Mountain Ridges
Scrambles in Lochaber
The Ayrshire and Arran Coastal Paths
The Border Country
The Great Glen Way
The Isle of Mull
The Isle of Skye
The Pentland Hills
The Southern Upland Way

The Speyside Way
The West Highland Way
Scotland's Far North
Walking in the Cairngorms
Walking in the Ochils, Campsie Fells and Lomond Hills
Walking in Torridon
Walking Loch Lomond and the Trossachs
Walking on Harris and Lewis
Walking on Jura, Islay and Colonsay
Walking on Rum and the Small Isles
Walking on the Isle of Arran
Walking on the Orkney and Shetland Isles
Walking on Uist and Barra
Walking the Corbetts
  1 South of the Great Glen
Walking the Galloway Hills
Walking the Lowther Hills
Walking the Munros
  1 Southern, Central and Western Highlands
  2 Northern Highlands and the Cairngorms
Winter Climbs Ben Nevis and Glen Coe
Winter Climbs in the Cairngorms
World Mountain Ranges: Scotland

NORTHERN ENGLAND TRAILS
A Northern Coast to Coast Walk
Backpacker's Britain
  Northern England
Hadrian's Wall Path
The Dales Way
The Pennine Way
The Spirit of Hadrian's Wall

NORTH EAST ENGLAND, YORKSHIRE DALES AND PENNINES
Historic Walks in North Yorkshire
South Pennine Walks
The Cleveland Way and the Yorkshire Wolds Way
The North York Moors
The Reivers Way
The Teesdale Way
The Yorkshire Dales
  North and East
  South and West
Walking in County Durham
Walking in Northumberland
Walking in the North Pennines
Walks in Dales Country
Walks in the Yorkshire Dales
Walks on the North York Moors – Books 1 & 2

NORTH WEST ENGLAND AND THE ISLE OF MAN
Historic Walks in Cheshire
Isle of Man Coastal Path
The Isle of Man
The Lune Valley and Howgills
The Ribble Way
Walking in Cumbria's Eden Valley
Walking in Lancashire
Walking in the Forest of Bowland and Pendle
Walking on the West Pennine Moors
Walks in Lancashire Witch Country
Walks in Ribble Country
Walks in Silverdale and Arnside
Walks in the Forest of Bowland

LAKE DISTRICT
Coniston Copper Mines
Great Mountain Days in the Lake District
Lake District Winter Climbs
Lakeland Fellranger
  The Central Fells
  The Mid-Western Fells
  The Near Eastern Fells
  The Northern Fells
  The North-Western Wells
  The Southern Fells
  The Western Fells
Roads and Tracks of the Lake District
Rocky Rambler's Wild Walks
Scrambles in the Lake District
  North & South
Short Walks in Lakeland
  1 South Lakeland
  2 North Lakeland
  3 West Lakeland
The Cumbria Coastal Way
The Cumbria Way and the Allerdale Ramble
Tour of the Lake District

DERBYSHIRE, PEAK DISTRICT AND MIDLANDS
High Peak Walks
Scrambles in the Dark Peak
The Star Family Walks
Walking in Derbyshire

White Peak Walks
  The Northern Dales
  The Southern Dales

SOUTHERN ENGLAND
A Walker's Guide to the Isle of Wight
Suffolk Coast & Heaths Walks
The Cotswold Way
The North Downs Way
The South Downs Way
The South West Coast Path
The Thames Path
Walking in Berkshire
Walking in Kent
Walking in Sussex
Walking in the Isles of Scilly
Walking in the New Forest
Walking in the Thames Valley
Walking on Dartmoor
Walking on Guernsey
Walking on Jersey
Walks in the South Downs National Park

WALES AND WELSH BORDERS
Backpacker's Britain – Wales
Glyndwr's Way
Great Mountain Days in Snowdonia
Hillwalking in Snowdonia
Hillwalking in Wales
  Vols 1 & 2
Offa's Dyke Path
Ridges of Snowdonia
Scrambles in Snowdonia
The Ascent of Snowdon
Lleyn Peninsula Coastal Path
Pembrokeshire Coastal Path
The Shropshire Hills
The Wye Valley Walk
Walking in Pembrokeshire
Walking in the South Wales Valleys
Walking on Gower
Walking on the Brecon Beacons
Welsh Winter Climbs

For full information on all our guides, and to order books and eBooks, visit our website:
www.cicerone.co.uk

Walking – Trekking – Mountaineering – Climbing – Cycling

Over 40 years, Cicerone have built up an outstanding collection of 300 guides, inspiring all sorts of amazing adventures.

Every guide comes from extensive exploration and research by our expert authors, all with a passion for their subjects. They are frequently praised, endorsed and used by clubs, instructors and outdoor organisations.

All our titles can now be bought as **e-books** and many as iPad and Kindle files and we will continue to make all our guides available for these and many other devices.

Our website shows any **new information** we've received since a book was published. Please do let us know if you find anything has changed, so that we can pass on the latest details. On our **website** you'll also find some great ideas and lots of information, including sample chapters, contents lists, reviews, articles and a photo gallery.

It's easy to keep in touch with what's going on at Cicerone, by getting our monthly **free e-newsletter**, which is full of offers, competitions, up-to-date information and topical articles. You can subscribe on our home page and also follow us on **Facebook** and **Twitter**, as well as our **blog**.

Cicerone – the very best guides for exploring the world.

CICERONE

2 Police Square Milnthorpe Cumbria LA7 7PY
Tel: 015395 62069 info@cicerone.co.uk
www.cicerone.co.uk